THE FIGHTING CAPTAIN

THE FIGHTING CAPTAIN

Frederic John Walker RN
and
The Battle of the Atlantic

by
Alan Burn

with a Foreword by
Admiral of the Fleet Lord Lewin

LEO COOPER

First published in Great Britain 1993 by
LEO COOPER

an imprint of
Pen & Sword Books Ltd,
47 Church Street, Barnsley, South Yorkshire S70 2AS

Reprinted 1998, 1999

A catalogue record for this book is available from the British Library

ISBN 0 85052 555 1

Typeset by Yorkshire Web, Barnsley, South Yorkshire
in Plantin 10 point

Printed by
Redwood Books, Trowbridge, Wiltshire

CONTENTS

DEDICATION

In World War Two, the Blockade of Britain nearly succeeded. This book is dedicated to the 35,000 Merchant Seamen and 51,578 men from the Royal Navy who gave their lives to keep the shipping lanes open, the people fed and the factories at work.

Say not the struggle nought availeth,
The labour and the wounds are vain,
The enemy faints not, nor faileth,
And as things have been they remain.

If hopes were dupes, fears may be liars;
It may be, in yon smoke conceal'd,
Your comrades chase e'en now the fliers,
And, but for you, possess the field.

For while the tired waves, vainly breaking,
Seem here no painful inch to gain,
Far back, through creeks and inlets making,
Comes silent, flooding in, the main.

And not by eastern windows only,
When daylight comes, comes in the light,
In front the sun climbs slow, how slowly!
But westward, look, the land is bright!

Arthur Hugh Clough

FOREWORD

By Admiral of the Fleet Lord Lewin, KG, GCB, LVO, DSC.

In World War Two as in World War One, for the Allies the availability of merchant shipping was the vital factor, and in both wars a ruthless enemy nearly succeeded in bringing us to defeat. From 1939 to 1945 the shipping war continued without respite, from the first day to the last. It was global in extent: from the Barents Sea off North Cape to the seas south of the Cape of Good Hope and in all the Oceans from the Pacific to the Caribbean, ships were attacked and sunk by submarine, warship, aircraft or mine.

The greatest threat was from the submarine and the fiercest battles were fought in the Atlantic, across which had to be carried the food, fuel, men and materials needed to sustain these Islands so that they could act as the springboard for victory. Reducing the conflict to its essentials, if the submarines could sink merchant ships faster than they could be built, we would lose. If the submarines could be sunk faster than they could be replaced by new boats with trained crews, we had a chance.

By the time Johnny Walker went to sea in November, 1941, in command of HMS *Stork* and the 36th Escort Group we had already lost over 2,000 merchant ships totalling five million tons, the number of operational U-Boats had nearly doubled and was rising rapidly. I was serving in a North Atlantic convoy escort at that time; our spirits were not high, the balance of sinkings was clearly against us and the weather was uniformly appalling. There seemed to be no light on the horizon.

On his first encounter with the enemy Walker's Escort Group sank four U-Boats in five days. The word got round, it could be done. Again and again Walker and his band of brothers showed the way and this book describes how. The tide could turn and turn it did, although it was a long hard slog.

Walker's success was founded on two outstanding qualities: professionalism and leadership. He was a dedicated Anti-Submarine Warfare specialist; besides knowing his job thoroughly he was an innovative thinker. But his professionalism would have gained him nothing had he not been able to inspire others with his aggressive spirit and to earn their devotion. Many Captains gain the trust and respect of their own ship's companies; for Walker to be able to transfer to other ships in his Group, displacing their Captains, and to be accepted not with grudging suspicion but with wholehearted warm support marks him as a leader of the calibre of Nelson.

Captain Johnny Walker's contribution to the winning of the shipping war was immeasurable.

ACKNOWLEDGMENTS

There are many quotations in this book from the men who served at sea under the command of Captain Frederic John Walker, and who have written to me recounting their memories of that great Naval Officer. Most of them are members of the Captain Walker's Old Boys Association which holds its reunions annually in Bootle, where still today the opening and closing of the Bootle Council's official sessions are marked by the ringing of H.M.S. *Starling's* ship's bell. The magnificent Council Chamber carries on its walls the crests of H.M. Ships which were based in the neighbouring docks and whose ship's companies enjoyed the unfailing hospitality of the area, which never faltered even in the worst days.

The Association has allowed me full access to its archives, and the assistance given to me by its secretary, Walter Riley, has been invaluable.

Bryan Carter, the Chairman and his Committee have given their full support to the writing of this book, under the watchful eye of their Treasurer, Tom Adams.

I am particularly indebted to George Dyson for the use of the vivid and unpublished writings of his time in *Stork's* and in *Starling's* engine and boiler rooms, to Clem Bray for his tales of life on the lower deck, to Captain Andy Palmer RN for his description of how to ram your Senior Officer's ship, and to many others whose stories find their way into every chapter and nearly every page of this book.

Starling's Deck Logs have gone adrift, last heard of when she paid off at the end of her first commission in 1945 in Newcastle, but Arthur Ayers, the Navigating Officer, scrupulously recorded many of the vital events for the talks that he gave in wartime to new joiners as they came on board. His records are to be found in the C.W.O.B.A. archives and are as accurate as his navigation of the Group in the wastes of the North Atlantic Ocean and the Norwegian Sea, before the days of armchair satellite navigation.

I am most grateful to the Naval Historical Branch who were extremely cooperative, to Mr. Coppock, to Fred Lake and particularly to Alan Francis who set me on the right track in my search for Captain Walker's original Reports of Proceedings and scores of other relevant documents in the Public Records Office.

Gillian Walker, Captain Walker's daughter was a WRNS driver in Liverpool at the height of the battle and Nicolas Walker, his son, served in *Woodcock*. Their help and recollections of their father have been invaluable, as have my colleagues' and contemporaries', John and Wendy

Filleul, Ceri and Vicky Fisher, and Bill Johnson.

The book has been brought to life by the people listed below, most of whom served in ships under Captain Walker's command and have written or spoken to me about him and life at sea in the Battle of the Atlantic:

Granville Allen	Lady Gretton	David Page
Derek Bagshaw	Mrs. Clive Gwinner	John Parnall
Derek Banham	Jack Hackman	W. Paton
Ken Bates	Ken Hawkins	Richard Phillimore
F, R, & J. Beckett	G. Hewett	Cliff Profitt
Jack Bishop	Alec Hinton	Derek Race
Frederick Bond	Stanley Hoare	Fred Glyn Samuel
Clem Bray	Danny Hogan	Sammy Saunders
L.C. Chappell	George Illston	Dudley Searcy
Frank Clarke	Lionel Irish	Tony Snelling
Fred Close	Tom James	Joe Smith
Denis Connolly	Eddie Keating	Richard Smith
Peter Davies	William Lethbridge	Bert Stanford
Bob Davis	Dennis Logan	Tom Teece
Alan Dewhurst	John Lownds	Fred Terreta
J. Dickie	R.S. Lumber	Tom Tribe
Reg Durrant	John Marston	Jim Trickett
Du Vivier, Captain, RN	Allen Martin	Peter Vanneck
Bert Entwistle	Leslie Martin	Gavin Wemyss
Peter Eustace	Len Matthews	Alfie West
Gerry Fitzgerald	Bill Mckay	Jimmy Westwood
Peter Francis	Conrad Meyer	George Wilson
John Gilligan	Gerald Mitchell	John Winslade
Patrick Glennie	Jack Moss	Ernie Woods
Cyril Gould	John Northmore	F.A. Woods
Albert Gore	Fred Orchard	Bill Wright
Ernie Green	Les Owen	Ron Young

The verse quoted on Page 24 was written by Frank Thompson, a Winchester scholar who left the school in 1939. During the war he was dropped into Europe to help the Bulgarian resistance, was captured and shot. He was the son of the First World War poet Edward Thompson.

I am particularly indebted to Captain Tony Sainsbury, RNR, for his contributions and corrections to the account of Convoy H.G. 76 in Chapter Two.

INTRODUCTION

Many people who read this book will have enjoyed the hospitality of the ships of the Royal Navy on Navy Days and on their visits to ports throughout the world in the course of their duties.

They will have been struck by the absence of portholes or indeed any openings through which the modern sailor can look out to the seas around him or to the coasts along which he is sailing. Only from the narrow slits of the enclosed bridge can the outside world be seen. The visitors will have seen the Commanding Officer's chair in the Operations Room, where he can sit in the centre of a platform insulated from vibration and survey a mass of instruments and screens which enable him to make the instant technical decisions which are vital in modern warfare. From this position, the whole operation of the ship is controlled.

The engine rooms are not manned when the ship is at Action Stations. The great brass telegraphs which conveyed the orders to the waiting stokers in the boiler rooms have gone. The weapons are directed and fired, and in most cases are even loaded and reloaded, by remote control. As they walk round the deck the visitors will have seen many notices, 'DANGER. THIS WEAPON MAY ROTATE AND FIRE WITHOUT WARNING'.

They will have been amazed at the mass of aerials attached to the tripod mast, some static and some rotating day and night, even when in harbour. Instead of a substantial wooden wheel with spokes to steer the ship, the coxswain uses a little joystick, but most of the time the course steered is automatically controlled, like an aircraft. To the old sailor, the only familiar pieces of equipment will be the compass repeaters and the signal lanterns, but he will be told that today these are very much the last resort for communication. If they should dare to touch them, they will find that their operating handles will be heavy and unresponsive from lack of use.

The modern frigate leaving Devonport in the dusk is a dark and menacing sight. Except for the bare minimum of navigation lights required of all ships by International Law, no glimmer of light can be seen from the grey hull as she eases her way past Devil's Point and down the deep-water channel to the open sea.

Captain Walker's ships were commanded from open bridges with no protection from the elements. The armament was manned, loaded and served by seamen exposed to spray, green water and sometimes snow and sleet. The stokers and engine-room crews worked below the waterline, behind double-clamped water and airtight doors. In action, Walker and his commanding officers were rarely absent from their crowded open bridges, except for visits to the plot in the wheelhouse to consult the navigator. In darkness, even these visits had to be kept to a minimum, for fear of losing night vision.

On many occasions, Walker and his key men transferred at sea from *Starling* to other ships of the Group. The only way to do this was by the old Montague Whaler under oars, pulled by five seamen, with a leading seaman at the helm. These sea boats were hoisted and lowered by manpower alone, with all hands tailing on to the falls.

Today's ocean racer has much better electronic navigation equipment and foul-weather gear than was available even to the Royal Navy in the Second World War, but otherwise will have no difficulty in imagining these conditions which were little different from those in which he now pursues his perverted sport.

GLOSSARY

Action Stations: complete readiness for immediate action.

Adrift: late or absent from place of duty.

Asdics: see Appendix 5, The Asdic System. Same as Sonar.

B-Dienst: Beobachter Dienst: The German counterpart to Bletchley Park.

Belay: make fast.

Belay the last pipe: ignore the last order.

Black Flag: hoisted by a ship running in to make a depth charge or Hedgehog attack.

Bletchley Park: the headquarters of the Government Code and Cypher School (GCCS) teams who worked on the decyphering of the German cyphers. See **Enigma** and **Ultra.**

Blind Period: see **Asdics,** Appendix 5. The period during which the attacking ship loses contact with the U-boat and the charges explode at the depth set.

Bogey: Enemy aircraft.

Boatswain's (Bosun's) Mate: quartermaster's assistant at sea and in harbour.

Buzz: Any rumour, however unreliable.

Bullring: The large fairlead on the very foremost point of the forecastle.

C.A.M.: Catapult Assisted Merchant Ship. A ship able to launch a fighter aircraft for a single flight, at the end of which the pilot had to ditch and hope to be picked up from the water.

Carley Float: unsinkable life raft. Sloops carried only two seaboats (whalers) which could be used as lifeboats, but which had a carrying capacity of only fifteen people in calm weather. In an emergency most of the remaining couple of hundred crew depended on Carley floats.

Cats: see **Foxers.**

Chernikeef Log: a retractable spinner protruding below the bottom of the hull which showed the distance run and the speed through the water.

Chippy: ship's carpenter: a useful accomplice in purveying **rabbits** qv.

Condenseritis: A recurring disease suffered by all ships when salt water penetrated the boiler tubes, making it necessary for the ship to return to harbour for repairs. Thought to have been used by Captain Walker as an excuse when nothing much was happening and he wanted to get back to put some forceful points requiring urgent action to his Commander-in-Chief.

Convoy Code: British and Allied Merchant Ship Code (BAMS). From the first day of World War One, the Germans were able without much interruption to decypher the wireless traffic going to and from Allied merchant ships which was hand-encyphered by out-of-date methods, a deadly advantage that they held until the summer of 1943 when at last the Admiralty changed its code.

Clear Lower Deck: the order given when all hands except those on watch were required.

Creeping Attack: see Appendix 6.

CWOBA: See p.189

Deckhead: ceiling.

Derby House: the headquarters in Liverpool of the Western Approaches Command.

D/F: direction-finding giving the bearing of wireless transmissions. See also **HF/DF**, high frequency direction-finding, one of the Allies' most powerful weapons which enabled them to locate the talkative U-boats.

Doppler: alteration in the pitch of the Asdic echo, indicating whether the U-boat was coming towards or going away from the attacking ship. A skilled Asdic operator, in good conditions, could give a subjective judgement of the course of a submerged U-boat and detect evasive action as it occurred.

Director Tower: the action station situated above and behind the bridge from which the guns were directed and fired.

Easy Item Turn. Method of altering course when disposed in line abreast. see note 11, chapter 9.

Enigma: the highly ingenious machine developed by the Germans and used by them for encyphering most of their enormous volume of wireless traffic. It was considered by them to be totally secure. Dönitz never believed that the Enigma codes could have been broken and put down our knowledge of his U-boat dispositions to long-range radar and aircraft sightings and to shore and ship-based D/F fixing of daily U-boat reports.

Fighting Lights: recognition lights on the crosstrees, used in emergencies to establish identity or whereabouts.

Fog Buoy: towed astern in fog or bad visibility to enable ships to keep in station with minimum risk of collision.

Force: see **Weather**.

Foxers: Noise-makers that could be towed astern as decoys for acoustic torpedoes (Gnats). These can be seen lying on top of the depth-charge racks in Plate 10. Later replaced by **Cats**, a more refined version.

Grey Funnel Line: The Royal Navy.

G.I.: Gunnery Instructor/Chief GI: The Senior Petty Officer in the gunnery department. Sometimes referred to as 'Chief Gunner's Mate'.

Guzz: Devonport.

Heave to: Hove to: Bringing a ship up to the wind and sea, with minimum speed to keep steerage way. The final resort in particularly vile weather and sea conditions, where survival and prevention of damage override all other priorities.

H.O.: Hostilities Only. Ratings or officers serving for 'the duration of the present emergency' (which, as far as the author knows, is still going on today).

HF/DF: See D/F.

Hooky (Killick): Leading Seaman with an anchor on his arm.

HSD: The highest ranked anti-submarine rating.

Jago's Mansion: Devonport Barracks.

Jury Rig: an emergency rig, for example to bring a damaged ship home.

Killick: see **Hooky**.

Kye: Standard Pusser's cocoa. Reputedly it should have enough body to enable the stirring spoon to stand up by itself. Has been described thus: 'Ah, luxury! Thick as the dimmest Ordinary Seaman.' Ranks next to **Nelson's Blood**, qv.

Masters-at-Arms: Formidable monsters with great disciplinary powers encountered in Big Ships, and shore establishments.

Mess Jug: each mess possessed one of these large cooking receptacles, used for all manner of eating, drinking and cooking purposes. In emergencies it could be put to other less conventional uses.

Nelson's Blood: a tot of rum. Twelve tots go to a bottle.

Number One: Jimmy, Jimmy the One: the First Lieutenant. The Senior Executive Lieutenant and second-in-command in the smaller warships.

Number Ones: best dress with gold badges, donned on ceremonial occasions or when going ashore.

Officer of the Watch: (O.O.W.): The officer in full charge and with full responsibility for the ship at sea, until formally relieved by a senior officer.

O.I.C.: Operational Intelligence Centre. The Admiralty intelligence centre to which all information, including **Ultra**, was sent. Duplicated in Liverpool.

Plaster: a variation of the creeping attack qv. See Appendix 6.

Pennants: the ship's identifying letter and numbers (painted on her side).

Piping: transmitting orders or marks of respect by means of the bosun's call. A pipe is the naval term for an order.

Plot: The minute-to-minute record kept of the ships' position and any attack or search. The Admiralty Research Laboratory (ARL) Plot did the basic work automatically, tended, augmented and interpreted by a team headed by Pilot, fed by information from the Asdic, the radar, and the HF/DF team.

Quartermaster: Steered the ship at sea and manned the gangway, running the ship's routine in harbour.

Q-Attachment: the beam of the basic Asdic projected in an almost horizontal plane below the hunting ship, like the fingers of a hand pointing diagonally downwards, giving a fairly accurate bearing and range of underwater objects, but no firm indication of the depth of the target. The Q-attachment was used as the range shortened: it transmitted a narrower beam in the vertical plane, from which could be deduced the depth of the target. Walker was offered the use of this latest development. Initially he resisted its installation in *Starling* because of the risk of breakdown of a newly introduced piece of equipment at a vital moment when in action at sea, but was using it effectively in his creeping attacks in early 1944.

Quarterdeck: the after deck. In escort vessels, almost entirely covered by depth-charge rails and throwers, ready-use racks and anti-aircraft armament.

Rescue Ships: vessels in the convoy which were specially equipped and manned to succour survivors picked up from torpedoed ships. Also fitted with HF/DF equipment for pinpointing U-boats gathering to strike. The target was to have one such vessel attached to each convoy.

Roll on my twelve: A naval prayer heard several times daily from long-service ratings looking forward to the end of their period of service.

Rabbits: items acquired for personal use by unorthodox and unofficial methods.

S.A.P.: semi-armour-piercing shells used against surface targets.

Ship's Company: Throughout this book this term has been used to indicate all officers and other ranks in the ship, but see *Admiralty Manual of Seamanship* (1951) p.753.

Snowflake: A powerful illuminant, issued to merchant ships as well as escort vessels. If the cloud base was not too low, snowflake rockets turned night into day, but could be extremely dangerous if used indiscriminately, since the firework display gave away the position of convoys and provided good aiming points for submerged U-boats.

Sonar: same as **Asdics**. See Appendix 5.

Splice the Mainbrace: 'The custom (dating back to 1756) of issuing an extra ration of spirit on occasions of particular arduous service or exposure': *Admiralty Manual of Seamanship* (1951) Vol. 1, p.265. Walker ordered the ships involved on each occasion that a U-boat was sunk to splice the mainbrace as soon as he was convinced that the job was done. *Starling* managed to take advantage of this privilege twice in one day on 24 June, 1943, after ramming *U-119* and after *U-449* was sunk, before setting off home, damaged, but in good heart. See Chapter Five.

Stringbag: An affectionate nickname for the antiquated Swordfish aircraft flown by Fleet Air Arm heroes from aircraft carriers. They were about all the Navy had in 1939. They were still in action in 1941, when they were responsible for crippling *Bismarck* by a torpedo hit on her steering gear and propellers, a fatal blow which led to her eventual destruction. The torpedo that disabled the most powerful battleship in the world was fired from a

Stringbag and has too often been referred to, even in responsible newspapers and publications, as a lucky hit. Where is the luck in achieving a defined objective, at the risk of one's life?

Stripey: an Able Seaman with three good conduct badges. A rare specimen of incalculable worth to any ship's company. His three badges seldom survived a really good run ashore.

T.B.S.: Talk between ships. Radio communication in plain language between ships. Used extensively by Captain Walker when directing creeping attacks.

Thrower: depth-charge throwers, four of which were positioned on the quarterdeck of each sloop, throwing charges out on either quarter to complete the pattern.

Three-Badger: see **Stripey.**

Tonnage: the tonnage of a warship is the amount that the vessel and everything on board weighs (displacement). The tonnage of a merchant ship is the amount that she carries (deadweight). The tonnage of a passenger ship is based on the enclosed space (gross registered tonnage).

Ultra: the highest category of secrecy for intelligence reports. Most information derived from Bletchley Park's deciphering of Enigma signals (q.v.) was in this category, usually restricted in ships at sea to a small list of selected Flag Officers. Walker was not on the list and received only heavily disguised information filtered through the Admiralty. This was subject to unavoidable delays in the process of interception, deciphering, translation and interpretation; the information had then to be re-enciphered in a lower category code and transmitted to the ship, where the wretched doctor or Captain's secretary would be dug out of his bunk to decypher it. This intelligence could be of great value, but rarely for operational purposes due to the time lag.

V.L.R.: Very Long Range Reconnaissance Aircraft.

Watches: The ships' companies were divided into watches. Ships were usually in three watches, called Cruising Stations, or at Action Stations. In harbour, a four-watch system was often used to allow everyone the maximum time ashore or on leave when the opportunity occurred.

Whaler: The Montague Whaler was the standard twenty-seven foot seaboat in the sloops and in most destroyer escorts. In these ships the term 'whaler' and 'sea boat' were interchangeable.

Weather: Wind Speeds are measured on the Beaufort Scale from 0 upwards. Force Eight is a Full Gale. In this wind force it is impossible, during gusts to walk across Liverpool's Prince's Pier in a naval great coat. Force Ten is a Hurricane as described in note 3 to chapter six. If you didn't wish to experience these conditions you should never have joined.

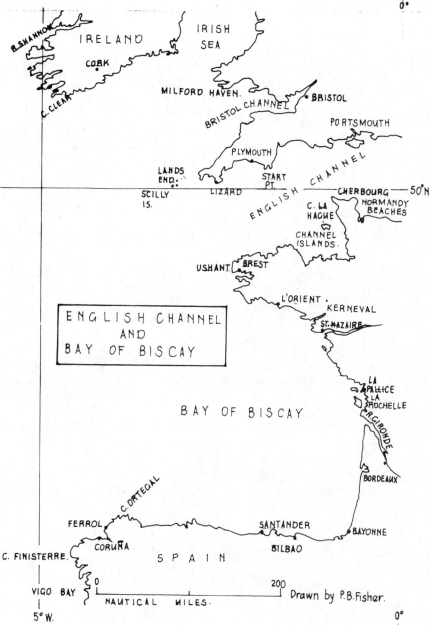

ENGLISH CHANNEL
AND
BAY OF BISCAY

IRELAND

IRISH SEA

R. SHANNON
C. CLEAR
CORK

MILFORD HAVEN.
BRISTOL CHANNEL
BRISTOL
PORTSMOUTH
PLYMOUTH
LANDS END
STILLY IS.
LIZARD
START PT.
ENGLISH CHANNEL
CHERBOURG — 50°N
C. LA HAGUE
NORMANDY BEACHES
CHANNEL ISLANDS.

USHANT.
BREST
L'ORIENT
KERNEVAL
ST. NAZAIRE

BAY OF BISCAY

LA PALLICE
LA ROCHELLE
R. GIRONDE
BORDEAUX

C. ORTEGAL
FERROL
CORUÑA
SANTANDER
BAYONNE
C. FINISTERRE.
BILBAO
SPAIN

VIGO BAY

0   200

NAUTICAL   MILES.

Drawn by P.B. Fisher.

5° W.   0°

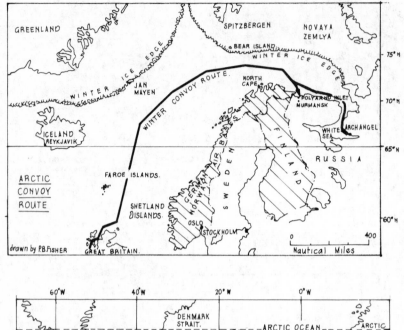

GREENLAND SPITZBERGEN NOVAYA ZEMLYA

BEAR ISLAND

WINTER ICE EDGE

WINTER ICE EDGE

JAN MAYEN

WINTER CONVOY ROUTE

NORTH CAPE

POLYARNO INLET
MURMANSK

ICELAND
REYKJAVIK

WHITE SEA ARCHANGEL

FINLAND

RUSSIA

ARCTIC
CONVOY
ROUTE

FAROE ISLANDS.

GERMAN NORWAY AIR BASES

SWEDEN

75°N

70°N

65°N

60°N

SHETLAND ISLANDS

OSLO STOCKHOLM

drawn by P.B.Fisher

GREAT BRITAIN.

0   400

Nautical Miles

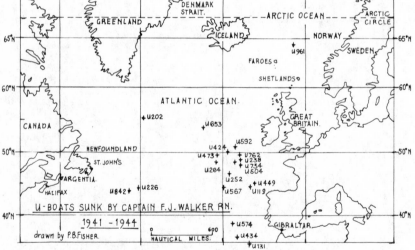

60°W   40°W   20°W   0°W

DENMARK
STRAIT.

GREENLAND

ARCTIC OCEAN

ARCTIC
CIRCLE

ICELAND

NORWAY

65°N

SWEDEN

✝U961

FAROES

65°N

SHETLANDS

60°N

60°N

ATLANTIC OCEAN.

GREAT
BRITAIN.

✝U202

✝U653

CANADA

U424
U592

NEWFOUNDLAND

U473✝

✝U762
✝U238
✝U734
U604

50°N

50°N

ST. JOHN'S

U204

✝ARGENTIA.

U252

✝U449

✝U842 ✝U226

U567 U119

HALIFAX

U-BOATS SUNK BY CAPTAIN F.J. WALKER RN.

40°N

1941 - 1944

✝U574

GIBRALTAR

40°N

drawn by P.B.Fisher.

0   600

NAUTICAL MILES.

✝U434

✝U131

PROLOGUE

On the morning of 31 January, the sloops were sweeping ahead of the carriers at twelve knots, one mile apart, in the order from port to starboard, *Wild Goose, Magpie, Starling, Wren, Woodpecker*. The two aircraft carriers were zigzagging 7½ cables apart and two miles astern. At 1015 the carriers were taking advantage of a break in the weather to operate their aircraft: *Nairana* was heading out towards *Wild Goose* as she turned into the wind. *Kite* had just caught up with the group and was closing from astern.

At 1015 Wemyss was below in the chart house with his navigator when his Asdic operator picked up a doubtful echo at the end of one his sweeps, on his starboard beam, half-way between *Wild Goose* and *Magpie*.

If this was a U-boat, it had nearly slipped through the sloops' line and was already in position to loose off a torpedo at *Nairana*.

Before Wemyss had reached the bridge, the echo had been classified as 'Submarine' and *Wild Goose* was turning to starboard under full wheel: the Officer of the Watch had immediately dropped her speed to seven knots to avoid attracting a Gnat while she was beam on and had warned off the carriers by R/T.

Wemyss had a few seconds in which to make up his mind. As soon as he was bows on to the bearing of the U-boat, he increased to full speed and went straight in for an immediate attack. As the black flag, signifying 'Attacking', broke out from the crosstrees, the aircraft carriers heeled over and scuttled off to starboard. Walker detailed *Kite, Wren* and *Woodpecker* to shepherd them away, while *Magpie* and *Starling* came in to join *Wild Goose* who was already dropping a pattern of charges to drive the U-boat down.

It was touch and go. The carriers and the sloops in the attack were all fine targets and within range of a Gnat, but *Wild Goose*'s immediate reaction and attack might just have put the U-boat off its aim or delayed the firing for long enough for the carriers' alteration of course to take effect.

Six minutes later, *Magpie* came with another attack, using her Hedgehog.

Neither of these attacks were successful: but the immediate danger to *Nairana* was past, and she had survived by the narrowest of margins.

'Unquestionably *Nairana* was saved by *Wild Goose*'s exemplary speed and decision. Another minute or two and she would have been a sitter.... *Wild Goose* handed me Asdic contact with the Boche on a plate. I could ask nothing better than to take the field again partnered by this doughty well-trained warrior.'

Conditions for Asdics were good, but the wind was rising and the sea was beginning to get up. This would not affect the U-boat, which had dived deep, but in these conditions time was on the side of the Germans. Walker called *Wild Goose* alongside. Communications between these two veteran ships was so good that by 1040, nineteen minutes later, the two ships had stationed themselves astern of the U-boat and *Starling* went in to attack.

The long series of twenty-six explosions started and continued at five-second intervals as the heavy charges rumbled down the rails and curved out from the throwers on either quarter.

A few seconds after the fourteenth charge disappeared over the stern, there were two almost simultaneous explosions: the first was part of the normal pattern, set to explode seven hundred feet down and not very dramatic. The second was far more frightening, heavy, inexplicable and totally unexpected, throwing up a huge hill of water, ten yards from *Starling*'s starboard quarter.

The great mass of water climbed higher than the ship's masthead and seemed to hang for seconds over the quarterdeck. The ship jerked unnaturally as if she had come up all standing on a rock. A fully primed depth charge was hurled over the side and another fell five feet onto the steel deck. Neither exploded. All the electrical switches were thrown in the power room.

Tons of solid green water began to descend on top of the depth-charge crews. As the water cascaded over the side, they emerged soaked, shaken, some badly bruised but still pushing out the remainder of the pattern.

Starling shook herself. The quarterdeck emerged from the water. Depth charges continued to leave the ship in the strict pattern of the creeping attack. There was no hitch or delay in the drill.

At 1132½ John Filleul was able to report that the pattern had been fired. He didn't sound excited or upset, but at that time he didn't know that the explosion had shattered the contents of the wardroom wine store (a repetition of *Deptford*'s escapade with *Stork*).

This was a remarkable effort by the depth charge crews carrying out their drills amidst feet of swirling water thrown on board by the explosion. But the successful completion of the attack was only made possible by the gallantry of Stoker Wilfred Mockridge, battened down below in the bowels of the ship in the power room with the watertight doors shut all round him. He was knocked off his feet: when he got up he saw by the dim emergency lighting that the main electrical switches had been thrown open by the shock. On his own initiative he immediately put them all back and so restored the ship to normal in a few seconds.

Three minutes later the Asdic team reported a heavy underwater explosion, just before *Wild Goose*'s follow-up pattern started to explode.

There were tapping and banging noises and two more explosions. Oil, wood, coats, books, clothes and human remains came up to the surface, to be collected by *Wild Goose*. The Asdic echo faded as the remains of *U-592* and its crew went on its long journey to the ocean bed 2500 fathoms below.

CHAPTER ONE

INTERWAR YEARS

At the outbreak of World War Two, Commander Frederic John Walker had devoted the thirty years of his naval career to the development of anti-submarine tactics and weapons. He believed that the outcome of the struggle would depend on the defeat of the German U-boats under Karl Dönitz. The Navy had not recognized Walker's outstanding personal and professional qualifications until the end of 1941 when he went to sea in command of the small sloop *Stork*. From then on, his impact on the war against the U-boats as a Fighting Captain was immediate and dramatic. He was considered by his Commander-in-Chief, Admiral Sir Max Horton, and by the Admiralty to have done more to win the Battle of the Atlantic than any other officer at sea.

Karl Dönitz was *Führer der U-Boote* and remained in active control of the U-boats throughout the war, even when he became an Admiral and Commander-in-Chief of the German Navy. He was a submariner, and believed passionately that Germany's only hope of ultimate victory lay in the destruction of the Allied shipping on the Trade Routes leading to the United Kingdom. Only the U-boats could achieve this. He was single-minded, unswerving and ruthless in the pursuit of this one objective. Had he been permitted by Hitler, and if the German High Command had granted the priorities in men, materials and air support that he demanded, the course and even the outcome of the Battle of the Atlantic could have been very different. However, he was frustrated by Hitler, the Naval High Command, and particularly by Goering in failing to provide the air support that he needed. He was able to inspire blind courage and loyalty from his U-boat commanders and men. 40,000 of them served at sea in the most appalling conditions. 28,000 of these were casualties, many of whom suffered ghastly deaths.

This is an account of the life at sea of Frederic John Walker, who dedicated his life to defeating the Germans, and Dönitz in particular, by containing the U-boats, wearing them down, and sending them scurrying back to their bunkers. Walker resembled Dönitz in that he shared a single-minded belief in the importance of his mission and inspired total loyalty. He differed in many ways, not least in his deep respect for the lives of British seamen.

Only three of the scores of warships that came under his command were lost. In the ships and men of the Second Support Group which he led during his greatest successes, there were no casualties at all due to enemy action, either in the warships or the merchant ships which he was defending.

Johnnie Walker was born on 3 June, 1896, and entered the Royal Navy on 15 June, 1909. He made an impressive start to his career, passed out top of his class at the Royal Naval College at Dartmouth, received the King's Medal and did well in his examinations in the training cruiser. In June, 1914, he went to sea as a midshipman in the battleship *Ajax* and stayed with this ship until his promotion to sub-lieutenant on 1st January, 1916, when he moved to a smaller ship, *Mermaid*, based on Dover. In 1917 he moved on to *Sarpedon*, a destroyer whose main function was to screen the big ships in the Grand Fleet from submarine attack. Thus, at the age of 21, in the First World War, he became involved in the battle against the U-boats. Anti-submarine warfare, (and small ships when he was allowed to serve in them), were to be his two main interests for the remaining 27 years of his life in the Service.

In October, 1918, a promising young German U-boat commander lost his U-boat, *UB-68*, in the Mediterranean during its first operational cruise under his command. During an attack he surfaced out of control in the middle of a convoy, was holed by an escort's gunfire, abandoned ship, and was picked up with all his crew except his engineer officer whom he had ordered back into the boat to open the vents.

He remained in captivity for some months after the end of the war in a prisoner-of-war fortress in Malta and finished up in England, first in a camp near Sheffield and then in the Manchester Lunatic Asylum, according to the British Intelligence file.[1] His name was Karl Dönitz.

Dönitz returned to a defeated Germany in July, 1919. There had been a mutiny in the German Navy in 1918 and Dönitz was personally involved in 1920 in putting down a particularly unpleasant incident which involved bad feelings between the ratings and the officer class. He was given command of a Torpedo Boat, `ᴠ` *157*, one of the twelve allowed to the Germans by the Versailles Treaty. Morale was at rock bottom except in these flotillas, whose crews considered themselves to be a cut above the rest. Through this involvement, in 1922 he was already leading the rebirth of the U-boat fleet, which was to be centred round a nucleus being surreptitiously constructed in Holland.

In 1919 Johnnie Walker married Eilleen Stobart. It was to be a very happy marriage, but from then on his wife and, in due course, his three sons and his daughter competed for his time and his loyalty. He came from a naval family. His father, Frederic Murray Walker and his brother William Baggot Walker (who married Eilleen's sister Peggy), were also Captains in the Royal Navy.

As the First World War drew to its close, he was sent back to the battleship *Valiant* as a watchkeeping officer. In 1921, making a determined effort to learn more about the subject which he had identified as the key to any future naval conflict, he was one of the first volunteers to go to the specialist courses at the newly formed anti-submarine school, HMS *Osprey*, at Portland. It was a courageous and far-sighted decision because, between the wars, this was not a fashionable or glamorous branch and was the least likely route for promotion to high rank. It was considered by many to be a bit of a backwater, rather like being an officer in the engineering branch, sometimes referred to in those days as 'plumbers'.

When he had completed this course the Admiralty sent him off to sea for six years (1925-31) in the largest ships that they could find, as far away from home as possible. He was appointed Fleet Anti-Submarine Officer in the Atlantic and the Mediterranean Fleets. First he went to the battleship *Revenge*, then to the Flagship *Nelson*, and finally the battleship *Queen Elizabeth*, and in these appointments he became increasingly disillusioned with peacetime service in the Big Ships.

It was not until 1933 that he was given a break. He was promoted at the last moment to Commander and to his delight was given command (albeit at the advanced age of 37) of *Shikari*. This destroyer was fitted with Asdic, the Royal Navy's anti-submarine detection equipment, on which the Naval Staff pinned their firm belief for the protection of convoys against submarines. Once again Walker was involved with the latest thinking on the subject of his choice but this time, best of all, in a small ship, under his direct command.

However, this appointment lasted for only six months, and in 1936 he was appointed to command the sloop *Falmouth*, used as the Commander-in-Chief's yacht on the China Station. This was an inspired bad choice of appointment. It might have been the perfect job for a bland, diplomatic officer and a driving ambitious wife with social aspirations, but Commander Johnnie Walker and Eilleen had none of these characteristics.

Nevertheless, he had to spend three years in this ship, moving his command around to suit the convenience of the C-in-C. His character was too strong to allow him to make a success of this job and during these important years he had little hope of a normal family life with his wife and family. Eilleen had been seriously ill when in China and had to submit to two major operations. Even though Timothy had got a scholarship to Eton, Walker was broke. In 1936, at the age of forty, he was a frustrated man, and the last thing that may have been held against him was his suggestion to the

6

Commander-in-Chief's wife that he would prefer to take his orders from the Commander-in-Chief direct.[2]

It was shortly after this that he completed his time in the Far East and returned home, preceded by unenthusiastic reports.

Sixteen years after he had left her as a Lieutenant, he was back where he started in *Valiant* but this time as her Commander.[3] During the interwar years, the Navy had been starved of funds. All ships wear out, particularly when inadequate funds have been allocated for their maintenance and improvement over a prolonged period, and *Valiant* was no exception. The job of the Commander of a battleship required total dedication, even if the ship was fresh from the builder's yard, but no one could have relished the task that now passed to Walker, entrusted with the thankless job of looking after an old ship for an ambitious commanding officer, Captain G.S. Arbuthnot, who was on the short list for promotion to Rear-Admiral.[4] When Walker left *Valiant* in early 1937, he had accumulated further bad reports.

In 1937 he became Experimental Commander in the Anti-Submarine School in Portland, and was responsible for research and development of anti-submarine materials and methods, an appointment which he held until the outbreak of the Second World War. This was without doubt the most important appointment that he had held in his naval career up to that time.

It was also one of the happiest periods in his life. Even when it became clear that he had missed the opportunity for promotion to Captain, his professional disappointment was offset by his responsibility for anti-submarine research, since it was becoming more and more likely that the Navy would shortly be in action again and that his specialized knowledge would be badly needed.

Just as important to him was the happiness of his home life. He and Eileen were both deeply religious and thoughtful people; they had three children at crucial stages of their lives. Timothy had joined the Roman Catholic Church and was going from Eton for training as a priest in the English College in Rome.[5] Nicolas was thirteen and Gillian was twelve. For the first time he was able to take a family house and return to his wife and children in the evening. For a Naval Officer, this was a dream not often fulfilled.

In spite of the Treaty of Versailles, secret plans to renew construction of U-boats had been put in hand by the Germans in 1922. This was done, with great stealth initially, using a Dutch shipbuilder, Ingenieurkantoor voor Scheepsbauw (IvS), funded by the Germans, and run by German shipbuilders and 'retired' German naval officers. Contracts were made for the construction of U-boats in Spain, and U-boats were delivered to Turkey and Finland manned by German crews who then carried on with the training. In this way the technical skills of construction, of equipment development and of crewing were kept alive and the development of the U-boats so successfully used in the First World War was continued.

There was nothing very secret about this activity after 1927 when the whole picture was exposed to the world by a German newspaper, the *Berliner Tageblatt*, which published full details of the companies involved and the fact that they were financed by the German High Command.

At that point, anyone who could read a German newspaper could see plainly how the Treaty of Versailles was being broken and the U-boat fleet being rebuilt. A few people in the German Defence Ministry were sacked or hidden for a while, or sent to sea, but it is difficult to understand why British diplomats at the highest level continued negotiations right up to the date when the Treaty was formally repudiated in 1935, and seemed to put faith in the words spoken and the bits of paper signed.

All these plans for the continued construction of U-boats were made and implemented long before Hitler had become the power in the land.

In 1936, when Dönitz took up command as *Führer der U-boote* (FdU), he set up an intensive training campaign for his future U-boat crews in the Baltic. He did not share the British Admiralty's great faith in the much-vaunted Asdic system, but treated the U-boat as a fast torpedo boat with an extensive endurance and the convenient ability to disappear below the surface of the sea during daylight hours. At night it could surface in an attacking position, almost invisible to the cumbersome merchant ships, manoeuvre at double their speed and disappear at the approach of enemy escorts. So, with minimum facilities, Dönitz was able to practise the tactics which he had evolved for the wolf packs using his fleet of torpedo boats in the Baltic.

Hitler described 18 June, 1935, as the happiest day of his life: on that day he had signed the Anglo-German Naval Agreement. This permitted the Germans, with few restrictions, to build warships, including submarines, to the limit of their capacity and beyond, an Agreement described by Churchill as 'the acme of gullibility', against which he protested twice in vain. The Admiralty appeared to have borrowed Nelson's blind eye at this time. When this Treaty was signed, Admiral Beatty told the House of Lords that 'There was at least one country with which Britain need not fear an armaments race'. The Chief of the German Naval Staff said that this Treaty rendered a repetition of the former rivalry with the Royal Navy impossible and forbade any reference being made to a future conflict with Britain, even in contingency planning.

By 1939, the British had completed the process of reducing their escort fleet to 201 from 477 in 1918.[6] There were only 100[7] destroyers left, barely sufficient to screen the battle fleets, and there were only 101 escort destroyers and sloops to defend the vast fleet of merchant ships needed to supply

Britain. At any one time there were 2,500 of these spread over the oceans of the world. As we shall see none of these escorts were fit for the tasks that they were required to perform and only a few of them could hope to face up to Atlantic Ocean weather conditions. There were no plans to build and man the numbers of escorts that would be needed.

British naval strategy was based on the assumption that there would be an Anglo-French Alliance, with a friendly and effective French Fleet lined up against Germany, Italy and Japan. The Asdic system would provide adequate protection for the Allied merchant ships in convoy.

German Naval strategy was based on Hitler's fantasy, the Z plan, envisaging an additional six 56,000 ton battleships, twelve 30,000 ton battle cruisers, eight aircraft carriers and 249 U-boats, all to be commissioned over the next ten years. Dönitz was not consulted about the strength of the U-boat arm and Hitler repeatedly told Admiral Raeder that he would not want this fleet before 1946.

Thus it came about that neither the British nor the Germans were ready for a naval conflict. The British convoy escorts were totally inadequate and the German construction plans were based on fundamental mistakes about the timing and need for a new fleet and its composition.

Nevertheless, on 3 September, 1939, the signal 'Total Germany' went out in plain language to the British Fleets. It was intercepted by the Germans and handed to Dönitz and to Raeder. They were both shattered. Raeder's reaction was that the Kriegsmarine could only show how to 'die with honour'. He had told the officers of the U-boat arm on 22 July, 1939, that war with Britain would mean *'Finis Germaniae'*. Dönitz had been more realistic: he had already deployed his entire operational fleet of fifty-seven U-boats in the waters surrounding the British Isles.

They had instructions to observe the Prize Regulations. These Regulations laid down that a U-boat should surface and then halt and examine its prize and cargo. If satisfied that it was entitled to sink the ship, it should first ensure the safety of those on board.

Ignoring these orders, on this first day of the war, *U-30* torpedoed and sank the liner *Athenia* without warning. There were 1100 passengers on board of whom 300 were Americans.

Of the 112 people who lost their lives, 28 were Americans. This was a mistake, and in flagrant disobedience of orders by the U-boat commander, but on return to harbour the matter was hushed up and the U-boat's log was doctored.[8] A series of conflicting instructions poured out from Hitler to the U-boat commanders, but within weeks it was clear that unrestricted submarine warfare was coming back.

The initial impact of the U-boats in the opening months was quite spectacular. The Royal Navy's aircraft carrier, *Ark Royal*, was attacked (and saved by the first failure of the Germans' faulty torpedoes). *Courageous* was sunk with a loss of over 500 of her ship's company. Scapa Flow, the base of the Home Fleet , was penetrated and the battleship *Royal Oak* went down at her moorings, sunk by *U-47*. On their return to harbour the whole U-boat's crew were taken up to Berlin to meet Hitler and every one of them received an Iron Cross. In the first three months, 114 Allied merchant ships of 421,156 tons were sunk, for the loss of nine U-boats.

The Battle of the Atlantic, which was to last 68 months, had been joined. It has been described as:

'One of the most vital, protracted and bitterly fought sea and air campaigns in which the British Empire and her Allies have ever been engaged.'[9]

Walker was appointed Staff Officer Operations to Vice-Admiral B.H. Ramsay based at Dover, responsible for the safe passage of the British Expeditionary Force and all its supplies and vehicles across the English Channel. When this had been achieved, he had the same responsibility for the 200,000 men crossing the Channel in each direction on leave. By June, 1940, about half a million men and 89,000 vehicles had made the journey without loss. Initially the main threat came from the U-boats, but once the Channel was blocked they were barred from using the Straits of Dover as a route for leaving their German and Baltic Sea bases on their way to their operating areas in the Atlantic Oceans and beyond. Only one got through.

While the 'phoney war' simmered ashore, the Norwegian campaign hit the Royal Navy. This was the first clash between the surface forces of the Allies and the Germans and resulted in the loss of fifteen Allied warships, including one aircraft carrier, one sloop and seven destroyers, and a further ten damaged. Our escort forces were thus deprived of eighteen vessels.

These losses were serious enough, but much worse was to follow. The Navy was still deeply involved in the Norwegian campaign when Hitler opened his campaign in the Low Countries and by the middle of May the Dutch had surrendered. Vice-Admiral Bertram Ramsay, Walker's boss, was Flag-Officer, Dover, in charge not only of the evacuation of the B.E.F. via the ports of the Lowlands, Dunkirk, Calais and Boulogne, but also of the demolition of the ports of the Lowlands, and the provision of naval covering fire.

It is beyond the scope of this book to attempt to describe this evacuation, but the effect on our already depleted force of destroyers and escorts, and so on the Battle of the Atlantic, was devastating. Of the 338,000 troops brought out, 103,000 were carried by the destroyers. The Royal Navy paid for this by the loss of another sloop and nine destroyers sunk, and nineteen more damaged. So, in these two months, forty-seven escorts were put out of action, of which the effect is best described in the words of the official historian.

> 'The Destroyers led the operation with selfless gallantry and suffered most heavily. And those losses were felt grievously during the anxious months that followed, when every flotilla vessel was needed in the struggle for control of the ocean communications.'[10]

The last ship to leave Dunkirk at 0340 on 4 June was the destroyer *Shikari*, which Walker had commanded in 1933.

For Walker at Dover the evacuation was followed by an intense period of activity scouring the small commercial ports and fishing centres for trawlers and drifters to set up a system of patrols whose task was to make quite certain that no surprise crossing in strength could take place. If an attempt was made, it could not be prevented, but at least the landing force would be detected before it could establish a foothold on the coast. By 10 July Churchill felt able to announce that the Admiralty had over a thousand armed patrolling vessels (the Auxiliary Patrol). Of these thousand vessels, two or three hundred might be at sea at any one time covering the hundreds of miles of coast line from Flamborough Head to Plymouth. Their armament was comparable to that of the Home Guard. Never before in the history of conflict has so much been said about so little.

In these tasks Walker saw the emergence of air power as the dominant factor in naval sea power in all its branches and he also came into contact with the huge mass of reservists who would come to man the ships which he would command in the Western Approaches. There was a sparse scattering of fine experienced seamen amongst the reservists, but they were untrained in the skills of war and the ways of the Service, and lacked the discipline of the regulars who had been his constant companions during the whole of his working life in the Big Ships, the Fleet Flotillas and the shore establishments of the Royal Navy.

In the four months between June and September, 1940, two priorities competed for naval facilities already stretched close to breaking point. One was to concentrate the available naval strength in a defensive role to repel an invasion, at the expense of defending our vital fuel and food convoys. The other was to apply such strength as we had to the protection of our ocean convoys and the destruction of U-boats, and to risk the Germans getting a foothold on the south coast of England.

The Admiralty could not possibly meet both these immediate threats. In the event, the defence of convoys was sacrificed, and sinkings of Allied shipping rose to horrifying levels. The U-boats achieved nothing at Dunkirk, but immediately afterwards, in the month of June alone, merchant ship sinkings rose to 585,000 tons (140 ships). Although there was only an average of fifteen U-boats operational in the Atlantic, they nevertheless sunk half this tonnage.

Walker tried every way to get to sea. The whole of his naval career had been devoted to preparation for this emergency and for the fight against the U-boat. It was no time to be shore-based in Dover, passively submitting to bombardment from the German guns firing across the Straits from their positions on Cap Gris Nez.

Fortunately he was under the command of Admiral Bertram Ramsay. Ramsay, who had not only seen Walker's performance under pressure during the evacuation from Dunkirk (for which he was mentioned in despatches) but who was also sympathetic to his cause since he had himself been retired early from the Navy during the inter-war years because he was not permitted to get on with the work that he had been given to do. Like Walker he was put to one side in peace time and became essential in war.

Walker also made a journey to put his case to his old friend and colleague, Captain George Creasy, the Director of Anti-Submarine Warfare, who knew best of all how badly the battle against the U-boats needed senior officers with Walker's deep technical knowledge of this specialized type of warfare.

It took a long time for his pleas to take effect. There were very few ships in 1940 and 1941 and many officers who could not wait to get back to sea, but at last Walker's name came to the attention of Admiral Sir Percy Noble, the Commander-in-Chief Western Approaches who had moved his Headquarters to Liverpool. In September, 1941, Commander F. J. Walker RN was appointed to command HMS *Stork* based in Liverpool under Sir Percy Noble.

The men in Walker's family now went to sea, with Timothy, back from Rome, now an ordinary seaman, Nicolas a midshipman and Commander Walker the Commanding Officer of His Majesty's Ship *Stork*.

And through the heat of conflict, keeps the law,
In calmness made, and sees what he foresaw . . . .
This is the happy Warrior, this is He
That every man in arms should wish to be.

CHAPTER TWO

WALKER GOES TO SEA

Stork was one of the Black Swan class sloops, built to prewar specifications and well suited to the job of ocean escort. At the same time Walker was to assume command of the 36th Support Group, consisting of two sloops and six corvettes.[1]

He had sought this challenge, but before his Group went off to their sea duties, each ship except *Stork* and the Group as a whole was put through an intensive working-up programme. The wisdom of the Royal Navy, accumulated over the centuries and reinforced by experience hard-won in 1939 and 1940, had shown that the best results were obtained when ships in a Group trained and worked together in conditions that were as close as possible to those that they would experience in action, even if the abilities and capabilities of the individual ships varied considerably. By going through this training together with their ships' companies, the commanding officers got to know each other.

To bring each ship to the highest state of efficiency possible in the short time available, Commodore 'Monkey' Stephenson had set up a training base, HMS *Western Isles*, at Tobermory on the west coast of Scotland.

As a rule, every ship in the Western Approaches Command spent a very uncomfortable month working up under this 'retired' Vice-Admiral[2] and his eager staff before taking up their ocean escorting duties. During this month every moment was deliberately packed with tension and exertion. Damage control crews learnt the position of every valve, so that they could be located blindfolded in the total darkness of a closed compartment below the waterline. Guns' crews learnt to get off six broadsides in thirty seconds, on a rolling wet deck with another turret firing over their heads.

Towing warps were rigged and taken over to 'damaged' flotilla mates in sea-boats under oars.

Steering engines broke down. All electrical circuits failed. The cypher officer lost his cypher books. The galley stove was put out of action. High-pressure hoses knocked ammunition parties off their feet. The ship's boats fell off their davits. Heavy depth charges were manhandled from ship to ship. Ladders between decks went missing.

'Stand by to ram. Where's the Officer of the Watch's kye? Roll on my Twelve. Fire in the Transmitting Station. Fire Number one thrower set to shallow. Torpedo starboard! Lower the port seaboat. Rig scrambling nets. Clear lower deck, hoist the starboard whaler. Wire round the port screw. Ship not answering her helm, – head paying off to starboard. Stream a fog buoy. Echo-sounding broken down, take a sounding with a lead line and report the nature of the bottom. Depth charge adrift on deck starboard side aft.

'Doctor required for an emergency operation in another ship. Rum jars broached by a near miss, what's your first action? Periscope to starboard. How far? Thirty yards. Open Fire! five rounds bearing green five-oh. Starboard bridge oerlikon jammed. Up Spirits! Belay the last pipe. Action Stations. Away boarding party, carry out 'Operation Haggis'.[3] Man the side, Captain's coming on board. Moor to twin anchors in position X. There's somebody there already. Motor boat's gone adrift. Away U-boat boarding party. Recover that torpedo.

'Take a fix on that light. Fighting Lights – Move! What's the recognition signal? Which side do I leave that boom defence vessel? Man Overboard – submarine echo bearing 065°, range 700 yards. Launch two Carley floats. B magazine flooded. No reply from the after steering position. 'Officer of the Watch sir, I've just shot a prisoner by mistake.' U-boat crews boarding over the quarterdeck. Officer of the Day, there's a large drunken three-badged able seaman about to hit you.

'The Captain's car has just arrived alongside. Where's the quartermaster? In the Captain's bath. Helm's jammed to port – She's broaching. What's our longitude? Sorry, the chronometer wasn't wound up. Where's Ordinary Seaman Burn? Fallen down the funnel, sir. Get him out. Board that merchant ship. Recover the sea-boat, holed on the rocks up the river. Weigh anchor by hand. Rig a jury wireless mast. Signal log gone over the side. Prepare gear and take on fifty tons of oil fuel and thirty depth charges from that tanker.

'And when you've done that lot and are climbing into your hammock – Get out and do it again, but this time faster. You heard the pipe, get fell in.'

For the young recruit who had just completed his three months' shore training, it might have seemed that the instructors were being unnecessarily bloody-minded, but at this stage of the war there were enough people around him who had seen and heard a tanker go up in a sheet of flame, or had been picked out of a freezing bog of oil-fuel on a dark Atlantic night, to convince him that the effort was worthwhile.

'There is no better bailer than a frightened man with a bucket.'

Walker accepted that this battle school made a major contribution to the efficiency of the ships in the Western Approaches, but the ships which he personally commanded, *Stork* and *Starling*, never went to Tobermory, because he was not prepared to delegate this function outside the ship itself. He trained his own men through his own officers and never relinquished this responsibility.

As soon as the training of the officers and ships' companies at Tobermory came to an end, Walker took his ships to sea and set about developing and practising Group tactics, aiming to build up an empathy among his commanding officers which would enable them to act on their own initiative in any circumstances without the need for long-winded instructions.

In contrast, Dönitz required his commanders to report in daily and to await his final decision before launching their attacks on the convoys. When we come to look at the effect of Ultra on the course of the campaign, it will be seen that this German principle of centralization came to be a major factor in the initial containment and final defeat of the U-boat offensive.

At the end of November the 36th Escort Group sailed from Liverpool with a convoy bound for Gibraltar and ran into a series of particularly ferocious gales. This introduction to the grey hostile element of the Atlantic Ocean was extremely unpleasant, but for a new group of ships, manned by many inexperienced ships' companies, it had advantages because the effectiveness of U-boat operations was very much reduced by bad weather conditions.

Most of the German training, although excellent in many ways, was carried out in the enclosed waters of the Baltic, the only area available to them, but very different from the Atlantic conditions. The U-boats had very little freeboard when surfaced. In quite moderate ocean conditions their decks were washed from end to end. The lookouts and the officer on the conning tower had to be lashed to their stations to prevent them being carried overboard. The driving spray rendered their binoculars useless for most of the time and visibility was very limited. When submerged in bad weather, it was more comfortable but observation through the periscope was quite ineffective, so that the boats were operating blind.

Because of the atrocious weather, the ships of the 36th Escort Group were not bothered by the enemy during their journey down to Gibraltar in November, 1941. The training on board continued without relaxation, under very real sea conditions. Naval guns' crews and the crews loading and priming depth-charges had an additional complication with which army gunners do not have to cope. They handled their ammunition from a platform which was never still, never on an even keel, and was intermittently covered with swirling water. By the end of this period, Walker's sailors had begun to find their sea-legs. For the unfortunate minority who still suffered from the hell of seasickness, there was little, too little, sympathy. Able Seaman Clem Bray remembers that he was sick as the proverbial parrot for three days and that he wished with all his heart that he had been torpedoed.

The next few weeks were occupied in patrolling the Straits of Gibraltar, which, in the absence of any contact with the enemy, gave further opportunities to exercise ship-handling and Group manoeuvres, this time in quite restricted waters.

Walker and his ships were now ready to take their place on the Gibraltar run. This was the route which was now under the greatest threat. Convoys bound for Liverpool (code-named HG) had to pass first up the length of the coast of Portugal and Spain. In peacetime they would have hugged the coast of Portugal as far as Cape Finisterre, before striking out across the Bay of Biscay, but this shortest route was now barred to them by the threat from the U-boats based in the Bay of Biscay ports, stretching from Brest, Lorient, and St Nazaire down to La Rochelle and Bordeaux. Focke-Wulf patrols based in the Bordeaux area operated outside the range of the Allied patrols from the British Isles and could pick up the convoys and guide in the wolf packs stationed by Dönitz in a line right across their route home. Commodores of convoys dreaded the sight of a shadowing aircraft hovering out of range just above the horizon, which was the first physical warning of a probable massed attack.

From the autumn of 1940 the number of U-boats coming out of the German yards had started to rise. After June, 1941, the rise was dramatic. Fortunately for the Allies, there was a long delay before these boats reached operational standards. By December, 1941, there were 88 operational boats out of a total U-boat fleet of 268, (in spite of losses of 47) and a further 19/20 per month were planned for 1942.[4]

With this increase in the number of operational U-boats, Dönitz had planned to bring into full operation the strategy which he had developed and practised in the Baltic in the years immediately preceding the war. He had trained his commanders to carry out mass attacks in wolf packs. They were to position themselves during daylight hours at speed on the surface and attack at night. Patrol lines of U-boats were to be disposed along the most likely routes of the convoys. The first boat to locate a convoy would shadow outside visibility distance and call in any others in the vicinity. On the Gibraltar run the wolf pack would be backed up by Focke-Wulf Condors, and the whole operation would be centrally controlled by Dönitz himself and his small staff at Kernéval in Lorient.[5]

Dönitz' plans were thwarted by three main factors, the difficulties experienced by the German and Italian armies in North Africa, the breakthrough by the cryptanalysts in Bletchley Park and Hitler's diversion of the U-boat effort from the Atlantic Trade Routes to the Mediterranean.

By the winter of 1940 the Italians were in danger of total defeat on the African mainland. They had to be backed up by German troops under Rommel who had some initial success but later came under pressure because his lines of communication were under continuous threat from the Royal Navy and from aircraft based in Malta. In July, 1941, 70% of the shipping supplying the Afrika Korps was being sunk and the Germans were facing a disaster. They were short of fuel after their efforts in Greece, and in any case the Italian fleet was incapable of standing up to the steely strength of Admiral Cunningham and the accumulated experience of the Mediterranean Fleet. In their two-man submarines they carried out deeds of incredible daring, but when Dönitz tried to work with Italian submarines, his efforts met with complete failure.

Inevitably Hitler stepped in. He ordered the diversion of operational U-boats from the Atlantic into the Mediterranean and the first twelve of these reinforcements started to arrive in September, followed by four more in November. The orders from the German Naval High Command instructed Dönitz to keep fifteen of his operational U-boats 'permanently astride' the Straits of Gibraltar, and a further six in the eastern Mediterranean. This diversion had the effect of causing a lull in the Atlantic for seven vital weeks while the U-boats tried (with little success) to get through to the Mediterranean, and to concentrate on the sea approaches to the west of Gibralter.

The battle between the cryptanalysts had swayed to and fro. Sadly the German B-Dienst organization had been decyphering the Admiralty's convoy code since the outbreak of hostilities. Our only advantage was that we suspected this. The main breakthrough by Bletchley Park started in March, 1941. Since the settings were changed daily, and the volume of traffic was enormous, there were initially some delays, but these had been reduced to a maximum of 72 hours by August, 1941, at which time we were able to read the whole German naval wireless traffic in Home Waters and the Atlantic, including the cypher used by the U-boat Fleet.[6]

The impact on the U-boats operations was dramatic. In the early part of the year they had been operating successfully in the more distant areas, off Freetown, using a fleet of supply ships dotted around the mid-Atlantic. These supply vessels were based in the Canary Islands replenishing an average of six or seven U-boats with fuel, food and torpedoes and so increasing their effective range by as much as 4000 miles.

Bletchley Park broke the Naval cyphers so effectively that these supply vessels were located and eliminated by the end of November. The final blow to the U-boats' distant operations was the interception of signals ordering a group of U-boats to refuel from the German raider, *Atlantis*. The raider, which had itself been operating under conditions of strict wireless silence, was sunk by the cruiser, *Devonshire*, in the South Atlantic on 22 November. These U-boats were way beyond their normal limit of endurance, some without enough fuel to get home.

After a dispiriting and prolonged period during which sinkings had fallen to their lowest, the psychological effect on the U-boats of the failure of their source of supply to turn up was considerable. The operational impact was also dramatic. There were instances of U-boats wallowing around in the middle of the Atlantic Ocean completely out of fuel, which Dönitz himself found embarrassing.

Another immediate result of Bletchley Park's breakthrough was an increase in the efficiency of the evasive routeing of the convoys and a consequent reduction of sightings by the Germans.

These factors combined to force Dönitz to halt all operations in the North Atlantic. By the middle of December six boats from Newfoundland, all boats operating in the mid-Atlantic, and all the boats ordered to the Mediterranean had either converged on the area to the west of Gibraltar, or were on their way through, having refuelled and replenished their torpedoes and supplies in the Biscay ports or in Vigo and Cadiz.

The Submarine Tracking Room, using Bletchley Park's information, pieced together the whole disposition of the U-boat fleet and identified the abandonment of the Atlantic in favour of the Mediterranean and the concentration off Gibraltar.

To restore morale and to achieve any results against the supply routes to the British Isles, Dönitz had to hit the next Gibraltar convoy.

The Germans had little difficulty in telling the departure dates and times of Gibraltar convoys. They could learn the time at which the convoy sailed from the observations of their agents in Algeçiras. In the autumn of 1941 they had even started installing heat-detection stations either side of Gibraltar in case convoys slipped out at night or in bad visibility.[7]

In the case of convoy HG 76, all they had to do was look through their binoculars to watch the merchantmen and their escorts assembling.

The convoy had been delayed until a strong escort could be assembled to fight it through the expected attack. Walker had under his command not only the two sloops and seven corvettes of the 36th EG, but also three destroyers, *Stanley*, *Blankney* and *Exmoor* detached from the Fleet at Gibraltar. But the most important ship in this force was *Audacity*, a German prize seized off San Domingo, towed to Jamaica and converted to become the first of the Allied escort carriers, able to fly off six American Mk II Martlet fighters, (Grumman Wildcats), rugged aircraft with specially strengthened undercarriages, six Colt-Browning machine guns and folding wings. They had four functions: the first was to protect the convoy from bombing by the Focke-Wulf Condors: the second was to prevent them shadowing and reporting the convoy's position, course and speed: the third was to reduce the mobility of the U-boats by locating and attacking them whenever they surfaced: and the fourth was to circle or drop markers on the diving position of U-boats so that the surface escorts could finish off the job.

Thus for the first time a convoy was able to put up powerful aggressive air patrols from its own resources when it went beyond the range at which it could be given shore-based air protection. The long-range Focke-Wulfs based on the Bordeaux airfields were not going to have it all their own way for once, and the U-boats were not going to be able to take up their attacking positions unmolested.

Audacity was commanded by Commander D. W. Mackendrick, himself a Fleet Air Arm Swordfish pilot. He had sailed from the Clyde on 13 September and had already gained experience and made a name for himself in the successful defence of the two previous Gibraltar convoys, OG 74 and 76 as well as the Sierra Leone convoy SL 91.

Before his appointment as Senior Officer 36th Escort Group, Commander F. J. Walker had last been to sea as the Commander of the battleship *Valiant* in 1937.

Suddenly he was back in the thick of it with a force under his control which might well have been a Flag Officer's command, moving into an area where a pack of U-boats, supported by land-based Focke-Wulfs, was known to be waiting for the convoy.

Furthermore the escort carrier *Audacity* had demonstrated to the U-boats and Focke-Wulfs right from the start of her first commission that there was now a new element in the battle to prevent them from cruising unmolested on the surface when outside the range of Allied shore-based aircraft cover. At the end of October and in the early part of November *Audacity*'s Martlet fighter aircraft had driven off the Focke-Wulfs that were trying to home U-boats on to convoys, and had shot down two of the six enemy aircraft. *Audacity* had already been marked by Dönitz and his commanders as the top priority target.

There were thirty-one merchantmen and *Empire Darwin* a (Fleet Auxiliary) in the convoy when it sailed on 14 December, 1941. The centre column of nine was led by the Commodore, Vice-Admiral Sir Raymond Fitzmaurice R.N. (retired) on board *SS Spero*.

The corvettes formed the first line of defence, stationed round the perimeter of the convoy, while the Support Group, consisting of the faster destroyers *Stanley*, *Blankney*, *Exmoor*, and the sloops *Stork* and *Deptford*, were stationed at visibility distance on the outer screen. Walker had ordered them to zigzag and weave continuously, so that it would be impossible for shadowing U-boats to assess accurately from their movements the precise course and speed of the main body of the convoy.

The Commodore was in command of the merchantmen in the convoy. Commander Walker in *Stork* was in command of the escorts.

For three days the convoy could expect limited air cover from shore-based aircraft operating out of Gibraltar: thereafter air cover would depend on the aircraft from *Audacity* until the convoy came within the range of the Liberators flying from UK bases.

The Commanding Officer of *Audacity* was responsible for stationing his carrier, bearing in mind the need to manoeuvre while launching or landing aircraft from his flight deck. The operation of merchantmen converted to aircraft carriers sailing with a convoy was new to the Royal Navy. His orders stated that 'the best course of action must depend on a number of factors and can only be decided by the Commanding Officer of the auxiliary aircraft carrier'. Over to you, Captain.

To limit the time that the Focke-Wulfs would be able to stay with the convoy and guide the gathering wolf pack onto its prey, course was set initially to the south-west, and then straight out to the west. It was a slow convoy with a maximum speed of 7½ knots but helped by the unusually calm seas in which they were now sailing.

The first grumble of the storm to come was heard on the evening of the first day at sea, a long way from the position of the convoy. Several U-boats had been replenishing fuel, ammunition and food in Spanish ports on their way down to the Mediterranean. One of these, *U-127*, was sighted coming out from the Spanish coast late on the 14th by a Sunderland from Gibraltar. It was picked up the following day by the Asdics of the Australian destroyer *Nestor*, and despatched with short shrift at 1100 that morning, 37 miles from Cape Finisterre, thus depriving the wolf pack of one of their potential reinforcements before it had a smell of its intended victims.

Just after midnight on 15 December the convoy made its first contact with the waiting pack. A patrolling Swordfish picked up a U-boat by radar on the surface just ahead of the convoy. The Swordfish attacked with three depth charges, dropped flares and tried unsuccessfully to warn *Stork*. However, *Stork*'s lookouts had seen the flares and heard the explosions, and she was already making for the spot at full speed with *Rhododendron* in pursuit.

Neither ship established contact in spite of a long search, but the Swordfish attack, followed up by the searching surface escorts scurrying around, forced the U-boat not only to submerge but also to stay down. Driven mercilessly by their Commodore, exercising emergency turns and other naval manoeuvres to keep them on their toes, the merchantmen steamed on unmolested.

There were mumblings amongst the merchant seamen. The ships were manned by seamen from all over the world who were used to independence. They did not like to be subjected to Home Fleet manoeuvres:

'What does he think we are? Grey Funnel bloody Line?'

By now well aware of the position of the convoy, seven U-boats were concentrating across the course line, to be reinforced by three more U-boats from the Biscay bases sent out on an interception course.[8]

HG 76 had now moved beyond the cover of the aircraft from Gibraltar and must now rely for air cover on *Audacity*'s Martlets. Her normal complement was six aircraft with ten pilots but this newly commissioned and innovative ship was on her fourth convoy. She had no hanger accommodation − the aircraft were maintained and repaired on the flight deck in the open. In these circumstances it was not surprising that only four were operational at this stage.

Stanley had sighted a Focke-Wulf during the day, which confirmed that the Germans were in touch and positioning themselves for an attack. With the good visibility and fine weather, flying was therefore kept down to a minimum to preserve resources for the battle that lay ahead.

The Escort force now consisted of:-

Sloops and Destroyers	Corvettes
Stork	*Samphire*
Deptford	*Rhododendron*
Stanley	*Vetch*
*Exmoor**	*Penstemon*
*Blankney**	*Marigold*
	Jonquil
	Convolvulus

Auxiliary Carrier −*Audacity*

*It was known that the fuel limitations of *Exmoor* and *Blankney* would make it necessary for them to leave the convoy on the 18th.

U-boats operating in wolf packs would be planning to stay on the surface at night and use their speed to take up favourable positions ahead of the convoy's line of advance, before daylight came. Thereafter, in fine weather, once ahead of the convoy and outside the range of the land-based aircraft, they would withdraw until they could just see the tops of the masts of the escorts' outer screen. In fine weather they could then continue to track the convoy without much danger of being seen themselves, because they lay so low in the water.

To break this pattern of surveillance, Walker asked *Audacity* to fly a search round the convoy at dawn on the 17th. He hoped to surprise any shadowing U-boats and to have a go at the Focke-Wulf that could be expected at first light.

This was a good guess. *U-131* had sighted the convoy on the afternoon of the 16th and had dived with the intention of shadowing from ahead. According to one of her crew, its hydrophones were not working, and they surfaced in the middle of the convoy, narrowly escaping an early death by accidental ramming, dived again and surfaced clear of the convoy and escorts before resuming the shadowing from the port beam.

Amazingly all these exciting activities went on without being seen or reported by any of the merchantmen or the ships of the close escort.

At 0918 one of *Audacity*'s Martlets spotted a U-boat on the surface 22 miles away on the port beam of the convoy and called up the escorts. Walker immediately set off in *Stork* and sent on *Blankney* and *Exmoor*, his two Hunt class destroyers, and *Stanley*, an ex-US Navy 'four-stacker'. These were his three fastest ships, but the corvette *Penstemon* was the ship nearest to the aircraft's sighting and she also joined in the chase.

Walker now guessed that the U-boat would be continuing submerged in the general direction of the convoy's route to the west, and formed up his ships to carry out a systematic search down its probable course line, starting at the position of the Martlet's report and working out to the westward in line abreast, one mile apart, out on the convoy's port bow.

However, the persistent Baumann of *U-131*, having been forced to dive by *Audacity*'s Martlet, had out-guessed Walker and altered course sharply towards the convoy. He evaded Walker's search line, but ran straight into *Penstemon* coming out to look for him. His hydrophones were still defective and he didn't hear *Penstemon*, now joined by *Stanley*, coming in to attack. His first knowledge of their presence was a pattern of depth charges exploding close around his boat, causing damage that convinced him that he would have to surface quite soon.

By the time he had completed some temporary repairs and sorted himself out, *Penstemon* and *Stanley* had lost contact with him and since no evidence of destruction had appeared, were reluctantly leaving the area to rejoin the rest of the ships in accordance with their orders. Baumann assumed that they might be waiting for him when he came up and made off at the maximum submerged speed to get away from the area. He was a determined and experienced commander, and when he found no one after him, surfaced to reposition himself.

Walker, whose own Standing Orders to his Commanding Officers emphasized the safe and timely arrival of the convoy as the main objective of the ships under his command, was now running out of time. He had to be back in position with all his force disposed around the convoy before darkness came. It was time to catch up with his flock and make ready for a bad night.

It looked as if this first test of the idea of offensive tactics by Support

Groups had not worked out. He would have to give up the chase and work back to the convoy.

There was a flicker of light from the far ship of the line, picked up and repeated from ship to ship. Long before it reached the next ship, Roland Keyworth, Yeoman of Signals, standing behind the lantern, was bellowing: 'From *Stanley*, sir, object on the horizon to starboard.'

Walker immediately ordered in the patrolling Martlet to attack on the bearing given and put all ships up to full speed.

Bellow again from the Yeoman: '*Stanley* confirms surfaced U-boat.'

The U-boat was still seven miles away, making off at speed on the surface. End on at seven miles, the guns' extreme range, it made a very small target. But up above the bridge, John Filleul, the gunnery control officer in *Stork*, could see the Martlet going in, straight as an arrow, diving down on the conning tower and into the solid lines of tracers floating up from the U-boat.

A plume of smoke floated out from the cockpit and the Martlet, all guns firing, flown by Sub-Lieutenant George Fletcher of 802 Squadron, went on into the sea.

It was a full twenty minutes before a number of hits from the four ships penetrated the hull eight times.[9] These hits, the fear of further air attacks and a continuous barrage of near misses making the conning tower untenable, convinced Baumann that the time had come to abandon ship and scuttle.

U-131 had disappeared and was on her way to the bottom before any of the ships could get there, leaving fifty-five men swimming and shouting for help. This was always the most dangerous time for the escorts. To haul the Germans out of the water with the ship stopped, lifeless and motionless in the water, was a risky business. There was a real danger that the full attention of the ships' companies would be focused more on the survivors than on the threat from another lurking U-boat or a surprise Focke-Wulf attack out of the clouds.

With the convoy steaming into the danger area where the rest of the wolf pack were waiting with their torpedoes, *Blankney* and *Exmoor* lowered their boats and pulled all the German survivors they could grab out of the oily wreckage-strewn water into safety.

The rescuing ships cleared lower deck to hoist the sea-boats and rushed off back to the convoy to take up their night stations. They were in a hurry and they took the fastest route because interrogation of the prisoners had revealed that there were other U-boats in the area. At 1401 that afternoon a signal had been received that the convoy was still being shadowed by a U-boat out in front whose transmissions had been D/F'ed. There was no doubt that this was the boat that was guiding in the wolf pack lying ahead and that a big battle could be expected.

Walker's hunting force came back and started to take up their stations on the deep screen. Darkness came down. It hid the emergency turn of the merchantmen as they altered course 80 degrees to the north, and settled down to enjoy their last night of unmolested passage. No problems, even in the darkness: they had done it all before during the Commodore's manoeuvres.

Commander Walker had passed his first practical test with flying colours. He had shown that it was possible to take half the escort force away from the convoy on an offensive strike for eight hours during the day, destroy the enemy, haul the German prisoners out of the water and still be back in station before dusk.

The Royal Navy is famous for its brief and dramatic war signals which contrast with the long harangues that went out from Dönitz to his commanders. In contrast, during the afternoon the Commander-in-Chief, Western Approaches, Admiral Sir Percy Noble, summarized all this success in a two-word signal: 'Well Done'.

Walker had the Commander-in-Chief's support. The Commodore sent him a rather more interesting signal at dawn: 'Never mind the gathering storm. With the score at one to nil, the convoy is in good hands.'[10]

The Commodore was a Vice-Admiral, Walker had his confidence too.

Among the wreckage of *U-131*, was Sub-Lieutenant Fletcher's body, still supported by his flying jacket. He was buried at sea the next morning. Each ship in the convoy, and the escorting warships lowered their ensigns in recognition of a brave young man.

> 'Write on the stone no word of sadness,
> Only the gladness due
> That we who asked the most of living
> Knew how to give it too.'

Overnight five U-boats had gathered in position for a full-scale attack with another three on their way to intercept.[11] This was a particularly important confrontation. It was the first new-style set battle. On the one hand the U-boats and the Focke-Wulfs, on the other the slow and cumbersome merchantmen, screened by the close escorts, the Support Group and the Martlets from an escort carrier.

Walker now had his chance to test at sea his long-held belief that the offensive use of an air/sea striking force would give the best chance of doing the maximum damage to the U-boats while still providing the maximum protection to the convoys.

He had already deduced that the crunch had arrived, and his appreciation was confirmed by further signals from the Admiralty during the night. The reliability of these Admiralty appreciations were still, and would always remain, heavily disguised for fear of blowing the secret that Bletchley Park was now again regularly decyphering the two-way traffic between the U-boats and their headquarters.[12] The numerous signals to Walker were sprinkled with phrases such as:

'Indications of homing' and — '5 or 6 U-boats appear to be hunting HG-76', and in the afternoon from Flag Officer Commanding Northern Atlantic — 'Well done, keep it up. More birds about, I hope you have got your loader with you'.

The ships were still steaming in exceptionally calm weather with excellent visibility. These unusual conditions led to an error in judgment by Heyda of *U-434*. He had picked up the convoy at midnight, and remained in touch all night as shadower. When dawn broke he was on the surface ten miles out, having fallen back on to the quarter because of the convoy's kink to the northward. From this position, in this visibility, he could observe the tops of the masts of the merchantmen and their close escorts and shadow without danger of being spotted himself. As the light grew, he made a final check. He was in no hurry to close his hatches and dive: it looked like being a nice day and he needed to make up some distance to get into a commanding attacking position. He could make more speed on the surface, circulate a bit of fresh air down below and conserve his batteries.

Stanley was Walker's fastest escort, zigzagging in the deep field on the port side of the convoy. During the day she would move in closer to the merchantmen to give some additional anti-aircraft protection. Meanwhile, because of her defective Asdics, she was definitely vulnerable herself and more than usually aware of the need for an exceptionally good all-round lookout, which was about the only contribution that she could make at this time.

Stanley's masthead lookout wiped off the lenses of his standard Barr and Stroud binoculars for the hundredth time: they weighed 3¼lbs, but they seemed to double their weight every five minutes of a long watch. He tried resting his elbows on the rim of the crow's nest. It didn't work. At these engine revolutions the whole ship vibrated. All the Officer of the Watch had to do was go up a couple of turns. Dozy dope, he ought to try a trick in the crow's nest.

He tucked his elbows into his chest, raised the glasses and took another look, allowing the slow turn of the ship in her interminable weave and zigzag to sweep his field of view along the flat surface of the sea.

What were those V-shaped ripples, breaking up the glassy surface of the sea? He blinked and looked again. There they were, and where they joined together, a silver shape! He trembled all over. Up went his left hand arm on the bearing.

'U-boat Red 150! On the surface!'.

Sudden activity on the bridge below, and half-a-dozen binoculars followed his outstretched arm.

'Full ahead, Hard a'port! Call the Captain.'

Alarm rattlers sounding. Deck alive with half-dressed matelots doubling to their action stations. *Stanley* heeled over to starboard as she built up to full speed in an attempt to get in a depth-charge attack before the U-boat dived. Strange situation: a U-boat without hydrophones trying to get away from a destroyer without Asdics.

Walker sent in *Blankney* and *Deptford* to join her. *Exmoor* was already on her way, but *U-434* had woken up, and dived about three miles ahead of *Stanley*, who reduced speed and circled round the diving position dropping single depth charges by eye to keep the U-boat down and mark the position.

Blankney was the first to get a firm Asdic contact. She hoisted a black flag to signify that she was attacking, and went straight in with a five-charge shallow pattern. When she regained contact she directed the 'blind' *Stanley* over the top of the U-boat, telling her the course to steer, the depths to set and the time to drop her full pattern of fourteen charges. The surface of the water hadn't had time to settle before she followed up with a further full pattern of her own. In a very short time *Stanley* had dropped thirty-three charges (one misfire), and *Blankney* had dropped ten which caused one of the U-boat's torpedoes to explode in its launching tube.

More of Walker's doctrine. Hit them as quickly and as often as possible before they had time to think and work out evasive action.

These accurate and concentrated attacks, following quickly one upon the other, damaged *U-434* beyond all hope. Heyda had no alternative but to blow his tanks, surface immediately and scuttle.

Luckily for him, *U-434* responded, coming up with a rush at a steep angle. As the crew poured out of the conning tower and over the side in a frantic effort to get clear, they found themselves only a mile ahead of *Stanley* and *Blankney*. Almost immediately, 49 minutes after being sighted, the boat rolled over and sank, much to the disappointment of the destroyers who were hoping to board her. The crew were picked up by *Stanley* and *Blankney*, helped by *Exmoor* who had arrived on the scene just too late to take part in the attack.

While the rescue of the German survivors was taking place, Focke-Wulfs appeared, circling low on the horizon, out of range of the escorts' guns, but clearly visible from their bridges. Their job was to stay with the convoy, transmit homing signals to the wolf pack, and, if they got the chance, pick off any defenceless stragglers. When *Audacity* flew off two Martlets, and they saw them coming out after them, the Focke-Wulfs showed no stomach for the fight and managed to escape in the clouds when the guns of the aircraft jammed.

Loaded up with ninety-three German prisoners, *Exmoor* and *Blankney* came to the end of their reserves of fuel and had to return to Gibraltar, with heartfelt expressions of frustration at having to leave Walker and HG 76 as the convoy steamed into the thick of it.

The first sighting was made by that ever vigilant corvette *Penstemon*. Gentelbach in *U-574* had been following HG 76 since the night of the 16th. During the next 48 hours, he had drawn up on the port side of the convoy and found himself ahead on the port bow when the convoy had turned to the westward. The convoy's alteration of course had put him in a strong position for an attack on the night of the 18th. As the light faded, he reckoned that the Martlets would have returned to their carrier, and he could afford to come up for another look. He was immediately spotted against the sunset by *Penstemon*.

Walker ordered *Convolvulus* to join her and *Stanley* was already on her way. As they came up to the diving position, *Convolvulus* picked up the sound of torpedoes with her hydrophones and, a moment later, the lookout bellowed, 'Torpedoes to port, sir!'

'Hard a'port! Full ahead together!'

Corvettes were fine sea-going ships with good reliable engines but they were never very handy. As the noise of the torpedoes on the loudspeakers increased, *Convolvulus'* head paid off slowly, oh so slowly, to port. The two torpedoes, their tracks clearly visible to the men on deck in the calm conditions, came in from the port bow and converged towards the port quarter.

They must hit the stern. Sluggishly, under full wheel, the stern swung out to starboard. They missed − by a mere twenty feet.

After loosing off the two torpedoes from periscope depth, Gentelbach took *U-574* down as deep as he dared and sat there, undeterred by the three escorts scurrying around above him. They knew he was there: there could be no doubt: but they could find no trace: no echo and no sound on the hydrophones. After two fruitless hours searching, they were forced by the gathering darkness and the threat of further massed attacks on the convoy during the night to return to their defensive stations. This they did at maximum speed by the most direct course.[13]

When the sound of the hunting escorts faded in the distance, Gentelbach blew his tanks and followed at speed on the surface. He could see the escorts in the gathering darkness and they provided an easy solution to the problem of relocating the merchantmen. In this weather he had the legs of the corvettes and had no difficulty in keeping them in view.

The evolutions that Commodore Fitzmaurice had exercised in the quiet period of the 15th, in broad daylight, paid off in the darkness of the long midwinter's night of the 18th. With the precision of a much-drilled flotilla of Fleet destroyers, the convoy made a massive alteration of course back to the north at 2200. *Stanley* on the port quarter, and Walker in *Stork* on the starboard quarter, brought up the rear.

The hours drifted into the middle watch from midnight to 0400. The night had gone pitch black. The sky was overcast: there was no moon, no glimmer of light from the stars or the great body of ships in the convoy. Only the slow roll and the flicker of phosphorescence from the bow wave or the wake astern told the Officer of the Watch that his ship was moving through the water.

On the bridge of *Stork* only the insistent ping of the Asdic transmissions, relayed on to the bridge loud speakers, and the occasional movement of a black shadow as the lookouts changed over, broke the monotony. One of those shadows was the Captain, who had been there since before dusk on the previous evening, ten hours before. He had scarcely moved, and took no part in the running of the ship, as she weaved and zigzagged behind her flock, and the watches changed.

'Kye's up sir'.

The Officer of the Watch heaved a sigh of relief: 'Bosun's mate, call the Navigator and the Gunner. Tell them it's a cold night. Call the morning watchmen.'

A roar up the voice-pipe: 'From *Stanley*, submarine in sight!'

'Sound Action Stations!'

Alarm bells and heavy boots pounding down the decks.

'From *Stanley*, torpedoes passing from astern.'

Walker was up behind the binnacle, passing out a string of orders:

'Where the hell is *Stanley*? Tell her to fire starshell.'

'Ship to port sir, signalling.'

'Officer of the Watch, Fighting Lights.'

'Yeoman, make our Pendants.'

A great pyramid of flame, hundreds of feet high, erupted from the sea astern, followed by a deep boom and a prolonged roaring sound. *Stanley*'s death throes.

The convoy broke into one enormous show of pyrotechnics. All the merchantmen now fired their snowflakes. In his Report the Commodore said, with remarkable restraint: 'One could not help being acutely aware that all ships of the convoy were vividly lighted up and shown to any other submarine that might be waiting to see its target.'

From *Stork* the whole skyline to the north appeared as a brilliantly illuminated panorama, punctuated by perfect silhouettes of the merchant ships in their compact lines, stretching right across the horizon.

To the south and quite close, a cloud of dense black smoke was already snaking up from the oily waters and towering above the blazing wreck of *Stanley*.

'Echo, Sir. Red Four Oh.'

'Hard a'port. Full Ahead Together.'

'Submarine. Drawing left. Marked high Doppler. Range 700 yards.'

Stanley's men were in the water not far away. Flames from the oil spillage still blazed just beyond. The U-boat was too close for a systematic attack, but a moment of hesitation could give it a chance to turn the tables by another attack. Having just accounted for one, its Commander would be looking for a second victim, this time *Stork*.

Walker already had the wheel hard over and *Stork* was heeling to starboard as she went in to drive it down by an immediate attack with charges set shallow.

With the water boiling from the last pattern, *Stork* turning at speed under full wheel, and the wreckage of *Stanley* still sinking through the water, the chance of success was very slim and the danger of losing contact was high. The U-boat would be taking full evasive action under the surface to hide behind the echoes put up by the last attack. But Michael Impey was right behind Darby Kelly on the Asdics, and between them they very soon picked out the U-boat's echo from all the other distractions as *Stork* opened out the range and came round to line up for another attack. This was a time when the experience, skill and the uncanny anticipation of the Walker, Impey, and Kelly team made the difference between regaining or losing contact.

Stork came out of her turn and returned for a copybook attack. Darby Kelly, from his caboose in the forward side of the bridge, kept up a running commentary, interpreting the confused noises that came back to him over his headphones. The best man in the Royal Navy.[14]

'Explosions.'

'Very heavy explosions.'

'She's blowing her tanks. Coming up!'

U-574 surfaced about 200 yards ahead, too close for the guns to bear and made away on the surface, as *Stork* tried to ram her. No drills or exercises could have prepared the ship's company, from Commanding Officer downwards, for the next few minutes which Walker describes in his report:

'As I went in to ram, he ran away from me and turned to port. I followed and was surprised to find later, by the plot, that I had turned three complete circles, the U-boat turning continuously to port just inside *Stork*'s turning circle at only two or three knots slower than me. I kept her illuminated with snowflake and fired at him with the four-inch guns until they could no longer be sufficiently depressed. After this the gun's crews were reduced to fist shaking and roaring curses at an enemy who several times seemed to be a matter of feet away rather than yards.'

After eleven minutes of these manoeuvres, *Stork* clobbered the U-boat with a glancing blow on the starboard quarter, rolled it over and dropped a shallow pattern for luck as the grey shape disappeared in the wash astern.

Lieutenant Gray, the First Lieutenant, had kept up a deadly stream of fire over the side of the bridge at the conning tower with a machine gun. When he ran out of ammunition, he rushed off the bridge to chivvy the sea-boat's crew, who were scrambling into their boat with all their boarding gear, ready for 'Operation Haggis'.

On his way past he hurled the machine gun to the Yeoman, who burnt his hands badly on the red-hot barrel.

With *U-574* on the way to the bottom, the sea-boats from *Stork* and *Samphire* set about the highly risky operation of picking up survivors in the hope that someone from *Stanley* might still be alive in the water after the awful initial explosion. The first batch to be brought on board were Germans but, in all, the two ships picked up twenty-eight British and eighteen Germans.

The unfortunate hands who had kept the middle watch from midnight on the 18th and been through the sinking of *Stanley* (at 0415), and of *U-574* (at 0449), were still at their action stations when the sad news percolated through that the *SS Ruckinge* had been torpedoed (at 0515) on the port bow of the convoy, so removing any hope that the pressure might be reduced.

The rescue efforts were interrupted next morning by the appearance of two Focke-Wulfs on the horizon, continuing their job of shadowing the convoy and mustering another concerted attack. *Audacity* sent off her Martlets to deal with this threat.

The weather had now broken and the crews of the escorts were treated to the sight of an exciting game of hide and seek as the Condors tried to hide in the clouds. One of them succeeded, but two were shot down in the course of the day, Walker reported:

'The resulting battle was pretty to watch. The two Martlets dived and climbed at him alternately as he attempted to escape to the clouds and then to the water. They presently returned leaving a very dead Wulf.' [sic]

The Germans were paying a high price for these attempts to shadow from the air. Not only had they lost four of their available long-distance planes, but any attempts to carry out their usual leisurely observation of the convoy's course and speed had been frustrated by these vicious and highly successful strikes by *Audacity's* aircraft. The Martlets had driven away or destroyed the shadowers, and at the same time they had kept the U-boats off the surface from dawn until dusk, thereby much reducing their ability to take up the optimum positions for their night attacks.

Walker left *Samphire* to complete the rescue and steamed at full speed to rejoin the convoy which had gone on to the north. After a few miles he came across *SS Ruckinge* still afloat, with a large hole in her side and, close by, a lifeboat containing the Master, Chief Officer and twelve of the crew, who were taken on board. The rest of the crew had been picked up by the *SS Finland* who had missed the Master and his party in the dark.

Ruckinge was too badly damaged to salvage: she was left for *Samphire* to sink on her way back to her station. *Samphire* found that the boiler room, engine room and number two hold were flooded, that she had a list of 25 degrees to port and that the water was rising.

This inspection and the final sinking took most of the day, and she was not back with the convoy until after dark. However, the boarding and the consequent delay in her return was not without value. She found the Confidential Books on deck in a weighted bag, and five bags of diplomatic mail, all probably thrown from the bridge as she heeled after she had been hit, landing on the main deck.

At this stage Walker was no longer able to send out fast destroyers to follow up the aircraft sightings. *Stanley* had gone down and the other two had returned to Gibraltar for fuel. *Stork* had lost her Asdic dome, her speed was reduced to a maximum of ten knots, and the damage sustained in ramming *U-131* had so bent her bows that her fuel consumption had doubled. *Deptford* was off hunting another sighting with *Marigold* and *Convolvulus*.

As the day of 20 December wore on, gloomy reports continued to filter through from all sources. Martlets reported U-boats ahead and on the port beam, but Walker had no ships to follow up these sightings. A signal from *Blankney* came through to say that the prisoners rescued from *U-131* knew the course and speed of the convoy and the name of the escort carrier. The three reinforcements that Dönitz had sent out from the Biscay ports could reach attacking positions at any time.

Walker assessed that the main threat from the wolf pack lay on the port bow. Hoping to gain just one night's respite, the convoy's course was altered fifty degrees to starboard at nightfall, from 330 to 020 degrees.

This would be the seventh day and night during which the merchant ships and their escorts had been continuously shadowed and under attack from a concentration of Focke-Wulfs and U-boats and it was not surprising that the tension on board all the ships was high. When *Deptford* returned with *Marigold* and *Convolvulus* from their fruitless chase *Deptford* was mistaken for a U-boat and 'the evening bout of pyrotechnics ensued', providing perfectly illuminated targets for any U-boats in the vicinity.

Apart from that, the night passed quietly. The final test had yet to come.

The action started at 0900 on the 21st, with a report from a Sub-Lieutenant E.M. Brown in a Martlet that two U-boats had been sighted on the surface, twenty-five miles astern of the convoy. They were lying alongside each other, and one of them appeared to be holed. They had been transferring men from one boat to the other across a plank when a burst of fire from the aircraft caught them unawares, blasting three of them into the water. When attacked, they broke off at slow speed on the surface, but Martlets subsequently sent up from *Audacity* to deal with them could find no trace.

Walker faced a difficult decision. His guess was that at least one of them had been damaged in a previous attack or a collision, and was probably unable to dive. He had no fast destroyers to follow up this very excellent opportunity, but it was astern and the convoy was plodding on towards home. Should he go for this chance or use his depleted escort force to maintain his screen round the convoy at maximum strength?

His decision was to send back the sloop *Deptford* and the corvettes *Penstemon*, *Vetch* and *Samphire*. It was a bold decision. These four escorts would be parting company astern of their convoy at a separation speed of twenty knots. If he let them hunt for too long, it was going to be very difficult for them to get back in station before nightfall. Without any doubt there was a trap waiting for him ahead of the convoy, and he was going to need them.

At this point he asked for further air cover from long-range aircraft from the UK bases, since the convoy would now be just inside their range of operation. But none were immediately available, and at 1126, since no further contact or trace could be found of the U-boats astern, he turned round the pursuing force to rejoin the convoy at their best speed.

He signalled the Commander-in-Chief advising him that the convoy had been shadowed continuously by submarines and Focke-Wulfs since leaving Gibraltar, and seemed likely to remain so. He therefore intended to shorten the voyage as much as possible by proceeding home by the most direct route.

Ten minutes later he spotted another U-boat at a range of about 12 miles ahead. In his report of proceedings he says:-

'The net of U-boats around us seemed at this stage to be growing uncomfortably close in spite of *Audacity*'s heroic efforts to keep them at arm's length.'

In spite of his signalled intentions (one wonders whether he was gambling on the chance that his signal would be intercepted and decyphered by the Germans), Walker carried out a diversion shortly after nightfall. He ordered *Deptford* to stage a mock battle with starshell, snowflake and depth-charging to the north-east while the convoy did a major alteration of course through ninety degrees to the north-west. The plan was to turn the convoy away from the wolf pack, putting the threat astern and so making it impossible to catch up and attack before daybreak, without travelling at high speed on the surface.

Just before this diversion was due to start one of the merchantmen loosed off a snowflake. When the planned mock battle started, the whole plan was ruined because every ship in the convoy put in a competitive firework display. Once again the merchantmen and the positions of their escorts were illuminated and silhouetted for all the lurking U-boats to see.

Stork, while this was going on, had stationed herself astern of the convoy, which was Walker's chosen position. After ramming *U-574* he had no Asdics but from this station he had the maximum opportunity to rush to support and direct any action around the convoy.

At 2033, the flash and roar of an explosion from a ship on *Stork*'s starboard bow announced the next stage of the battle. The ship torpedoed was the Norwegian *Annavore* of 3324 tons, carrying iron ore from Spain. She was the rearmost ship in the centre column. He ordered the escorts in the vicinity to start firing snowflake to starboard, to force the attacking U-boat down and to try to pick him up on their Asdics.

In his report Walker says the order was an error. He should have ordered them to fire astern of the convoy.

This was a bad start to an awful night.

Audacity was the first escort carrier to work with convoys. Before taking part in convoy work, the C-in-C Western Approaches had 'indicated', on 8 November, that he would 'recommend' that the carrier should either remain inside the convoy, or leave at dusk, operating at high speed, zigzagging continuously with two escorts, not less than 30 miles from the convoy. He warned that to be outside the convoy was dangerous if U-boats were shadowing or homing on to the convoy, unless operating with adequate speed and adequate escort. Only in special circumstances, such as a small convoy with an exceptionally high number of escorts, should the carrier leave the convoy.

Audacity's Commanding Officer was Commander Mackendrick. His seniority was 31/12/37. Walker had been promoted to Commander six years earlier than him, on 31/12/31 and was therefore the senior officer. In addition the C-in-C had indicated that the commanding officer of a carrier had the responsibility for stationing his ship and informing the senior officer of the escorts of his intentions. Not a very clear chain of command.

Every evening before darkness *Audacity* had left the convoy and zigzagged away from its vicinity with a corvette as escort. Since she was constrained by the maximum speed of the corvette, she could scarcely zigzag at speed as recommended by the Commander-in-Chief.

On the afternoon of the 21st Walker had signalled his night intentions and *Audacity* had asked for an escort before pulling out on the starboard (eastern) side of the convoy. Walker had only four escorts in close defence and had, reluctantly, to turn down this request. At the same time he suggested that the port side would be safer because he expected that the attack would come from the starboard side. *Audacity* was not happy to be on the side towards which the convoy would be making an emergency turn after dark, and he had also to consider the best position from which to fly his aircraft on and off. Perhaps he did not relish the thought of the thirty-one merchant ships in nine columns turning towards him at 7½ knots in the pitch blackness.

Audacity set off to the eastward, at dusk, on her own, and started zigzagging at her best speed twenty minutes after she had left the convoy.

U-571 (Bigalk) had been shadowing on the surface and was closing from the starboard side. The torpedoing of *Annavore* had once again lit up the night, and he was looking towards the shapes of ships and escorts perfectly silhouetted against the activity in and around the convoy.

When he set course to join in the attack, the great bulk of *Audacity* making off at speed to the east came between him and the convoy at short range.

His first torpedo crippled her and he made doubly sure with two more. She listed to port and went down in ten minutes at 2210.[15]

Penstemon was trying to pick up survivors from *Audacity*, swimming in the water, amongst whom was her Commanding Officer. There was a swell running and he was washed away from the scrambling nets. Lieutenant Williams went into the water after him with a line, but tragically the line that he got round Mackendrick was lost and he was carried away in the darkness and never seen again.

In her short months in commission, *Audacity*, under his command, and her brave young pilots had demonstrated the way in which victory over the U-boats would eventually be achieved. Her aircraft had delivered sharp reminders to the Germans that they did not enjoy undisputed air superiority on this convoy route. But there was a heavy price to pay for this experience: her Commanding Officer and eight officers and sixty-three men of her complement of 400 were lost .

Meanwhile *Marigold* had sighted a U-boat on the surface on the port side of the convoy. *Samphire* and *Deptford* were in Asdic contact with another on the starboard side, plastering their contact mercilessly, and very conscious of the convoy drawing steadily away from them. In the darkness they could see no signs of wreckage but when they left they were confident that they had given their target a very sore head.

At that time, they were not to know that this was another milestone in the Battle of the Atlantic. They had put an end to *U-567*, commanded by Endrass. In his memoirs Dönitz says, 'among our casualties was one of the best and most experienced of our U-boat Commanders, Lieutenant-Commander Endrass'.

The night was not yet over. The escorts were beginning to resume their stations around the convoy. *Stork* was bringing up the rear, and Walker was in his sea cabin taking advantage of the lull in the activity to catch up with sleep lost during five nights on the bridge.

He was aroused by a resounding crash. Looking over the port quarter, the startled Officer of the Watch could make out a great black shape looming over the low deck on the port side aft, and behind that the dim outline of a ship. The intruder's bow was one third of the way across *Stork*'s stern.

Stoker Petty Officer George Dyson had climbed into his hammock fully clothed. He had not taken his lifebelt off. Those were the orders and he stuck to them.

'There is a saturation point for fear, and I fall asleep. A heavy crash jerks me into action and brings me back to the present. All the lights are out; the motion of the ship is peculiar; a strange hop, skip and jump, which doesn't seem to make any sense to me. We have a permanent list to starboard, which delays me getting up the ladder. As I climb out of the hatch, a terrific explosion tears through the ship; awful naked fear grips me as I stagger along the passage in the dark. Suddenly I am all alone except for the alarm bells. What are they saying – 'Abandon Ship'? Three more rending crashes tear through the ship. The deck is trembling like a jelly and I'm flat on my stomach, beyond any thought now. The heaving and erratic motion has ceased and I stagger along the passage which will bring me to the quarterdeck. Suddenly I run straight into a solid wall that isn't supposed to be there. I feel along with my fingers to find a solid steel barrier with rows of rivet heads. Water is splashing over my feet and up my legs. Warm blood is running down my face from my bleeding nose and into my mouth; now there is a horrible grinding noise all round me. I run my hand sideways along this barrier and as I extend my arm the whole damn wall starts to move sideways, grinding and tearing along. As the last edge disappears. I realise that I'm on the edge of a hole, and beyond there is just cold night and sea, and the bow of a ship just dropping slowly away.

A shout comes over the loud-hailer across the water, "Goodbye *Stork*, and Good Luck!"

I feel awfully lonely by myself and work my way back to the centre of the ship, avoiding the huge long gap of gaping metal. I'm feeling better now, so I go below and tell Taff what has happened.'[16]

Deptford, racing back to fill the gap she had left in the defensive screen, had run up *Stork*'s stern. With unerring aim she had run straight into the compartment aft where the German survivors were imprisoned. In his full report, Walker said:

'The damage was serious enough but not vital, since the main engines, and steering gear by an inch or two, had not been touched. The after cabin flat was wide open to the elements but the wardroom flat and the tiller flat were tight .... There were five Boches pulped literally into a bloody mess.'

Ten minutes later *Stork* was under way at ten knots and Stoker Petty Officer George Dyson was to lose a few more hours of sleep clearing up the mess and shoring up the bulkheads.

Deptford had been depth-charging a contact on the night of the 21st, some miles astern of the convoy, but had to abandon her attacks because the convoy was steaming on ahead and she had to get back in station. The ships' companies of the escorts by this time were all extremely tired, having been under threat and at action stations for much of the past seven days and nights. During this time their Commanding Officers had rarely been able to leave their bridges, making the best of an occasional catnap in the wheel house, if they were lucky, or else propped up in a corner of the open bridge. As *Deptford* made her best speed to get back in her station on the screen round the convoy, Lieutenant-Commander H. R. White, was persuaded by his Number One, Lieutenant E. Palmer, to get a few hours' shuteye in his cabin while things were quiet.

Captain Andy Palmer RN remembers:

'We set off at our maximum speed of sixteen knots to rejoin the convoy. After a while our primitive fixed aerial radar gave a small echo but with that set it was uncertain whether the echo was ahead or its reciprocal, astern. I decided that it was most likely ahead and probably a U-boat on the surface (possibly the one we had lost contact with) trying to overtake the convoy.

'While I was telling the OOW to call the Captain, the radar operator called up the voice pipe, "Contact closing rapidly!"

'I shouted, "STAND BY TO RAM!" and rammed.

'Only in the last few seconds could I see in the dark that the object I was ramming was not a U-boat, but an escort vessel. "Full Astern!" and "Hard a'starboard" had no time to take effect – these sloops had tiny astern turbines and therefore feeble astern power in any case. Two depth charges, primed and ready to attack U-boats, were dislodged by the impact; they exploded under the stern as the two vessels lay stopped and locked together. A calm voice called out of the darkness,

"What ship is that?"

"*Deptford.*"

"I'm very sorry, *Deptford.*"

'I had rammed my Senior Officer's ship, *Stork*. But that was the only reproof that I ever had from F.J.W.

'A chunk of plating about six foot square was torn from *Deptford*'s bow about four feet above the waterline. *Stork* was struck about two-thirds of her length aft, just above the break of the boat-deck. At deck level she was cut almost to the centre line, and only the rake of *Deptford*'s stem prevented damage to her port propeller shaft. Some U-boat prisoners on board *Stork* were killed by the impact and two others appeared, terrified, on *Deptford*'s forecastle, having seized the deck's edge and hauled themselves up on to her foredeck.

'The awful grinding of the tortured plate as the two ships moved in the slight seaway is in my ears still. *Stork*'s rum store was flooded and her ship's company never forgave me.'[17]

Deptford made port safely. When she arrived in Liverpool the Commander-in-Chief was walking up and down Prince's landing stage awaiting her arrival.

'So was my wife, then a Petty Officer WRNS. As the ship loomed out of the mist the C-in-C stopped near her and said to his Flag Lieutenant, "Look at that bow!" His Flag Lieutenant said, "She must have rammed a U-boat. There'll be a DSC for this." There wasn't. I was lucky that everybody was too busy to court-martial me.'

Naval Officers are not renowned for over-lengthy descriptions of their trials and tribulations. At 1053 on 21 December the Commander-in-Chief received the following signal from Walker:

'*Annavore* sunk last night. Probably three submarines last of which beaten off by *Deptford* without loss. All well depth charged. Have collision damage aft but am reasonably seaworthy.'

Next morning, when there was enough light for the other ships to see the condition of *Stork*'s bow, there was a further exchange of messages by signal lamp.

'What have they done to your nose?'

'That's nothing. You should see what they have done to my arse.'

The situation on the morning of 21 December was gloomy. *Stork* had no Asdics, her bow was bent to port, her maximum speed was nine/ten knots and the few depth charges that she had left were piled up on the bow to lessen the strain on her damaged stern. Walker had lost *Stanley* and no longer had the protection of *Audacity* and her aircraft. *Deptford*'s self-inflicted wound had reduced her maximum speed to eleven knots. Most of the radar sets in the escorts were out of action.

At 1115 a Focke-Wulf appeared and circled monotonously out of range of the escorts' guns. There was no Martlet to deal with it. After two hours, Walker interrupted his walk up and down the after end of the bridge:

'Yeoman! Tell that damned aircraft to go round the other way.'

The aircraft complied without a murmur.

At 1600, any thoughts that the convoy might have passed through the danger zone were dispelled by a report of two U-boats ahead of the convoy's route on the port bow. The only good thing on this cold winter's day was the arrival of a Very Long Range (VLR) Liberator which had covered the 800 miles from its base to spend two and a half hours in company. When the Liberator arrived, the Focke-Wulf left. The arrival of this solitary aircraft from home, the convoy's first contact with the British Isles, did a great deal to lift the morale of the dog-weary crews.

In Walker's report he said: 'There was one thing not be done – continue on the same course and passively await attack.' His attempted ruse on the previous evening had not paid off. He described it as 'a flop'. Nevertheless, he did not give up. He decided to try again, signalled his intention to the Commander-in-Chief and got on with the job.

He did not expend his wrath on the merchantmen for the premature firework display of the previous night. He did consider asking the Commodore to have all illuminants ditched, but later relented and emphasized that there was to be no firing of snowflake that evening.

His plan this time was to carry out not one, but three major alterations of course after dark, the first two to bring the line of advance in two bites 100 degrees to port on to 327 degrees. There would then be a fake battle by *Deptford* and *Jonquil* at 2225, in the position where the convoy would have been if it had not altered course. At midnight the convoy would alter course back to 047 degrees which was the course for home. The effect of these course alterations would be to displace the whole convoy thirty-two miles to the north-west of the original line of advance. This was a great deal to ask of a fleet of merchant ships of mixed nationalities travelling at 7½ knots at night without lights and all very tired after several days and nights under attack.

The night of 22 December was going to be another tense and sleepless period. The tactical plan was designed by Walker, but the success would depend on their Commodore's orders and the willingness and skill of the Masters of the Merchantmen. They were being asked to carry out manoeuvres at close quarters that would have taxed a flotilla of nippy trained fleet destroyers. A small error of judgement or timing, momentary bad station keeping or a poor lookout could result in collision, detection by the wolf pack and sinkings.

Fortune favoured the brave. The night passed quietly and Walker remarked: 'I hope there were some very angry U-boat Captains on the morning of the 23rd.'

Dönitz had chucked it in. In his memoirs he blamed it on the fine weather. He might have been more realistic and blamed it on the excellence of the handling of the anti-submarine forces. In retrospect, the German Naval History (Gunther Hessler) said:

'The chief reason for their [the U-boats'] serious failure was the extremely skilful handling of the A/S forces.'[18]

Dönitz had lost five U-boats (including *U-127*, sunk by HMAS *Nestor*) and four Focke-Wulfs. The convoy had lost two merchant ships and *Stanley*. But the worst blow was the loss of *Audacity*. She was the first escort carrier in action. Only two were lost during the whole campaign.

The passage of HG 76, under Commander Walker's orders, had proved that the combination of continuous air support with adequate surface escorts could fight a convoy through a concentration of U-boats with limited losses to the merchant ships and unacceptable losses to the U-boats and their air support.

This convoy defined the shape of the convoy escorts which in 1943 would begin to drive the U-boats inexorably away from the Trade Routes of the Atlantic. Each convoy needed a close escort, a support group in the deep field, an aircraft carrier and aircraft to keep the U-boats submerged and drive off the German shadowers.

This had been an arduous patrol for Walker and his exhausted ships' companies. At first the sheer exhaustion of working up a bunch of reservists to an efficient fighting force, then getting to know the commanding officers of the ships in his Group, then the bitter battle against the Atlantic weather and finally one of the hardest-fought and most significant victories over a wolf pack supported by Focke-Wulfs.

Stork staggered slowly back home: in her battered state she would have had little chance of surviving even a half-hearted attack. Even in calm weather, her maximum speed had been reduced to ten knots.

As the convoy steamed out of the danger area and came under the protection of shore-based aircraft, Walker received a signal from a retired Naval Officer, Vice-Admiral Sir R. Fitzmaurice R.N., the Commodore of the convoy, who had shared the rigours of the last few days with him, and contributed so much to the success: "You have won a great victory".

Decorations and distinctions would be awarded to Walker in profusion from now on. But in truth this signal was all the recognition that he sought.

CHAPTER THREE

PROMOTED TO CAPTAIN RN

Commander Walker went off for a few days' leave, and learnt of the immediate award of a DSO. The great advantage of ramming as a method of destroying the enemy was the high chance of the ship spending a few weeks in dock, during which time the officers and both watches of the hands could take it in turn to go on leave. Walker was not so lucky. After a short week at home he was summoned to appear at the Admiralty to present his Report of Proceedings and to make his recommendations to the C-in-C Western Approaches, the Director of Anti-Submarine Warfare, Captain George Creasy, and other senior officers. He was one of the few senior officers who could speak from successful practical experience about the protection of a convoy by a combination of escort groups, support groups and aircraft operating from an aircraft carrier and the shore. He, of all people, also knew both the theoretical and practical strengths and weaknesses of the Asdics and depth charges with which the escorts were armed.

In his Report of Proceedings he had shouldered full blame for the loss of *Audacity*, saying 'I should finally have ordered her either on to the port side or the middle of the convoy and I feel myself responsible accordingly for her loss'. Admiral Sir Percy Noble commented that no blame could be attributed to Walker.

Although his damaged *Stork* would not be ready for some weeks he was back at sea by 10 January in temporary command of *Pelican* to continue the protection of the Gibraltar convoys. He met convoy CG 76 with his faithful corvettes of the 36th Escort Group. Without the strength of the two larger, faster and well-armed sloops *Stork* and *Deptford*, which were still in dock under repair from their experiences with HG 76, the Group had lost a lot of its striking power. By the 16th this convoy of twenty-six merchantmen and these little escorts were bashing into violent gales which scattered thirteen ships and damaged most of the escorts. The foul mid-winter weather continued until the 21st, when it was at last possible to get the convoy back into reasonable order. This was no easy task since the slow corvettes were bound by strict radio silence, and were operating in conditions of low visibility. Four merchantmen that had been blown away by the gales never rejoined, and limped into Gibraltar on 25 January, the day after the main body. There were no losses or engagements with the U-boats: perhaps on this occasion the weather was too rough for them.

Three days later Walker and his Group were on their way back to bring home another convoy, unmolested. In February he returned to Plymouth to resume command in his repaired *Stork*.

Walker now faced a period of hard slog. He could expect little else. Throughout the centuries the Royal Navy's wartime routine has been dominated by long periods of deadly dull routine, and by battles against the weather. The problem has always been to find the enemy and bring him to battle on whatever terms. Even the busiest and most often involved striking forces have rarely spent more than a small percentage of their time in action. Nelson travelled all the way round the Mediterranean before catching up with the French for his victory at the Battle of the Nile, and took his fleet on the long journey of nearly 7000 miles across the Atlantic and back again before he finally caught up with the French fleet off Cape Trafalgar. He once spent two years without setting foot on shore.[1] In the Battle of the Atlantic many spent the whole of their time at sea without any contact with a German U-boat, ship or aircraft. Their main memories are of a grey and featureless ocean, rarely blessed by a warm cloudless sky and never free from the long ocean swells. In spite of this, most ships built up a family spirit and high morale. Many friendships and internal loyalties were formed that would endure until the end of their lives.[2] Some groups of ships would develop a similar feeling of belonging to an elite corps, arising from hardships shared, battles lost and won and an acceptance of interdependence.

In the early part of 1942, the Battle of the Atlantic was nearly all bad news. On a wider scale, throughout the world, the Allied Forces, not yet enjoying the enormous support that would start to flow from the United States, suffered their greatest defeats. On the Home Front, every ship on its return to base found news of disaster and family death from air raids in its mail bag.

In ships and in the flotillas and fleets of the Royal Navy, the spirit reflected the ability of its commanding officer to lead. This was now Walker's main task. He and the officers and senior rates on board well knew how few ships were available and the weaknesses of their armaments. The ships were too slow: Asdics[3] were inaccurate and, in some water conditions, completely ineffective. Depth charges could not be set to the depth to which U-boats could and did dive: in any case ships didn't carry enough of them. The gunnery systems were based on subjective judgements: the maximum speed to which the instruments could be set did not even reach the usual speed of attacking aircraft. There were not enough aircraft allocated to convoy defence and reconnaissance duties: the pilots were not properly trained. As the convoys drew away from the land, the aircraft disappeared and there was a great gap in the middle of the Atlantic where they never appeared at all. The

U-boats somehow knew where to lie in wait for the victims and could follow them for days on end, but sometimes our own intelligence seemed to dry up.

Walker had a thousand British tars in seven seaworthy ships, and a sympathetic and supportive Commander-in-Chief. Supplies of rum never failed – except when smashed up by *Deptford* or by near misses or premature depth-charge explosions. The food was good and there was plenty of it. There seemed to be no shortage of ammunition or fuel.[4] He set about making the best of these resources.

In the months that followed the ships' companies had no time to relax or to think about anything except the ceaseless series of drills and manoeuvres, carried out by day and night in all the weather conditions that convoy escorts must expect.

Many of the officers and key rates in *Stork* were to stay with Walker and move from ship to ship with him for the rest of his career. One of them was a young Sub-Lieutenant RN, John Filleul, fresh from the life of a junior officer on a cruiser, who was to become his Number One (First Lieutenant) at the tender age of twenty-two. John Filleul was one of the many to fall under the spell of Walker's leadership and remained with him until he died.

Walker himself was especially involved in the development of the Support Groups as integrated fighting units. Ships thrown together and sent to sea without the understanding built up from operating together were not as efficient as they might be. They could and did run into serious problems. In the opening rounds of the Battle of the Atlantic this lesson, proven over centuries of sea fighting, had to be learnt again.

Communications at sea under action conditions were a major problem, and in many ways they had not improved since the days of Nelson. Convoys and their escorts endeavoured to observe radio silence, to avoid revealing their presence to the enemy. Most of the signals to manoeuvre these unwieldy masses of ships were therefore dependent on flags, signal lamps, sirens and even loud-hailers. Walker aimed for a higher standard than this. In his own ship he aimed to train his officers so that in action they would do exactly what he wanted them to do without any orders.

His further task was to achieve the same understanding between himself and the commanding officers of the ships in his Group, an understanding that would not break down even in action conditions when the ships were separated by several miles of fog or darkness.

On 9 December, 1941, the Japanese entered the war and on 11 December the Germans declared war on the United States, two events which completely altered the nature of the Battle of the Atlantic, opening up new opportunities for the U-boats which they seized with both hands. Dönitz now set his sights on the undefended American coastal traffic. However, he continued to maintain the pressure between Gibraltar, the coast of Portugal and the

Azores. Nine boats continued to threaten this area, *U-73*, *U-561* and *U-572* were patrolling off the coast of Spain: three were waiting for the right conditions to get through into the Mediterranean. Another three, *U-71, 571* and *93* were patrolling between Gibraltar and the Azores, with orders to attack convoy HG 78. The functions of these boats was to create an impression of maximum activity and to work with the Focke-Wulfs from Bordeaux so as to tie down escorts urgently needed on the other side of the Atlantic.

On 9 April the 36th Escort Group sailed from Liverpool with Walker in command in *Stork*. His force was reduced to *Stork* and the four corvettes *Penstemon*, *Vetch*, *Gardenia*, and *Convolvulus*: they went off for three days of exercises from Lough Foyle, before joining convoy HG 82 of sixteen ships bound for Gibraltar.[5] Nothing of interest had happened on the last several convoys on this route. There were no reports of U-boats in the area and all attention was focused on the other side of the Atlantic.

Walker had taken up his usual station astern of the convoy and had sent on *Vetch* to sweep five miles ahead. At 2130 on the 14th an Admiralty signal gave warning of a U-boat in the vicinity and, fifteen minutes later, *Vetch* picked up an echo on radar at 3¾ miles astern, between herself and the convoy. At first she was not alarmed, thinking it was *Penstemon* ahead of the convoy and leading the close screen. She turned immediately to investigate, albeit with some caution as she was not keen to run head-on into *Penstemon* or the convoy on opposite course.

The plot looked odd: the radar echo was going diagonally across and towards the front of the convoy.

Vetch fired starshell: in the flickering light she could see a grey shape: at first she thought it was a corvette but as she closed the range it dawned upon her that this was no friendly corvette but a U-boat on the surface heading straight into the convoy, in the process of firing two torpedoes at her as it dived.

As *Vetch* headed for it at full speed, the torpedoes passed down her side, missing her by 20 feet.

Vetch had made two reports on her sightings, but neither of them had made clear where she was. *Stork* was heading blindly towards the tracer that she had seen from her station astern of the convoy, but had no means of knowing whether or not this was another panic display by a ship in the convoy.

Walker was not at all pleased. This was a repetition of the events leading up to the sinking of *Stanley* on 19 December. Mistakes were inevitable, but to make the same mistake twice when in contact with the enemy was a serious matter and could be fatal.

Twenty minutes later, for no apparent reason, the U-boat surfaced again without warning less than a mile ahead of *Vetch* who went after it at full speed, illuminating the target and firing as fast as she could load. Her wildly excited gunners sent back enthusiastic reports to Walker, who was coming up from three miles astern, also blazing away with her four-inch guns and firing starshell. Neither ship was fast enough to catch up: *Vetch* saw the range opening and *Stork* could not do much better. After half an hour of this, the fire from *Vetch* (100 rounds) and *Stork* (73 rounds of four-inch and 26 rounds of starshell) became too hot for the U-boat which dived at 2239.

Walker had instilled in his Commanding Officers the need to give the U-boats no time to think, take evasive action or to carry out any running repairs. When *Vetch* picked up an Asdic contact at 1000 yards she attacked immediately with a shallow pattern three minutes after the submarine had dived. This pattern was fired: 'On principle, and for moral effect'.

Coming in behind, while the U-boat was still reeling from *Vetch's* attack, *Stork* put down another ten-charge pattern at 2253, went straight round and dropped another at 2259. *Vetch* came in for a deliberate attack at 2309, to be followed up by *Stork* two minutes later at 2311.

The U-boat had been under gunfire from 2208 until 2239. When it dived, it had been plastered with fifty depth charges in five separate attacks between 2242 and 2311, a very remarkable achievement by the attacking ships' depth charge and Asdic crews.

During the final attack, when the range had come down to 800 yards, Kelly reported that the character of the echo had changed to 'non-sub, probably wreckage'. Walker reported:

'I was tolerably certain that the Boche had been pole-axed as indeed he had. Wreckage boiled to the surface and in high delight I lowered a boat to investigate. Amongst the wreckage recovered was a pencilled chit from a trouser pocket, containing the number of the U-boat, and a human heart and lungs penetrated by splinters. The gruesome-looking heart and lungs were avidly seized by my Surgeon Lieutenant and put into pickle for the future pleasure of the Medical Branch.'

This was the end of *U-252*. *Stork* hoisted her whaler at 0038 on 15 June and was back in her station with the convoy at 0500, but the slower corvette *Vetch* had a much longer haul. During most of that night the convoy had gone on its way with just three corvettes to protect sixteen merchantmen.

In his report, Walker emphasized the value of the outer convoy screen to provide advance warning of probable attack, while admitting that the U-boat had been unfortunate in choosing the one sector of the outer screen that was occupied by the vigilant *Vetch*. He gave credit to all parts of the ship in this destruction of the enemy. He credited the guns with forcing the U-boat to dive, and for providing excellent illumination with star-shell, but doubted whether they had registered as many hits as they claimed. He emphasized the value of the Admiralty Research Laboratory Plot (ARL Plot) and the plotting team in tracking the U-boat initially and making it possible to keep continuously in contact during five attacks by two ships in twenty minutes.

In his recommendations for awards and decorations he acknowledged the genius of his Asdic team under Michael Impey and Darby Kelly, and of the depth charge crews who had achieved in action what they had practised so often as drill. He praised the engine room for producing 'more revolutions than the ship has ever done in her life before'.

He had two views on the value of radar, being highly delighted with *Vetch*'s Type 271 which picked up *U-252* on the surface at 7500 yards, thus preventing it from penetrating the screen, but lashing into *Stork*'s 286P set with which 'even in the hands of the Group RDF officer no contact could be obtained on the U-boat plainly in sight at a range of 1½ miles'.

In the section marked 'Lessons Learnt', however, there was a long list of the difficulties overcome, mistakes made and emergencies surmounted. He had given orders that in future his corvettes were not to fire depth charges set shallow at fifty feet,[6] because in one of her attacks *Vetch* had produced an explosion at least twice as heavy as usual from a charge set shallow from her starboard thrower. As a result her hull leaked at six frames. To keep pace with the water filling the bilges, she had to operate her pumps continuously. Three of her wheelhouse windows were blown in and the coxswain was wounded by flying glass. The key locking the rudder to the rudder post had been blown out, putting the steering completely out of action for an agonizing period. One depth charge had jammed in the rails. For a different reason, something had gone wrong with the firing mechanism on the gun, which from then on was operated by a leading signalman with a pair of pliers.

After long periods at sea, the firing bells were sometimes unreliable, and orders were often shouted down the voice pipes: two of these were close together. As they were running in to attack, a discussion between the Asdic officer and a colleague on the bridge about the time to fire was overheard by the communications rating on the quarterdeck. He heard the word 'Fire', passed it on, and a charge was loosed off prematurely.

In spite of all these tribulations, *Vetch*'s Commanding Officer, Lieutenant-Commander H. J. Beverley RNR, signalled at 0045: 'Let's have another one'. And at 0924, when he had had time to think and a bit of sleep: 'Permission to Splice The Mainbrace?'

Walker gave particular credit to *Vetch*, commenting on her Commanding Officer's exemplary initiative and dash, his bulldog tenacity, and finally saying: 'To him must go the Lion's Share of the credit'.

For no logical reason the sinking of *U-252* had a major effect on the deployment of the U-boats during the coming months. This U-boat was the last of a trio, *U-82*, *587* and *252*, which had been sunk by Allied escorts while shadowing convoys to the west of the Bay of Biscay. During the months of February, March and April these three had been making their routine daily status reports and each had suddenly gone silent. At Dönitz's headquarters, this silence meant that another U-boat had gone down.

Partly because he suspected some special trap, and partly because he preferred to concentrate on the easy pickings off the coast of America, (in spite of the long and time-consuming journey across the width of the ocean), Dönitz had ordered all U-boats leaving the Biscay ports, bound to or from the east coast of America, not to attack convoys in the area between ten and fifteen degrees west and forty-three degrees and fifty degrees north. This order took effect on 19 April and was in force for several months.[7] Several convoys were sighted but the U-boats continued on their way across the Atlantic without attacking or shadowing.

There was in fact no special trap. The U-boats had no more reason to be afraid of this large and rather important stretch of water than of any other patch in the Atlantic Ocean.

However, by May, 1942, as the Americans got their act together, the U-boats' easy hunting in the west was coming to an end and Dönitz once again switched his main focus of attack. The success of our landing in Africa depended on the regular convoys running between the Straits of Gibraltar and the UK. All this shipping had to cross the route of the U-boats going to and from the Biscay ports.

In this area lay opportunities for the Germans to pick off some rich prizes. The U-boats were not too far from base and within range of their own airfields in the Bordeaux region: they had full fuel tanks, rested crews and a complete new outfit of torpedoes. Dönitz now determined to renew pressure on these Gibraltar convoys, tying down escorts that might be diverted to strengthen further the system of overlapping convoys now operating from the Caribbean up to New York, and threatening the supply routes to the Allied Forces in Africa.

On 9 June, when German Intelligence reported that a convoy was setting out from Gibraltar, five U-boats were sent to take up station across its homeward route, and four more were sent out to form another line sixty miles further north.[8]

On the same day Walker sailed to meet and escort the homeward bound convoy HG 84.[9] The convoy consisted of twenty-three merchant ships, under Commodore H. T. Hudson in *SS Pelavo* which was the leading ship of the centre column. Only *Stork* and the three corvettes, *Marigold*, *Convolvulus* and *Gardenia*, the rescue ship *Copeland* and the *Empire Morn*, a Catapult Aircraft

Merchantman (CAM) were available to take on the nine U-boats drawn up across the convoy's track.[10]

This time Walker was without the invaluable help of *Audacity's* aircraft, constantly available to keep the U-boats at a distance and to drive off the shadowing aircraft. He could call on *Empire Morn's* pilot and single aircraft once and once only. When the decision was taken to catapult the aircraft off, its life was limited. As soon as fuel ran out, the pilot had to ditch in the sea and hope to be picked up. It required a brave man: however keen he was, and however hard he trained, he only had one chance to try out the ditching and recovery procedure. If the procedure didn't work, the pilot had little chance and in any case the aircraft were only capable of one flight before they were abandoned.

Three ships came out from Lisbon to join the convoy. The Focke-Wulfs followed them and so found the convoy on 11 June, and started relaying details of its movements. Throughout the next three days the convoy continued steadily north, with the sure knowledge that every alteration of course was being relayed to the waiting lines of U-boats. The only hope of evasion lay in the weather closing down to give the chance of a major change of course in low visibility. The wind and swell was bad enough to make it difficult for the merchantmen to maintain station, but unfortunately the visibility remained good enough for the shadowing to continue.

On 14 June the first group of five U-boats, code-named Endrass, was successfully guided in. Walker now had four escorts and one aircraft flight to defend a convoy spread over some six square miles of sea, with a perimeter of ten miles to defend. In reasonable weather his Asdic screen could cover an arc of three-quarters of a mile ahead and on either beam of each escort. The key place by day was the sector ahead of the convoy, and by night, astern. These were the positions occupied by *Stork*, but it took time to change stations and the corvettes did not have much advantage of speed over the merchantmen.

This was the third day that the ships had been watching the Focke-Wulfs dodging in and out of the patchy clouds. Walker reckoned that the crunch must come that night and that it was time to take the initiative, disturb the complacency of the German pilots, and get a short breathing space during which the movements of the convoy were not being relayed to the U-boats.

When the next Focke-Wulf was sighted about noon, Walker ordered off *Empire Morn's* Hurricane in an attempt to shoot it down. However, the low cloud gave the German the necessary cover and he made off, leaving the aircraft to complete its one and only patrol, ditch and disappear under the sea while the pilot was heaved out of the water. In his case it worked first time.

At 1600 the first U-boat sighting report in the vicinity of the convoy was picked up by *Copeland* by HF/DF. A single interception of this kind gave only a bearing on which the U-boat was transmitting and no reliable idea of the range. To make matters worse, in this case the bearing indicated that the U-boat lay somewhere astern of the convoy. If this bait was taken, half the escort would have to belt off at top speed in the opposite direction to the convoy which would then start to disappear over the northern horizon, separating from its escorts at a rate of more than a mile every three minutes.

Walker didn't hesitate. He called in *Gardenia* and set off down the line of the bearing. At the corvette's maximum speed it could be two hours before they reached the point from which the U-boat had transmitted. In that time, free from aircraft threat, it could be anywhere in a circle of thirty miles diameter, and the distance from the convoy would have increased by over forty miles. By the time that the two ships could rejoin, it would be dark.

The deathly hush on the bridge as the two ships surged along in line abreast was broken only by the monotonous noise of the Asdic pinger relayed on the bridge loud-speakers. In each ship, six pairs of binoculars swept slowly from side to side. The visibility was good but in the distance a grey watery haze joined the surface of the sea to the low clouds. As the ship rolled and pitched it was difficult to know where the sea ended and sky began.

A voice from aloft: 'U-boat, sir! Right ahead. On the surface!'

Stork's lookout in the crow's nest up above the bridge had spotted the grey shape of the U-boat's conning tower on the surface at the limit of his visibility.

'Alarm right ahead. Load with S.A.P!'

The U-boat was already turning away and making an attempt to escape on the surface, and at the same time draw the escorts farther from the convoy which it had been shadowing. It was well out of range of *Stork*'s four-inch guns and only *Stork*, not *Gardenia*, had a speed advantage of two or three knots. To pull down the range enough to get a reasonable chance of a hit would take an hour or two, and meanwhile the convoy was pulling away in the opposite direction into the trap. Walker thought again of *Audacity*'s Martlets and the way they had pushed the U-boats down below the surface so that he could get at them.

The range crept down to 14,000 yards. Another few hundred yards and John Filleul might be able to have a shot at it. The chances were very poor even then: firing at full elevation at a target twenty feet wide, six and a half miles away, with the ship rolling,[11] did not give the gunnery officer much of a chance.

At this point, the U-boat, which had worked slowly round to a north-westerly course, paralleling the convoy's course, dived. Walker in his report says:

'I estimated that the U-boat would make a violent alteration of course immediately after he dived. This could only be to port or to starboard. I opted for port, and thirty minutes later, at 1720, I picked him up on the Asdics.'

As Walker picked up this target astern of the convoy on the port quarter, the rest of the wolf pack started to gather ahead on the starboard side of the course line. *Marigold* was already chasing a contact reported some fifteen miles away, leaving *Convolvulus* as the sole protector of the convoy as it went on into the gathering darkness. Walker had no time to spare: he made five attacks in rapid succession before *Gardenia* arrived. He now had only eighteen depth charges with which to face the main battle which must soon be upon him. There was no chance of replenishing his supplies.

Walker now tried out the new form of attack that he had evolved to counter the normal evasive tactics that the U-boats used as soon as they heard an escort coming in to attack. While he remained almost stationary, in contact with and pointing at the U-boat, he guided *Gardenia* in to drop a ten-charge pattern at his bidding. When he had directed her right over the position of the U-boat as determined by *Stork*'s Asdic team, he ordered her to start firing the pattern as she ran down the course of the U-boat.

The results were spectacular, if unexpected. Just after the first charges rumbled down *Gardenia*'s rails there was an almighty roar from the stern and a huge flurry of foam. Her ensign dissolved into ragged strips. One of her charges had exploded prematurely, damaging her stern and leaving a badly shaken depth-charge party working to clear the buckled rails.

A few minutes later she was back in action, and Walker directed her in for more attacks. To his frustration none of these produced any definite evidence of destruction.

Meanwhile, left alone with sole charge of the sixteen ships in the convoy, *Convolvulus* had sighted another U-boat on the starboard bow and gone after it. At this time all four escorts were chasing after U-boats, leaving the convoy with no close escorts in station. Walker in *Stork* was left with no alternative. He left the hunt at 2200 to rejoin the convoy, leaving *Gardenia* still in Asdic contact, with orders to continue the attacks until successful or out of ammunition.

The hard-worked terriers had had a busy time. Of the five U-boats in the pack gathering to pounce on the convoy, three had been chased before they had made their first move, and two firmly nailed down in positions which made it impossible for them to get back ahead for an attack that night.

Stork and *Convolvulus* were back in station by midnight, *Marigold* was just coming back into her place on the starboard beam and *Convolvulus* had pressed on to clear the way ahead of the convoy. After a hectic day of chase and attack, only the damaged *Gardenia* was still astern trying to polish off her quarry.

They had performed miracles but it was too good to last. At one o'clock in the morning *U-552* broke through from the front and found the weakness of the defence – one corvette trying to protect five columns of merchantmen moving forward at seven and a half knots. Three ships, the Commodore's ship *Pelavo*, the *Etrib* (1943 tons) and the *Slendal* (same) went up in quick succession before the attacking U-boat withdrew at speed on the surface in front of the convoy. Walker ordered *Marigold* and *Copeland* to pick up survivors astern of the convoy.

At 0400 *Stork* spotted another attack coming in from the stern and dropped a pattern on a U-boat that had just dived, Walker wrongly thought this was a certain kill, but fortunately he did not stay to finish it off as the pack had meanwhile regrouped on the starboard bow.

The next attack came at 0430 sinking in quick succession the SS *Thurso*, an ammunition ship that disappeared in a few minutes after one huge explosion, then the *City of Oxford*, torpedoed in one of her cargo holds. Complete chaos took over when the whole convoy loosed off all their illuminants, silhouetting the rest of the ships and providing a selection of targets for the rest of the pack. This was a repetition of the disastrous night with HG-76, which had so infuriated Walker.

During the firework display, fully illuminated by the merchantmens' pyrotechnics, *Marigold* continued her task of picking up survivors. It was asking for trouble.

But nothing happened: the attacks of the previous day had driven the U-boats' first line of attack down and left them with enough running repairs to prevent them taking advantage of these vulnerable targets.

Walker remained on the bridge until the end of the morning watch. He was depressed by the loss of five ships: the prospects were worse: his convoy was clearly surrounded by U-boats: logically he could have little chance of defending it with his three undamaged escorts, all very low on depth charges. He had asked for air support, but so far none had appeared. With no air support, the U-boats could remain on the surface and move faster than his corvettes. He had a full two days more to go before he would be clear of the Bay of Biscay.

In *Stork*, the rest of the dark hours of the night had passed without incident, but *Gardenia*'s speed was now reduced to ten knots, she had fired all her depth charges, and her Asdics were out of action, *Copeland* and *Marigold* had performed magnificently: the corvette had picked up so many survivors that she could no longer find enough space on deck to work her guns. The 172 survivors on board, many of whom were in a bad way, outnumbered the ship's company by nearly two to one. *Copeland* on the other hand was one of the first convoy rescue ships designed and equipped specially with all the medical staff, equipment, and ship-borne hospital facilities to deal with large numbers of casualties.

Stork and *Marigold* dropped astern of the convoy. The three ships lay close together, unprotected, while the most serious cases were being transferred to *Copeland* and some of the others were being transferred to *Stork*, but this hazardous operation was interrupted when *Marigold* spotted a U-boat on the surface, some six miles astern, outside the extreme range of her single four-inch gun. She broke off the transfer to chase after it and drive it under the surface.

The U-boat showed the corvette a clean pair of heels on the surface, not even bothering to dive: it would no doubt continue to shadow the convoy at extreme visibility range during the rest of the day, sending out homing signals to the rest of the pack. When dusk came, it would position itself ahead of the convoy ready for a night attack.

Marigold came back to complete the transfer of the survivors and both ships then made their best speed to rejoin the convoy. It was going to be another long chase if *Marigold* was to get back level with the merchantmen on their starboard side. She had some way still to go when darkness fell and only ten depth charges left. With her better speed *Stork* was able to get back to her normal day position ahead of the convoy.

On the evening of 15 June, a Liberator joined the convoy and shortly afterwards *Stork* sighted a U-boat on the surface. The Liberator was sent after it and returned shortly afterwards to claim optimistically that they had registered seventeen hits and that their target had either submerged or sunk.[12] The aircraft had not been able to stay for long but its mere presence and this determined attack affected the mobility of the waiting line and gave hope to the escorts and merchantmen that they might break clear of the pack after the coming night.

Meanwhile the convoy was now facing its fifth consecutive night under threat and seemed to be surrounded. *Stork* took up her usual station astern, *Marigold* went back on the starboard beam, and *Gardenia* reappeared from astern after her long chase to catch up.

In theory the escort was now back to its full strength of one sloop and three corvettes. The night was full of false alarms and sightings, and the escorts scurried hither and thither, making as much fuss and covering as much of their sectors as possible. Neither the ships in the convoy nor the U-boats had any way of finding out that one of the corvettes was reduced to ten knots, with no Asdics and no depth charges, and that *Stork* and *Marigold* had only enough charges for one more attack. Only *Convolvulus* had a full load of depth charges and it was she who spotted and drove off the only U-boat that tried to attack from the starboard bow.

On the morning of the 16th a Catalina hove into view and started to lumber round the convoy. Catalinas were heavy and slow seaplanes with great endurance, sitting ducks for their German opponents, but the presence of even one aircraft transformed the picture by preventing the U-boats steaming unseen on the surface outside the range of the escorts' guns. To add to the strength of the air support, a Whitley bomber came out in the afternoon.

Encouraged by this show of air support, Walker seized the initiative. He called in *Convolvulus,* lowered his motorboat and proceeded to collect twelve depth charges from her — with much difficulty. It was most unusual to lower and hoist a cumbersome motorboat at sea but once in the water it cut down the time for the transfer journeys between the two ships carrying one depth charge at a time. This slow and hazardous exercise was carried out in full daylight with no form of Asdic screen around the two ships, outside the perimeter of the convoy which was known to be beset by U-boats on every side.

Under the cover of darkness the convoy turned for home. Walker was not to know that the Germans had called off the attack. According to the German Naval History:[13]

> 'Further attacks were prevented by the escorts which were stronger than expected . . . air cover forced the boats so far away from the convoy that contact was not regained . . . one by one they were frustrated by the A/S screen.'

Once again the Germans blamed it on the weather, claiming that, in the calm seas, the boats stood no chance against the strong air opposition!

Seven of the U-boats went on their way to refuel from *U- 459* and *U- 460,* milch cows stationed off the Azores in mid-Atlantic. None of them had fired any torpedoes except the very successful and well-handled *U-552* which put into her home base to replenish.

The following evening the convoy's protection was further reduced when one of *Stork*'s engines broke down, bringing her maximum speed down to nine knots. Until repaired, she limped along, just able to keep up with her charges. The only sign of the Germans was a single enemy aircraft late one night.

On 20 June the ships of the convoy and their escorts were steaming up the muddy Mersey to battered Liverpool, and for many, sad news of houses lost and loved ones missing.

It would not be long before Hitler would be saying that the only hope of victory was to massacre the Allied and neutral seamen who manned the merchantmen. Henry Kaiser's shipyards in America might turn out Liberty

Ships in six weeks but this production miracle would be of no avail if there were not the skilled and courageous seamen available and ready to man them. Five ships and their cargoes had gone down, but 172 seamen had been rescued by the escorts and brought safe home. Most of them would go straight back to sea to face the same perils, some twice or more. The ships were replaceable but the volunteer British and Allied seamen were not.

This was a fine example of handling an inadequate, slow escort force aggressively against a strong wolf pack attack supported by aircraft. Walker took risks which could have been disastrous and came out on top. With one exception, the U-boats ran away with their tails between their legs, and their unfired torpedoes still in their tubes. One of the boats ordered to the attack never got there.

The U-boats didn't try it again and Dönitz's order banning attacks on Atlantic convoys off the Bay of Biscay remained in force. On 24 June he ordered all U-boats to remain submerged when crossing the Bay of Biscay, thereby multiplying greatly the unproductive time spent on passage.

Walker said in his report, 'I am proud of the offensive spirit, initiative and sheer guts displayed by these corvettes'.

This convoy battle, during which three corvettes, one disabled, and one sloop drove off eight U-boats,[15] of which seven never fired a shot, took place at the time in the Battle of the Atlantic when the Germans were coming to the end of their unparalleled slaughter of the well-lit, undefended shipping in the Caribbean and the Gulf of Mexico. They were gearing up for their final drive at the Atlantic convoys. Much has been said about the tremendous morale and courage of the men in the U-boats, but this was certainly not an occasion on which they or their leaders showed any stomach for fighting a smaller force of British tars led by a man of Walker's calibre.

It was fortunate for Convoy HG 84 that the wolf pack was not led by a commander with the determination and drive of Walker. It would have been annihilated. Probably a greater victory than the sinking of *U-252*.

Walker had proved in the few months that he had been at sea in command of *Stork* and the Senior Officer of the 36th Escort Group that he was an officer of outstanding fighting ability. He had handled large and small mixed forces of escorts with uncanny skill. He had taken risks which had paid off. His ships had sunk five U-boats in four months. He had successfully conducted the defence of several convoys with great *élan* against the odds. He had built up a team bursting with pride and enthusiasm. He accepted no credit and took all the blame. His reports bubbled over with positive practical recommendations and read like *The Boy's Own Paper*.

The Commander-in-Chief was not slow to show his appreciation. In the mid-year list of 1942, Walker's name appeared at the head of the names of officers promoted to Captain, dating from 30 June, 1942.

CHAPTER FOUR

CAPTAIN (D) SECOND SUPPORT GROUP[1]

Liverpool at War.

Admiral Sir Percy Noble had moved the headquarters of the Western Approaches Command to Liverpool in February, 1941. In this month Hitler had issued Directive No. 23, concentrating the Luftwaffe's bombing on the ports, harbours and ship-building centres of the UK. Liverpool ranked first amongst these by a big margin. During the six years of war, the docks were to handle an average of 13,000 ships per annum and a total shipping tonnage of 120,000,000 tons, plus 23,000,000 tons of coastal trade, carrying 56,500,000 tons of imports. This included 19,000,000 tons of food and just under 74,000 aircraft and gliders. 4,700,000 troops passed through the port.

It is a great city and at that time it was at the height of its importance as a port. Unlike any other in the UK, it was closely linked to the industrial heart of the Midlands, populated by a complicated mix of nationalities and served by over 40 miles of docks and 120 miles of railways. Just across the muddy Mersey, linked by the road and rail tunnels and the ferries, lies Birkenhead and behind that the big complex of the Bidston Docks stretching back into the countryside of the Wirral. On the south bank lay Cammell Laird's great ship-building yard, turning out every type of warship from aircraft carrier to submarine.

The Commander-in-Chief Western Approaches was now responsible not only for the protection of shipping but also for the routeing of the convoys and for the working of the whole Atlantic convoy system.[2] He brought together in Derby House, close by the waterfront of the Mersey, the elements that controlled all the Allied forces in the Battle of the Atlantic. For the first time, Western Approaches Command, No 15 Group, Coastal Command Headquarters, and a duplicate of the Admiralty Trade Plot showing the movements of merchant shipping and convoys, were all housed under the same roof as one operations centre. They were connected by direct line to the Submarine Tracking Unit and the Operational Intelligence Centre at the Admiralty.

The centre of command had moved from Plymouth to a very different environment. Plymouth was a West Country port which had been for centuries a Naval base and a Royal Dockyard centre, steeped in the traditions of the Royal Navy.

By contrast, Liverpool, known at one time as the second city of the Empire, was a cosmopolitan city, inhabited by people originating from many different countries of the world, with a population four times the size of Plymouth. Liverpool and Birkenhead were commercial, not Royal Navy ports.

Noble needed further to strengthen his staff with senior officers with fresh experience of the war at sea, and with strong positive views on the deployment of the new forces that were about to come into play. So the wheel had come full circle. Walker had regained the rank denied to him in peacetime: his strong outspoken views and dedication to anti-submarine warfare, which had held up his progress in the inter-war years, now became his strength. He had been awarded two DSOs in the last year, had a recent record of success in action at sea, and was one of the few senior officers with practical knowledge of operating with an escort carrier in defence of a trade convoy. In the conduct of the actions against convoy HG 76, his sinking of *U-252*, and his defence of convoy HG 84, he had demonstrated how an inadequate force of poorly armed slow escorts could be used aggressively to fight off a powerful force of highly trained U-boats, at the peak of their form.

'He had salt water round his lug-'oles.'

Walker was brought ashore to a new appointment as Captain (D) Liverpool in October, 1942, when the Battle of the Atlantic had entered its most critical phase.

In September, 1942, Support Groups were being formed and by the end of the year six escort carriers, the successors of *Audacity*, would be at sea: the new British-designed ten centimetre short-wave radar and heavier depth-charges had been developed and supplied to the escort ships. In January the first escorts were fitted with the Hedgehog.[3]

The entry of the United States into the war at the beginning of the year had increased rather than reduced the load on the Atlantic escorts. The resumption of the Arctic convoys, the heavy demands for protection of the troop convoys to North Africa and the continuing shortage of escort vessels prevented the full implementation of the aggressive actions which Walker advocated and for which the new escort ships had been built and equipped.

This was not a marginal shortage. A combined assessment by the British and the Americans in March, 1942, showed that there was a need for 1315 escorts. Less than half of this number (505 ships) were then available.[4]

Nor was it a short-term shortage. The demands from America for the escalation of the Pacific War conflicted with the need for the ships, supplies and men needed to get the Allies back into Europe. Admiral King asked for, and received, help from the Royal Navy to build up his escort forces on the east coast of America, but the Allies could not release an aircraft carrier for the Far East, which he also needed and asked for. At the same time Stalin was insisting that we should increase our Arctic convoys and open a second front immediately. Churchill was not able to accede to either of Stalin's demands and got 'a rough and surly answer'.

Meantime the burden on the Atlantic escorts had increased enormously. The area to be defended now extended over to the east coast of America and down to the Caribbean and the Gulf of Mexico. The U-boat fleet had rocketed to 365 boats, of which about 195 were operational and 161 available for the Atlantic. Between July and October, 1942, sixty-one new boats had joined the fleet, and the Allies had sunk only thirty-two.[5]

In this year, as Dönitz's easy pickings in the Caribbean were brought to an end, the opposing wolf packs and Allied escorts finally came to grips in mid-Atlantic in their biggest convoy confrontations. By a stroke of ill fortune, the battle of the cryptographers had temporarily swung in favour of the Germans. They had reduced the delays in deciphering the Allied Convoy Code, and from the beginning of 1942 had also begun to read the traffic in Naval Cypher No 3, which was used in the communications between the Admiralty, the Canadians and the United States. To make matters worse there was a gap in the ability of Bletchley Park to read the Shark Enigma signals.

Allied losses in the Merchant Fleets were appalling.

In the four months from July to October the U-boats sank 396 ships, more than two million tons. During the whole of that dreadful year, we had lost the enormous total of 1,664 merchant ships, eight million tons.

Even more serious was the loss of their gallant crews. These merchant seamen were recruited not only from the Allies but from all the neutral seafaring nations. Many of them had now been in the forefront of the battle and under fire without cease since September, 1939, three years of constant exposure to death by drowning, burning or hypothermia. Although the shipowners were minting money, the seamans' pay was stopped at the moment when their ships went down.

Churchill said, 'The U-boat attack was our worst evil. It would have been wise for the Germans to stake all upon it .... It constituted a terrible event in a very bad time'.

Dönitz held the same view and fought Hitler all through the war to get absolute priority for his U-boats. Fortunately he was not successful.

Nevertheless, at this time the Germans were winning this battle upon which the whole outcome of the war depended. They were sinking merchantmen faster than they could be replaced and bringing U-boats into action against Allied shipping much faster than we could sink them. If this continued, fuel reserves would soon be exhausted and our fleets of warships and cargo vessels would be unable to leave port. Aircraft would be grounded. Munitions factories would run out of raw materials. The build-up for the second front would come to a halt and the basic food rations would be cut again.

Few British believed that the situation was that bad. They just soldiered on, driven by the blind belief, sheer obstinacy and sense of humour that had been their main support since the collapse of Europe under the Nazis.

The increase in the number of U-boats now massed in the North Atlantic and the success of their pack attacks required new thinking. The vital role of aircraft from escort carriers and the need to close the gap in mid-Atlantic were now recognized as absolute essentials. There was a need to handle much larger escort fleets and to work with carriers, and aircraft with widely different capabilities. This was a new type of warfare for the Royal Navy.

There were daily problems of communication with the mounting numbers of US escorts and with the Royal Canadian Navy which had increased from nothing to a major strength in the Atlantic and had now taken over the responsibility for the ocean convoys on the western side of the Atlantic. All the ships in the Western Approaches were manned mainly by Hostilities Only ratings and officers from the RNVR and RNR, who were serving in the Navy for the duration of the war only. Some of them were by now battle-hardened, but they had not got the background and years of training of the regular Royal Navy.

In an amazingly short time new ships would start to roll off the production lines in America, and these new ships must of necessity be manned by inexperienced ship's companies. Very soon, the most powerful of the long-awaited Support Groups,[6] in ships fitted with a range of new equipment and weapons would be ready for sea.

At this greatest crisis in our history, it was not surprising that Walker did not welcome his move to a shore appointment. There was, however, a real need to bring him back from sea for this change of duty.

The balance of priorities was shifting from lack of ships, aircraft and adequate anti-submarine weapons to even greater emphasis on the problems of new tactics, training and manning at all levels. Hitler foresaw with deadly clarity that the time had come when his most effective, perhaps his only counter to the huge production power of the Americans would be to kill off the maximum number of merchant seaman from the Allied Nations, and to so terrify the seamen from the neutral countries that they would back off from further sea service. For this reason he had ordered Dönitz to pick up only Masters and Chief Engineers from ships sunk, an order that Dönitz did not pass on, at least in writing. The American historian, Professor Morison, tell us of the very high rates of pay demanded by American sailors to persuade them to take part in the Arctic convoys and by those who had the misfortune to man the Allied bases in Russia.

In October, 1942, Liverpool had clawed its way back from a severe hammering from the German airforce. Raids had started in a small way in September, 1940. The first major disaster occurred in the early morning of 29 November. At 0155 the Junior Technical School, which was being used as the Durning Road public shelter was hit by a parachute mine. Of the 290 people in the shelter, 164 were killed and 96 seriously injured. The raids escalated and 702 people were killed in a raid along the docks on 20 December. This raid damaged Gladstone Dock, the Liverpool home and base of the Western Approaches' flotillas. The casualties to the civilian population in this one raid were equivalent to the sinking of a major warship.

Much worse was to come. On the night of 3 May, 1941, a series of night raids started, which were to continue without a break until 8 May. Nearly 3000 civilians were killed or seriously injured in Liverpool, Bootle, Wallasey and Birkenhead. There were hundreds of fires and a full-scale firestorm was only narrowly averted by the tremendous efforts of the fire-fighting services and the arrival of fire engines from all over the country. Had the wind blown harder that night, the whole city would have been destroyed by fire. The river entrances to the docks were blocked, ships were imprisoned and 80,000 tons of shipping sunk in the docks. Sixty-nine of the 144 berths in the docks were unusable. The famous overhead railway was down in several places.

At the end of this series of raids, Liverpool, the main port of the UK, was reeling. But the Luftwaffe had had enough. On their journey along the west coast and back, they had been worried by the fighters. Their aim had become remarkably inaccurate. Many of their bombs now fell on the decoy sites well away from the real targets and they even dropped a few on Dublin, killing and seriously wounding 115 Irish. They were also needed in Norway to protect Hitler from the invasion that he was convinced would be launched there – a continuous obsession that distracted him on several occasions.

The raids left behind horrible slaughter and confusion. 10,000 houses had been destroyed and 184,000 damaged. Bootle, the area along and behind the docks, was worst hit with another 51,000 homeless and 90% of the houses destroyed.

At the height of the raid the merchant ship *Malakand*, loaded with a full cargo of explosives and ammunition, blew up in Huskisson Dock, hurling steel plates and debris for two and a half miles.

My wife to be, then three years old, was asleep in the reinforced half-cellar of her parent's house in Everton Valley, one and a half miles away. Her mother was outside.

'The appalling explosion sounded as if it was in the next garden. I rushed down to the cellar: all the windows were blown in: the remains of the plaster, loosened by previous raids, was still showering down from the ceiling and the walls. The frame of the cellar window had been blown in at an angle over her bed. We lifted her over the fence into our neighbour's house. She was still sleeping soundly.'

Yet Carolyn maintains fifty years later that my snores wake her up!

The docks remained in action. By 9 May the dockers were back on full shift loading and unloading cargoes, and the port was approaching full capacity again by the middle of June.

Liverpool's victory in this battle was one of the most crucial in the whole campaign. It was just as vital to the eventual triumph in the Battle of the Atlantic as any of the hard-fought naval engagements out of sight of land. It was fought by civilian women and men in squalid and austere conditions with little glamour and swagger, and much unsung heroism. The Liverpudlians were stretched to their limit but they did not break.

Liverpool was always a lively, pleasant and welcoming place to the men coming in from sea. Although the pubs shut at 9pm for many months, there was singing and drinking in the Flotilla Club at Gladstone Dock close by the ships. A ghost train ran very late at night from Southport, which seemed far from the war. It was there, on a summer's evening in 1941, just after the bombing of Liverpool, that four of us seamen learnt in the bar of the Caradoc that *Hood* had been sunk. After a few more beers, we were staggering down the street in our bell-bottom trousers singing:

> Roll on the *Nelson*, the *Rodney*, *Renown*;
> You can't sink the *Hood*,
> But the bastard's gone down.

The theatres still operated. It was possible to sit behind the orchestra in the Royal Philharmonic Hall for a bob. The Grafton Rooms were full of life. Able Seaman Max Savage and I sat back-to-back on the floor, in the middle of the dance hall while the rest of the dancers wheeled around us with linked arms, singing:

> All the nice girls —
> love a sailor,
> All the nice girls —
> love a tar,
> Because there's something —
> about a sailor,
> And you know what sailors are.

Liverpool, with all its scars, was home to thousands of seamen, many of them cut off from their real homes in Europe by the Germans. We have all left a bit of our heart there.[7]

Birth of a Ship
The Commissioning of His Majesty's Ship *Starling*.

Captain Johnnie Walker was to command this ship for the rest of his life. He called her 'My Gallant *Starling*'. In one and a half years she would sink fifteen U-boats.

She was laid down in Fairfields yard in Glasgow at the end of 1941. In February, 1943, as she neared completion, an advance party of officers and key senior ratings joined the ship at the builder's yard. Our Navigator, Lieutenant Arthur Ayers RNVR, referred to from now on as 'the Pilot', remembers arriving at the yard on a cold February day. He describes the scene that met his eyes on 15 February, 1943, in filthy Scottish weather:

'As she lay there, all I saw was a mass of black plates, red lead and rust alongside the dock wall and it was there that I met the advance party from *Stork* which had just arrived. The first man that I saw was Chief Engine Room Artificer Eddie Freestone who seemed very unhappy about taking over the ship at five days' notice, but he managed.'

An all-night journey in an overcrowded and unheated train, sitting on a suitcase in the corridor, brought me to Glasgow. After a ride on the dirty and stuffy subway and an early morning tramp through the back streets, I finally reached the big main gates of Fairfields Yard.

Starling had not yet been given a name: she was just Job Number SL 11701, lying somewhere amongst the apparent confusion of a very big and busy yard in the midst of the wartime rush. Picking my way along the slimy roads between the great sheds, surrounded and deafened by the clatter and hammering of the riveters, I made my way to the dock where the ship lay. To the right and left, through the doors of the buildings could be seen vistas of great machines and spinning driving belts. Down the congested tracks between the sheds, long unwieldy lorries with overhanging loads fought for right of way with railway trucks full of rusty iron plates. On the edges of the dock, cranes trundled to and fro hooting officiously.

In the dock itself there was a confused jumble of stumpy naked masts sticking drunkenly out of grotesque top-heavy hulls. On board the half-built ships, piles of metalwork obscured the upper decks.

The embryo of *Starling* lay amongst this heap of junk, tucked away behind the towering hull of a cruiser. A cold drizzle cast a gloomy spell over this depressing scene. The little that could be seen of the ship looked more decrepit than the oldest coal-burning tramp that ever belched smoke from one east coast port to another. The acrid smell of the red-hot rivets did nothing for my breakfastless stomach and my head throbbed from the remains of an unenviable hangover after a short few days leave in London.

I went on board over the two planks that connected her with the dockside, and found my way on deck and into the passage way. The smell was even worse below: the air was cold, damp and foul, resounding with the clatter of hammers and the hiss of escaping compressed air. Ragged holes in the decks gave glimpses of machinery down in the bowels of the ship. Tangled knots of bare electric cables hung down from the deckheads. Men in cloth caps and overalls scurried backwards and forwards. In a compartment some shipyard workers whiled away their breakfast break playing cards on top of a packing case. It was quite clear that I wasn't welcome and I wandered back to look for the office, thoroughly deflated and dispirited by this first encounter.

The office wasn't too impressive either; the five of us in the advance party were jammed into a small wooden hut on the dockside. The Pilot had a great crate of charts parked outside. He honestly believed that he had first priority on any dry clean space and that the only decent table was his so that he could get all his charts up to date. For this he certainly needed space because *Starling* was a sloop and was therefore equipped with charts covering all the oceans of the world.

I made myself some coffee, sat on an upturned packing case, and put my cup down on the only table.

'Not there, Alan! Don't put your flaming coffee cup on my charts.'

How many times in the months to come would I hear this same despairing complaint.

In wartime officers and key ratings appointed to stand by ships in the last stages of their completion were there to act in an advisory capacity. They had no direct powers, but it was clearly in their interest to make sure that the ship left the yard as an efficient fighting unit, lacking only a trained crew. Their relationship with the builders was not easy. They had no ship-building training or experience. The yard was under enormous pressure to meet a completion date. Apart from the Pilot and his charts, the one man who already seemed to be part of the ship was Eddie Freestone, dressed in filthy working overalls covered in black grease. He never looked any different throughout the whole commission except when he got out his number ones for a rare ceremonial occasion or a run ashore. He was much too busy looking after his beloved machinery.

By lunchtime the first feeling of depression caused by the apparent confusion and squalor in the yard had been chased away by a rush of curiosity and, of course, 'bright' ideas. Although everything was being installed according to the Admiralty plans and drawings which covered each item in the ship, the team standing by had accumulated enough hard-won experience to be able to work out a few small details which would make the odd seconds difference in action. A switch moved a few inches, an instrument tilted through a few degrees, another hook to stow some gear that might otherwise fall and block a pump, these things must be attended to. There were the little bits of unspecified equipment that would give the ship a style of its own. Brass tampions with the ship's crest to fit into the gun muzzles when in harbour were not considered to be absolutely essential in wartime and so might be omitted from the official specifications, but they did something for the panache of the ship: and the man in the foundry might help, particularly if the gunnery officer didn't smoke and could spare him a tin of tobacco.

There was so much to be learnt in so little time before the ship went to sea: the operation and the layout of the complex multi-position telephone systems, the damage control systems, the boat-hoisting arrangements, the Asdic system, the gunnery system, the depth-charge and ammunition supply systems were just a few of the things that had to be mastered.

The key rating of every department joined the ship to watch and learn about the installation of his own equipment. More officers appeared and some were sent away on last-minute courses to cover the latest drills and routines for operating their weaponry.

The ship was, of course, uninhabitable, so we lived ashore in billets, flats or hotels. Days at sea on a draughty open bridge were replaced by hours in an office surrounded by piles of paper and the clatter of the typewriter. Instead of an unsympathetic able seaman pulling us from our bunks in the early hours of the morning with a bad weather report, our landladies shook us with cups of tea. For a week or two we enjoyed leisurely breakfasts and travel down to the Yard on the subway hidden behind newspapers, no longer bound by routine and unvaried discipline.

Very quickly, the jumbled mass of girders and plates was riveted and welded into place, and the ship began to take shape. Leisurely breakfasts became less and less common as the days of preliminary trials began. Stores had to be brought on board and mustered; soggy sandwiches replaced proper meals and very soon we realized with a shock that the great day of commissioning was only two weeks away.

Out of the blue we heard that Captain Frederic John Walker had been appointed to *Starling* in command and as Captain (D) Second Support Group. He was going to bring many of his officers and ship's company from *Stork*, which had gone into dock with her bows blown off during the African landings. On the one hand, *Starling* was going to have the great advantage of starting with an experienced ship's company, but on the other hand it was going to mean some very hard work for the team already standing by the ship. Most of the key ratings had to be sent back to barracks, and the new bunch from *Stork* brought up to date on their new home. The first two to arrive were Lieutenant Michael Impey, Walker's specialist Asdic officer, and John Filleul, who had been promoted to Lieutenant on 1 March, both of whom had served in Walker's team in *Stork*.

The last days before the final inspection by the Admiral Superintending Contract Built Ships were scenes of terrific activity in the Yard. Ship's Officers had now prepared the Watch Bills and each man's watch card which would tell him his part of the ship, his mess, where to sling his hammock, his locker, his Action Station and all the other details which would regulate his life for the coming months.

On the night before the inspection the last air pressure hoses and heaps of tools were taken ashore. The ship was almost complete structurally but still looked like a wreck recently brought up from the ocean bed.

As the last workmen left the ship a great armada of Glasgow buses drew up alongside and discharged an army of cleaning ladies, complete with the tools of their trade, and, just behind them, the painters. They worked all through the night in relays and when the morning came they had completed a magical transformation from a jumble of iron into a ship that looked as if she might one day be good enough to enter the Royal Navy.

Meanwhile, down in the barracks in Devonport, the loud-speakers blared out all day long, every day, the lists of ratings drafted to ships all over the world. These loud-speakers controlled the destiny of thousands of men who made up the floating population of this great barracks, commonly known as Jago's Mansion. This Mansion was supported by a number of barrack stanchions, who were long-service able seamen, nicknamed 'Stripeys' from the three badges on their sleeves, a band of men who did not want to go to sea. What is more they found ways and means of avoiding the drafts and the eagle eyes of the Masters-at-Arms. There were no personal feelings in these institutions; most nights were spent sitting upright in cold, damp air raid shelters; most days in unpleasant and boring jobs such as providing sentries or clearing bombed houses in the devastated city that was Plymouth.

For most people one day in Jago's Mansion was one day too many and any draft to any ship must mean an improvement.

Able Seaman Walter Riley had been listening subconsciously all day for his name; in the afternoon it came over the loudspeakers.

'The following report to the Master-at-Arms for draft to Job Number J11701. Able Seaman Walter Riley D/JX 178006.'

As the list was reeled off, a warm sensation of familiarity came over him. Most of the names were the old crowd from *Stork*! Up in the barrack messdeck, as he collected his bag and hammock, he found little knots of his old shipmates already collecting, discussing the latest buzzes and creating new ones. What was this "Job Number J11701"? Where were they all bound?

They boarded the special train and set off on an all-night journey in blacked-out carriages through blacked-out Britain. Thank God for the Salvation Army who appeared in unlikely places with cups of hot tea.

The day after the Admiral's inspection was Commissioning Day. To the Yard it was the end of seventeen months and four days of concentrated effort and coordination of innumerable activities and materials. In 1915, this great yard, Fairfields, had built a battlecruiser in just eighteen months, but there had been little money and little warship work between the wars.

The load now was the heaviest ever and would not end when Job Number J11701 was finished. J11702 (*Woodcock* to be) was lying in the neighbouring dock and was due for completion two months later.

But this was a very special ship, to be commanded by this man Captain Walker, who already had quite a reputation and a couple of DSOs. To him the ship was always to be 'My Gallant *Starling*'.

After this day the ship would cease to be a lifeless hulk resounding with the noise of riveting and welding, and would become a throbbing man-of-war, humming with machinery and alive with the talk, laughter and complaints of many men. This was the day when two hundred men shifted house at the same time and met the friends (and enemies) with whom they would live for months in the closest proximity and under the most exacting conditions.

The ship, its upper works still glimmering in its fresh paint, rapidly took on a new appearance as the first sailors came over the side. Bunches of men, staggering along with their bags on one shoulder and their hammocks on the other, followed the signposts down the narrow passageways, directed by harassed petty officers in their shirt sleeves. As the train disgorged more and more men to crowd down the gangways, it seemed impossible that any more could be crammed into such a small space; the mess decks, empty a few minutes before, lost their semblance of order and began to resemble an ant's nest in a treacle pot. Piles of kit bags littered the decks. Down below, the great competition for the best place to sling a hammock was in full swing. In the middle of this mêlée, others tried to find room to gulp down their first hot meal for twelve hours; an ex-policeman sweated gloomily alongside an ex-salesman as both tried to stow impossible quantities of badly folded gear into adjacent lockers while a cursing leading seaman climbed wearily over their suitcases.

In 1943, the proportion of regular naval ratings available for draft to any ship was small. Consequently the first few weeks of most ships' working-up period were often nightmares. The new Hostilities Only ratings, recruited from all the cities, towns, villages, factories and schools of Britain, arrived in their ships to find that not only were they going to live in an entirely different environment, but they were also expected to understand a new vocabulary, full of complex terms for which their short basic training had not been long enough to prepare them. They were thrown into close proximity with scores of others from every walk of life, with whom they had to eat, work, sleep and spend each minute of the day and night, with no hope of privacy, for many weeks on end.

Very soon the seaman learnt that the plain simple drills and skills set out in his *Admiralty Manual of Seamanship*, Volume One, dealt with only a small part of his life. He would need to turn his hand to any and every task; he would have to live and get along with others, whether he liked them or not.

Starling's commissioning went comparatively easily. There is no doubt that by inheriting a good proportion of the crew from *Stork* she started with a considerable advantage. The experience of these veterans, already used to working and living together in the hard conditions of the Atlantic in wartime, was invaluable to the young ratings going to sea for the first time; they had plenty of old hands[8] around them with plenty of sea time behind them. It might take them little time to acclimatize to the new ship and new colleagues, but the nucleus of *Stork's* crew brought with them a tradition of success and confidence in their Commanding Officer, born of experience.

The only difficulty was that *Stork's* men brought an old name to a new ship. *Starling* would have to sink half-a-dozen U-boats by ramming, depth charges and gunfire before the old hands really believed that their ship was now *Starling* and not *Stork*.

The first entry in the Ship's Log, (which sadly has now disappeared) was Monday 22 March, 1943. On the following day the real life of the ship began as hands set to, storing and victualling the ship. Two hundred and forty hungry men can get through a lot of food in six weeks.

The daily routine of the ship started with Hands Fall In at 0800 and finished at 2055 with Hands under Punishment to Muster (yes, even on the first day), before Piping Down. The next day a tug took us up to Prince's Pier to ammunition ship.

This is a big job in which every man in the ship is involved. It is also a good test of a ship's organization. Although it takes only a short while to blast off the whole stock of ammunition, it takes many hours to replenish and to stow. Each shell must be taken out of a lighter or railway truck, unscrewed from its special box, carried by hand into the magazines right down in the bowels of the ship and the box screwed up and returned to its transport. Every shell has stamped on it the details of manufacture, the type and date of the explosive filling and the batch number. The shells must be systematically stowed and systematically served up to the guns in action, so that each broadside is made up from shells from the same batch, thus minimizing the risk of error in range through variations in charge.

This was the Gunner, Stan Baulcomb's big day. He had drawn up a plan of the ship and detailed the exact station and duty of every man on board. Signposts were positioned to control the stream of men entering with their shells and going up for more. Cranes on the jetty were standing by to lift in the depth charges.

Additional gangways were secured opposite each ammunition hatch, ready for the off at 0800 sharp. A masterpiece of organization. But the train didn't turn up at 0800 sharp. It turned up at 1100.

Since we were due to go to sea the following day for trials, the hands worked in shifts throughout the day, the afternoon and on until midnight, first in the cold Glasgow fog and later in the dim blue lights of the vast shed in the black-out, until the many tons of explosives had been stowed safely below in their proper places.

No sooner had weary bodies settled into their hammocks than the air-raid sirens started their dreary wail and it was 'Fire Parties To Muster'. Guns and the gunnery officer had certainly started off determined to make themselves unpopular.

The only man excused this duty was the Pilot and his Yeoman, who were still trying to get their charts up to date. After all, we were to proceed several miles to the Tail of the Bank on the morrow.

Next morning, we slipped from the jetty and proceeded down the narrow dredged channel, under our own power for the first time. On the way we passed Fairfields Yard. Every foot of the jetty lining the river was packed with the men who had built the ship on which our lives would depend for the coming months. They watched her for the first and last time as she moved slowly downstream against the flood. I had seen *Starling* grow from a shapeless hulk with a number to a live ship with a name. They had seen her as a mere keel, growing to a ribbed skeleton and then to a top-heavy hulk on the slipway. They had seen her launched, waterborne, commissioned and taken over by the Royal Navy.

Now they stood in complete silence to see this new untried ship glide down the river with her white ensign fluttering out astern. We could feel the wish of 'Good Luck and God Speed' reaching out to us across the water.

They turned back; and soon in the distance we heard the hammering and riveting starting up again as they went to complete *Woodcock*. We went on down towards the Clyde and the open sea beyond.

Starling pushed her nose out beyond the boom defence vessels for the first time on 27 March to carry out gunnery and anti-submarine trials. These were followed by full-power trials over the measured mile. During full power trials there was some conflict between our engineer (Chiefie Bramble), who wanted to reach only the minimum speed required to get the ship accepted, and the Yard Management who wanted to show off. Chiefie, and his fellow engineers in the Yard, wanted to keep the speed as low as possible; they didn't want to see the spanking new boilers and engines pushed to their limits a couple of days after the ship had left the dock. Chiefie also wanted to have 'a bit in hand', so that in an emergency, he would be able to achieve the impossible in hot pursuit and acquire great glory.

We averaged nineteen and a half knots on the first runs and exactly twenty knots on the final runs. Our fuel consumption was 2.435 tons per hour and we developed 4300 shaft horsepower, with the port engine doing 295 revolutions and the starboard engine 305.

That night it blew hard; as the wind and tide tore at her, *Starling* shook and trembled as if keen to be away; she dragged her mooring wilfully all round the anchorage, and for the first of many times the duty watch had to turn out to drop a second anchor.

The Scottish weather dogged us right through our trials. Conditions throughout the ship were at their worst. We still had a team from Fairfields on board; there were no full watches being kept; the crowding in the messdecks gave a foretaste of things to come. Nobody had yet settled in, but somehow the old hands got the best billets.

By 3 April, twelve days after commissioning, most of the little jobs had been done. There was some sort of order on board and the last of the Fairfields party were going down the gangway on their way home. A huge clean-up, organized by the leading hands of the messes and backed up by the stripeys, swung into action down below, and at 0755 we weighed both anchors and were off down the Clyde on our way to Moville to take on oil. Thankfully we began to shake off the dust and grime of the builder's yard as we set off to Moville to oil and turned to the serious task of getting ready to face the Atlantic.

Ten minutes after securing to the oiler, a signal arrived directing us up to Londonderry to have the 291 radar set removed and the latest available HF/DF gear fitted, so back came our friends the dockyard workers. But this time they were Irish; there were plenty of eggs and chickens, a football ground within reach, dance halls and, above all, a very adequate population of WRNS.

This last-minute modification provided a good excuse for Walker. He believed very strongly that it was the task of the commanding officer, and nobody else, to train his officers and through them his men. For one flimsy reason or another, he managed to keep *Starling* out of the hands of the Western Approaches training base at Tobermory, although all the other ships in the Group went through the capable hands of Commodore Stephenson and his staff.

In this case the last-minute dockyard modifications took up the few days allocated for *Starling's* final sea exercises, and she did not go to Tobermory. She suffered from the lack of the formal working-up period that the other ships in the Group had just completed. When we did get away, the next few days were filled with headaches and frustrations. It was only possible to fit in three or four preliminary exercises to accustom the ship's company to the new gear, but in that short time we managed to get wires round both screws at the same time. We went out for anti-submarine exercises and were rammed by the target submarine, picking up a small hole in our stern. Our first gunnery trial attracted the wrath of the skipper of a small coaster hidden in the murk and a lady ashore in Northern Ireland was most embarrassed and indignant when her outside privy fell from under her, after a direct hit from one of our practice shells. (This was the start of *Starling's* rivalry with *Wild Goose*, about which more will be said. On this occasion *Wild Goose* did better than *Starling*; she bagged a hospital ship without increasing the number of casualties on board.)

Once at sea Walker quietly but firmly clamped down with an iron hand. He made it very clear that our task was to destroy U-boats and all that we did from then onwards was directed to this end. The first paragraph of his orders read:

SECOND SUPPORT GROUP OPERATING INSTRUCTIONS[9]
(Short Title – S.G.2)
OBJECT
The object of the Second Support Group is to destroy
U-boats, particularly those which menace our convoys.

There is a significant difference between these orders and the standard objective of an Escort Group, which was:

'The Safe and Timely Arrival Of The Convoy'

When the rest of the Group appeared, *Starling* was ready to take her place at the head of the line as Captain (D)'s ship – Walker's ship. Ready to seek out, wear down and destroy the attacking U-boats, while the close escorts looked after the defence of the convoy. The sloops first came together on 28 April, 1943, off the north coast of Ireland and started to take up station in line ahead. Each ship was fresh from their period of intensive working-up training under Commodore G. O. Stephenson, who had returned to the fray to set up and run the sea training of the Royal Navy's anti-submarine forces at Tobermory. 'Monkey' Stephenson was a formidable character whose name and presence left an indelible impression on almost every ship that operated in the Western Approaches. He was a Vice-Admiral (retired) who had taken charge of the evacuation off the beaches of La Panne, before setting up the training operation, through which nearly all Western Approaches ships passed (except *Stork* and *Starling*).

Captain Walker paused at the end of his short walk to the after end of the bridge. He looked back over the upper deck, past the starboard side of the funnel, over the twin oerlikons to the barrels of the twin four-inch guns on X gun mounting, pointing away from him over the stern. Beyond them, two cables apart, he could see the menacing line of the other five ships of his Group as they followed his wake round in a gentle curve. He could just see the six four-inch guns on each of the following sloops as they heeled gently to port and took up station on the new course. Away astern, the last of the sunshine picked out the line of the hills standing up from the haze on the horizon above Rathlin Island. A perfect end to a sparkling spring day. He imagined the young officers of the Watch in the ships astern peering over the windscreens on their bridges to pick out the tell-tale kink in *Starling*'s wake which would show them the exact moment to put the wheel over, so that each ship would follow precisely in his track.

He felt good. It had been a long haul, stretching back over thirty-four tough and often frustrating years. Today he had reached one of the high points in any Naval Officer's career. He had been entrusted not only with the command of his own new ship, but with a flotilla of six of the finest little ships that the Royal Navy had ever built, designed for the job that they had to do, and fitted with all the available equipment that three hard years of bitter war had shown to be necessary in the Battle of the Atlantic. Each ship had come straight from its intensive working-up training and was now ready for battle under his command.

Astern, the rest of the Group, His Majesty's Ships *Cygnet*, *Kite*, *Wild Goose*, *Woodpecker* and *Wren* fell into station. They looked for all the world like a squadron of little cruisers.

The Second Support Group

Abstract from Captain Walker's Group Operational Instructions[10]

OBJECT

'Our job is to *kill*, and all officers must fully develop
the spirit of vicious offensive. No matter how many
convoys we may shepherd through in safety, we shall
have failed unless we can slaughter U-boats.
All energies must be bent to this end.'

In March, 1943, our fortunes appeared to be at their lowest ebb. Dönitz's fleet of U-boats in commission had increased to 417, of which 229 were operational.[11] With his new influence as Commander-in-Chief of the German Navy, he was planning to launch a further twenty-seven U-boats every month in the second half of 1943. We had lost forty-one merchant ships in the first ten days and fifty-six in the second ten days of March, totalling more than half a million tons, of which two-thirds were sunk in convoy.

At this time, and right up to the summer of 1943, Beobachter-Dienst was able to decypher the Allied convoy code. In contrast, Bletchley Park had not been able to break the German U-boat cypher from 1 February, 1942, until 13 December, 1942. After that they had made steady progress, but, on 10 March, 1943, they had run into one of their 'blind' periods, when the Germans introduced a fourth rotor to the Enigma coding machine. For a vital period of nine days there was a blank in the decrypts and during this period convoys SC 122 and HX 229 were attacked by forty U-boats, 'the largest pack which has ever been collected together in one place for the same operation'. A major slaughter took place.

The situation at this time was so critical that the Naval Staff wrote of this period: 'It appeared possible that we should not be able to continue (to regard) convoy as an effective system of defence'. The Director of Naval Intelligence was forced to warn that the flow of information about U-boat movements would cease and might not be renewed for 'some time – perhaps even months'.

With a tremendous effort, and probably because they had anticipated such a crisis, Bletchley Park were able to break the new system and start to return to effective operation in nine days. By the end of the month they had re-established a steady flow of information.

There were so many convoys bashing about the Atlantic, so many operational U-boats at sea, so many escorts arriving on the scene, so much known to each side about their opponents' movements that it became less and less possible to carry out convoy evasive routeing with any degree of success. The First Sea Lord said, 'The Atlantic is now becoming so saturated with U-boats that the practice of evasion is rapidly becoming impossible'.[12] Consequently the balance swung back to the fighting will and effectiveness of the U-boats and Focke-Wulfs against the Allied warships, merchant ships and increasing air cover. This was only weeks before the full effect of the Support Groups, the escort carriers and the Very Long Range Aircraft finally tied up the convoy system and began to tip the balance decisively in our favour.

While the Allies were licking their wounds, they were not at the time aware that on 24 May the Germans had actually suspended all U-boat operations against North Atlantic convoys and were considering abandoning the Atlantic altogether. The sudden impact of air cover, the use of aircraft radar, and the increasing strength of surface escorts had resulted in a disastrous month for the U-boats. They had lost three of their four available U-tankers and were having great difficulty in getting to and from their bases. The sixteen boats with enough fuel moved down to replenish from U-tanker *488* and then resumed the attack on the convoys bound to Gibraltar from the United States, while twelve boats, low on fuel, wallowed about making decoy signals to give the appearance of strength on the North Atlantic convoy routes while awaiting replenishment.[13]

One of these was *U-202*, a veteran U-boat which had been in commission since 22 March, 1941. In the course of nine patrols since then it had sunk fourteen merchant ships. This was its fifth patrol from French ports since March, 1942.

The new escorts built in Britain and a steadily increasing flow of new frigates and British Destroyer Escorts built in Canada and the United States had started to appear.

The days of tight defensive screens, packed close round the perimeters of the convoys, were passing, as these new ships joined the escort fleets. Now at last it was becoming possible to realize Churchill's dream in which the convoy would no longer be thought of as a frightened and juicy prize but rather as a lure to draw the U-boats to their destruction. He said gleefully, 'We were now strong enough to form independent flotilla groups to act like cavalry divisions, apart from all escort duties. This I had long desired to see.'[14] He had for once been very patient, perhaps because he had no option.

The idea of the Support Group was not original but Captain Walker's short stay ashore in the centre of events at Liverpool, and his empathy with Admiral Max Horton, had given him the opportunity to push his conviction really hard and convert it from dream to reality.

No more suitable man than Walker could have been chosen to lead one of the first of these Groups to sea. He was the only full Captain in the Royal Navy at sea in a modest little sloop. Apart from his personal qualities, from which stemmed the happiness and loyalty of the people under his command, he had a great fund of technical knowledge on which to draw, both theoretical and practical. Coupled with this he had an uncanny instinct for the location of the wily U-boat and a boisterous delight in the destruction of the enemy which became the dominant spirit in the Group. There was a definite feeling in his ships that the tide was turning and that his drive and knowledge could be a decisive factor if he stayed at sea in command of the Second Support Group.

The next few weeks were very full. *Starling* had had no proper working-up period. After only three or four preliminary exercises to accustom the crew to the new equipment, she suffered badly: defects in construction, equipment and training showed up very quickly and with ghastly regularity. Much blood and bad language was expended before efficiency was attained.

In the first few practice shoots it was normal for the order 'Open Fire' to be followed by a horrid hush and the order 'Cease Firing' to be followed by a loud bang.

Our first patrol was fortunately uneventful and we had no contact with any enemy except the Atlantic weather. The wretched Officer of the Watch had very little peace from Walker. He would appear suddenly on the bridge and heave a life buoy over the side. 'That's a man overboard. Pick him up without lowering a boat.' On a peaceful afternoon, 'Order all ships to fire a depth charge set to 100 feet'. At night, on his way through the wheel-house, 'Quartermaster, report the wheel jammed hard a'port and keep it there'. When the bridge was fully occupied with the steering problem and the ship turning under full rudder, 'Illuminate with starshell on a bearing from 340 to 010 degrees'.

In all these tests and exercises, the Officers of the Watch were given a completely free hand; Walker never interfered except to make a quiet comment or give a word of advice at the end of the exercise. If it had gone really badly he would say without heat, 'I think we had better do that again'.

Depth charge and guns' crews were drilled without warning at least once every two hours in each watch. Every ship in the Group was expected to fire a ten-charge pattern by day or night within thirty seconds, to open fire with oerlikons or pom-poms within ten seconds and to bring the B four-inch mounting into action within thirty seconds.[15] There was never any possibility that any crew would fail these standards; they carried on drilling until they succeeded.

The weather was as usual cold and misty with a continual heavy swell running; these were not ideal conditions for exercises and practices, but at least they served to rid the younger ratings of their seasickness and to accustom them to the sort of conditions that they would experience. Even at the end of the first fortnight there was a noticeable change in the atmosphere on board. Friendships were formed and cemented and it became possible to gauge the suitability of certain men to certain jobs. We had our first few false alarms and were able to test the fighting organization of the ship under action conditions. The defects in training and equipment were eliminated, but the leaks in the deck-heads remained and grew steadily more persistent, rendering the conditions on the crowded messdecks and the officers' quarters damp and cold.

By the end of this first patrol, the standards of the Second Support Group were fixed and understood at all levels; a confidence and determination ran like wine through the sloops; every man knew his job at sea and did it well, not from fear of punishment, but with the pride of a craftsman. Each man had become his own most unforgiving critic.

The Glorious First Of June

The morning of the first of June dawned clear and sunny. For once the Atlantic was not grey and grim, but lay placid and blue under a brilliant hot sun shining from a cloudless sky. The faintest of mild airs ruffled the surface of the water. It was King's weather. The ship's company abandoned their salt-soaked duffle coats and appeared on deck at Hands Fall In, dressed in trousers and flannels. They set to, getting the salt off the guns and the paintwork.

The Second Support Group had left Iceland on 21 May and had since been scurrying around on various unproductive missions. The six sloops were now on course to pick up the next convoy.

Pilot finished his inspection of the plot and climbed up the ladder from the wheelhouse, pleased with himself. He had stowed away his sextant and had just finished working out and plotting his morning sights which were the first for several days without glimpse of the sun or stars. The Group's next job was to take up deep screening duties protecting convoy HX 241, homeward bound from Halifax to the UK. We should meet them head on, steering reciprocal courses, which made it even more important to know where we were, in case the visibility shut down. With these sights maybe he was a couple of jumps ahead of the navigators in the other ships.

'Signalman, ask the Navigator of *Wren* for his 0900 position.'

The clatter of the big signal lantern shutter disturbed the quiet of the bridge, and answering flashes came back across the water.

'Lootenant[16] Ayers, sir, *Wren's* navigator, reports that his estimated position at 0900 first June was 4100 yards north of *Starling*. Message ends.'

On *Starling's* bridge, John Filleul too was in good form. For some time he had been trying to organize a period of leave so that he could finalize the arrangements for his marriage to Wendy Taylor. On the last visit to Liverpool, Walker had stepped in with a signal of warning to Wendy so that she could make all the arrangements before the ship got in. To do this Walker had used official signal channels from sea and had been hauled over the coals for his breach of regulations. John just had sufficient time for the wedding and enough leave for a short honeymoon before going back to sea. On the bridge he was telling me the story. If Pilot could find the convoy there was a good chance that the Group would soon be on its way back to Liverpool and a little more time to enjoy married bliss.

Archie Pitt was not so happy. Nobody seemed to have much faith in his complicated bit of chicken wire up the mast. It got in the way of the guns and spoiled the neat outline of the ship's silhouette. He had somehow to find out the wavelength on which U-boat Headquarters were broadcasting their daily instructions to the North Atlantic U-boats. There was no lack of traffic, but the frequency was changed often and each time that happened he and his operators had a period of frantic search, because the U-boats reporting back stupidly used the same frequency. That was the time when he could pick up their bearing. It was easy to tell when Archie had gone 'blind', because his rather rosy face would turn white and strained, he would take no meals, speak no word to anyone except his own team, and answer no questions. He looked around the happy scene on deck, sniffed, scowled and went off down the ladder to his caboose under the HF/DF aerial.

The dozen U-boats lying in the North Atlantic short of fuel were still transmitting their routine daily status reports and manufacturing other spurious messages to create the impression of activity and so disguise the decision to suspend activity against the North Atlantic convoys. Dönitz, right up to the Nuremberg trials, in spite of many clues, strong suspicions and intensive internal investigations of security procedures, never accepted that their signals were being decyphered. These investigations had been extended to all headquarters staff, until eventually Dönitz had to accept that a leak could only be coming from himself or his Chief of Staff, Godt. His security specialists were so insistent about the invulnerability of the Enigma signals that he deduced wrongly that the Allied knowledge of U-boat locations could only be coming from aircraft sightings, aircraft and surface radar, or HF/DF bearings.

In this case, his deductions about the Allied use of HF/DF were certainly right. *U-202*, down to only thirty tons of fuel, surfaced on the morning of 1 June. It was a nice morning and the crew could do with a bit of fresh air after four weeks at sea in the squalor of a U-boat on patrol. Gunter Poser stayed in his bunk while the long signal was transmitted. On this last patrol he had had a frustrating and tiring time. He had noticed a radical difference in the pattern of his war, caused by a most unusual number of aircraft and escorts which forced him to dive time after time when attempting to shadow a convoy. He was now making his way back to base as fast as his depleted stocks of diesel would let him.

When the lookout reported the mastheads of ships in a convoy in sight he ordered the Chief Petty Officer on the conning tower to alter course towards, pulled on his boots, grabbed his binoculars and made his way up the ladder.

On *Starling's* bridge, at exactly 0930, the buzzer on the bridge and the voice of the HF/DF operator broke the peace of the morning: 'U-boat transmitting on bearing 311. Strong Signal. Estimated distance twenty miles'.

Four things happened almost simultaneously. The OOW ordered 'Full Ahead Together, Starboard Twenty, Steer 311. Captain, sir, HF/DF reports U-boat transmitting, strong signals'. A signal lamp from *Wild Goose* confirmed the bearing. Archie Pitt's beaming pink face appeared above the top rung of the bridge ladder to confirm the bearing. Captain Walker arrived on the bridge, miraculously preceded by the Yeoman, and started reforming the Group at right-angles to the line of advance.

The engine room telegraphs clanged. Immediately the tempo of the ship changed; *Starling* began to vibrate as the screws picked up speed. A thousand little fittings thrummed as the power came on. The bow began to pay off rapidly and the list increased.

'Action Stations, Number One. Yeoman, make to the Group:

"Take station abeam, distance apart 2000 yards. Submarine transmitting bearing 311. My course 311 at full speed".'

This is what we had been waiting for. The alarm rattlers sounded throughout the ship. The decks and ladders were immediately alive with seamen doubling to their action stations. On either beam the ships heeled under the wheel and pressed on at full speed to take up station on the new bearing. The gun mountings swung round, the depth-charge parties climbed about the quarterdecks checking their equipment and a steady stream of reports poured in to the bridge.

The minutes flew by. The broad white wakes of the six ships fanned out behind them, creaming up the surface of the water and disappearing behind the low swells astern. *Kite* started slowly to draw ahead.

'Ask the Chief if he would be good enough to come up to the bridge.'

The Chief Engineer appeared, sweating hard from the noise, turmoil and heat below in the engine room and the run up the ladders to the bridge, wiping the sweat off his face with the sleeve of his grimy overalls, happy to get a breath of clean air. Walker was up behind the compass, tense and grim, totally concentrated. Clearly not pleased.

'Chief, there's a U-boat out there. *Kite's* going well, isn't she? Watch her for a couple of minutes.'

Kite continued to draw slowly ahead. Chiefie was off down the ladder. The vibration increased perceptibly and *Starling* slowly pulled back on *Kite*.

Poser came up through the conning tower hatch, looked around, put the binoculars to his eyes, and started to swear hard and loud.

'Those aren't merchant ships, you idiot, they're destroyers. Dive, Dive, Dive.'

He wasn't too worried, because he thought that the escorts coming towards him would be unaware of his presence and wouldn't have been able to detect the low profile of his little conning tower at that distance. But for safety's sake he went straight on down to 500 feet and closed down all unessential machinery to lie doggo. It would be the sixth time on that patrol alone that he had been attacked by convoy escort vessels and he had survived the last five occasions without serious damage.

At 1005, after thirty-five minutes' steaming, *Starling's* lookout reported a swirl in the water. Walker dropped down to fifteen knots. At 1010 Petty Officer Kelly, the leader of the veteran team of Asdic operators who had come from *Stork* with Walker, reported, 'Echo bearing green 20'.

And a little later: 'Submarine'.

A hoist of flags flew to *Starling's* yardarm, and the information was passed out by T.B.S. to the other ships in the Group. *Starling* went straight in to attack, ordering *Wild Goose* and *Kite* to pick up and maintain the Asdic contact and to stand by in support. It was a common trick for one U-boat to lie deep and doggo while his mate stalked the attacking escort, but Walker was not going to be caught that way. He deployed *Cygnet, Woodpecker* and *Wren* on Operation Observant, a square patrol around the attack area.

For the first time in anger, *Starling* hoisted the black flag as she went in to attack. The first charges rumbled down the rails over the stern; on either side of the quarterdeck the four depth-charge throwers heaved out more high explosives in graceful curves. After a few seconds' pause, the whole surface of the sea astern, and *Starling* herself, shook and quivered as the pattern of ten charges exploded in sequence. *Starling* ran on clear of the churned-up water and the guns, loaded with armour-piercing shells, swung round on the bearing.

Every man on the bridge and the upper deck watched for the first sign of the U-boat as she surfaced. The great fountains of water settled back into the ocean. The chalky patch of disturbed sea merged slowly back into the deep blue of the surrounding water. A few small bubbles appeared.

We hadn't got her that time, but she was firmly held in Asdic contact by *Kite* and *Wild Goose* and, shortly afterwards, Darby Kelly, sweeping astern was also back in contact. More attacks followed but *U-202* was up to all the tricks in the book. Poser was weaving and dodging at the critical time just before each pattern was fired, when the attacking ship was committed to her final run. As soon as the charges started to explode he was then making big alterations of course while the water was stirred up by the ships and their depth-charge explosions, causing all sorts of false echoes.

After several attacks, during which contact was lost at 700yds, and no evidence of destruction appeared, Walker fell into deep discussion with Michael Impey and Darby Kelly. There was something uncanny in the conversation of these three specialists as they worked out their plans of attack from the front of the open bridge, just behind the small compartment where the operators controlled the Asdic instruments. All three of them had devoted the main part of their naval careers to the study of anti-submarine warfare; with three years of war experience behind them and several sunken U-boats to their credit, they made up a formidable combination.

They next put into action a new method of attack that the ships had

1. 'Captain Walker quietly but firmly clamped down with an iron hand' (see p.68).

2. HMS *Starling* taken from aircraft flying from HMS *Tracker*.

3. HMS *Starling's* Ship's Company in Scapa Flow.

4. Captain Walker introduces his officers to the First Lord of the Admiralty, Mr A. V. Alexander. Left to right: Lt A. C. Ayers (Pilot), Lt A. C. Burn, S/Lt Hutchins, Stan Baulcombe, Chiefie Bramble, Doc Fraser, Bill Johnson, Archie Pitt, Ceri Fisher, Snaps Parnell. Lt John Filleul (Number One), Lt L. C. H. Porter (Pinger) and Lt Lionel Ferguson are hidden behind the First Lord.

5. Some of the Key Men pose for the camera.
Back Row: Bill Johnson, Chief Yeoman Roland Keyworth, Chief Petty Officer Telegraphist Tom Teece.
Front Row: Ceri Fisher, John Filleul, Alan Burn.

6. Captain Walker, correctly dressed, carrying his gloves, steps ashore while Able Seaman Burnett presents arms.

7. 'At sea neither the Captain nor the officers nor the crew wore anything that resembled uniform' Walker directs a creeping attack from the front of the bridge, wearing his coat of many colours. Pilot holds on to his kye. The Yeoman watches the signal lamps (see p.106).

8. 'The Most Outstanding Performance of the War' Walker directs the fourteen-hour Asdic chase and eventual destruction of *U-202* by gunfire (see p.81).

9. Some of HMS *Starling's* Ship's Company at sea. No wonder the German prisoners never gave any problems once they were brought on board.

10. 'By this time, the men could sleep through the noise of depth
charging.' The ships of the Group dropped 252 depth charges and fired
forty-eight Hedgehog bombs to sink this U-boat (see p. 132). Note that
most of the men have their backs to the action and are watching John
Filleul who is giving the settings for the next pattern. Tubby Richards,
a three-badged Able Seaman on the starboard thrower (bottom left)
meanwhile finishes off his cup of kye.

11. 'There was a thunderous roar and *Kite* disappeared completely behind a pyramid of foam and water several times higher than her masthead'(see p.130). HMS *Kite*, with seconds to spare, counter-mines an acoustic torpedo aimed at her by a diving U-boat.

12. Refuelling at sea and replenishing stocks of depth charges. 'Signals came in with doleful tales of steadying lines wound round propellers and parted fuel hoses'(see p.132). Two men were lost over the side.

practised together during the working-up period. Walker stationed the two sloops on either beam of *Starling*, took over the contact by Asdic and ran straight over the top of the U-boat at five knots, with each ship dropping a string of charges set to 550 feet at five-second intervals. Whichever way the U-boat turned it was bound to run into this carpet of explosives.

Seventy-six charges were laid down the U-boat's course line in three minutes. In the second of these attacks *Kite*, running low on depth charges and with her gyro out of action, was replaced by *Woodpecker*. But even these demonstrations of massive fire-power failed to produce results.

Walker now decided to try another method of harassment. He called *Kite* and *Wild Goose* alongside and explained his impromptu plans to their Commanding Officers over the loudhailer. He then positioned *Starling* about 1500 yards behind the U-boat and directed the other two ships slowly towards the target. In this way he was able to guide the attacking ship silently over the position of the U-boat, at about five knots. The U-boat would not hear the normal sounds of the sloops working up speed and would have no warning of the impending attack and so no indication when to take avoiding action.

This U-boat was using Submarine Bubble Targets, which had been developed by the Germans in 1941. S.B.T.s were ejected from the submerged U-boat in tubes of chemicals to form areas of gas bubbles underwater, large enough to provide echoes on the escorts' Asdics which would conceal the U-boat itself and hopefully deceive the hunter into following a false trail. While the three sloops stalked from astern and manouevred at slow speed to get in position, *U-202* let off several of these screens, while twisting, turning and putting on bursts of speed. This was exactly what Walker wanted; *U-202* was using up her battery power and reserves of air, but failing entirely to confuse the experienced Asdic operators in the sloops.

All through the day the rumble and crash of depth charges continued as ship after ship went in. In spite of all Poser's endeavours, only once did *Starling's* operators lose contact when the equipment failed for a short while, but the U-boat was firmly held by the supporting ships and contact was resumed a few minutes later.

In the evening it became evident that this was going to be a test of endurance. Walker signalled his night intentions; he told the surrounding ships that he thought the U-boat would surface under the cover of darkness to loose off a few torpedoes; he reckoned that its batteries and air would run out about midnight and that he would make his break then.

The breath of wind that had blown all day fell right away: the ships steamed slowly in a flat calm. On *Starling's* bridge men stood in silence ready for the moment: on the guns the crews clustered round the mountings talking in hushed voices while the sun glowed blood red on the brass ammunition cylinders.

Above the bridge, in the director tower, the sound came up over the telephones of a party playing cards in the transmitting station, a man humming Bing Crosby and a candidate for Leading Seaman rehearsing his gun drill.

Backwards and forwards down the starboard side of the bridge paced Captain Walker. The shapes of the ships on either beam began to merge into the surface of the sea and a blue haze settled slowly down, blending the horizon and the darkening sky. The night grew dark; the faint murmur of conversation died. All was quiet, except for the soft creaking roll of the ship, the hum of the fans and the muffled reports of the lookouts changing watches.

Eight bells came and went. Tucked up in the starboard forward corner of the bridge, the signalman rested his elbows on the wind deflector and swept his binoculars towards the starboard bow. It was two minutes after midnight.

'SUBMARINE SURFACING BEARING GREEN 30 SIR!'

'STARSHELL COMMENCE COMMENCE COMMENCE'

The director tower swung onto the bearing as Petty Officer West trained right. The crash of metal on metal as the round went home was followed in a moment by the roar of gunfire as B mounting started to pour out starshell and spread the horizon with light. And there, just visible, right in the middle of the gunnery officer's binoculars, was the tiny silver conning tower and hull of the U-boat, shining on the glassy surface of the sea, a white wake already starting to foam out from its stern, water pouring off its deck as it gathered speed on the surface. Then the crash and flash of the broadsides from the four guns on the forward mountings. With the whole Group firing, the black night was lit up with flares, starshell and tracers all converging on the one point. A dull red glow leapt from behind the conning tower as the first shell struck home.

Starling trembled, heeled and seemed to rush and leap as she went in at full speed to ram. The range closed rapidly until the four-inch mountings could no longer be depressed enough to bear on the target, which now lay stopped and enveloped in thick coarse red smoke, the conning tower riddled with shell holes. *Starling* charged in to ram. At the last moment, some hundred yards short, Walker decided that there was no fight left in this former adversary and that there was no point in risking damage to his own ship. *Starling* sheered off to starboard and shaved past close alongside, raking the upper deck with converging fire from her port oerlikons, dealing the final blow by straddling *U-202* with shallow depth charges from the port throwers. The grey hull seemed to lift clear out of the water as the two tall plumes of water engulfed it. When the smoke and haze cleared, it could be seen settling slowly down into the water, waves pouring in and out of the shattered conning tower and the surrounding sea dotted with the crew abandoning ship.

The sea-boats manned by boarding parties ready for Operation Haggis[17], were already launched and on their way to attempt the capture of the U-boat, but the shattered hull was settling fast. Walker decided that he was too far from land to have any hope of bringing the prize back and that he was not prepared to risk the lives of British seamen in an attempt to capture a prize that was already on its way to the bottom.[18]

We turned back. The cries of the men in the water could be clearly heard through the cheering of our elated ship's company. *Starling* picked up two officers and sixteen men, *Wild Goose* two officers and ten men. Some of them were badly wounded. None of them were allowed on board until they had given the number of their boat and the name of their commanding officer, but once on board, the two doctors worked unceasingly to save their lives.

U-202 took forty minutes to sink. As the hull finally disappeared, lower deck was cleared to hoist the seaboats and the Group reformed to carry on with the interrupted patrol.

For the lucky ones there was a dry hammock and three hours' sleep after a chase that had lasted for fourteen and a half hours: the unlucky ones had to endure the torture of maintaining their vigilance for a further three hours until the end of the middle watch at 0400, a total spell on watch of eighteen hours. Doc Fraser operated for a further fourteen hours to save all but one of the Germans picked up by *Starling*.

Captain Walker wrote of this action: 'I am most grateful to *Kapitanleutnant* Poser for an excellent bit of Group training,' and in the forenoon hoisted the signal, 'Splice the Mainbrace'.

This was the Second Support Group's first kill and His Majesty's Sloop *Starling's* first contact with the enemy. Driven remorselessly by Walker, the ships had enjoyed barely enough time to settle down and attain a certain degree of efficiency in the detection, hunting and final destruction of a U-boat. Much valuable knowledge and experience had been acquired during the chase.

Every ship in the Group and every department in each ship had played their part. The Intelligence from the Submarine Tracking Room ashore had told the Group where they should be, and Pilot with his team on the ARL plot had got us there. Archie Pitt's HF/DF bearing, confirmed by *Wild Goose*, had pin-pointed the target when it poked its nose out of the water. The engine room crews had shown just that little bit of extra speed when it was needed, and had then sweltered below for many hours juggling to respond to the continuous stream of engine orders, well below the waterline with the roar of depth-charge explosions, some dangerously close, resounding through the plates of the ship's side. Underlying the whole operation was the extremely efficient communications team under the leadership of Petty Officer Telegraphist Tom Teece and Yeoman of Signals Roland Keyworth, who had brought several of their key men with them from *Stork*. They had the best jobs in the ship; they knew it, and aimed for perfection.

The guns' crews were especially delighted. The Captain and his First Lieutenant were essentially anti-submarine men who gave priority to the Asdic gear and depth charges. However, the combined efforts of all the ships' depth charges, the mass barrage attacks mounted by three ships simultaneously, the skill and tenacity of the Asdic operators were not sufficient to despatch *U-202*. It was the second broadside that did the trick, giving great satisfaction to the gunnery team, the largest number of men in the ship.

The German prisoners, once on board, gave no trouble. They were badly shaken and were suffering from reaction after their ordeal during the long hunt. They slept most of the time and sometimes sang, rather beautifully, sad sentimental German songs accompanied by an accordion lent to them. Most noticeable to the eyes of the British tar was the almost servile attitude that seemed to have been bred into them. If they met one of *Starling's* officers on deck they would spring to attention and order each other out of the way. This was less surprising when two of them told the interrogating officer that they were only in a U-boat because they had been forced below at the point of a gun.

Starling's people treated them on board as fellow men who had been beaten in a fair fight. The one German that Doc had not been able to save was buried with full honours next morning. One of the sentries was seen showing his loaded revolver to the officer prisoners, who had been allocated Fish and Archie's cabin, much to their fury.

'Just thought they'd like to have a look at it, sir.'

The following day the able seaman on sentry duty guarding the men in the depth-charge store left his post for an urgent call of nature. A smug German handed him back his rifle, which he had left propped up against the bulkhead while both his hands were engaged.

In the few days that it took to get back to Liverpool, there was little left to do but to sink the U-boat on paper, brush up the number ones for the first run ashore, and try to make the ship look a little less second-hand.

Our arrival at Gladstone Dock was triumphant. Walker had left many friends behind after his spell as Captain (D) Liverpool and his first return from sea in his own ship, in command of his own Group, laden with prisoners and with a scalp dangling from his belt was the signal for great celebration. Before the gangway was ashore, a great crowd of his friends from headquarters ashore and from the borough of Bootle had climbed on board to congratulate him. A number of staff specialists from Admiralty followed to question him about any new tactics used by him or by the U-boat, examining like terriers the failure of our depth charges to destroy a U-boat held remorselessly in ideal attacking conditions for such a long time.

Four vital lessons were learnt:

1. The 'creeping attack'[19] and the variations devised by Walker were shown to be a powerful new tactical weapon under action conditions.
2. Nevertheless, U-boats could dive deeper than our depth charges could be set to explode. Nearly four years after the start of the battle, the escorts still did not have a weapon capable of destroying a U-boat at its maximum depth.[20]
3. Time was essential to make quite certain of a kill.
4. There were signs that German morale was weakening.

After the tumult and the shouting had died, and the visitors had gone ashore, Walker produced from under his table two bottles of champagne with which his officers and his family drank to the further success and happiness of the good ship *Starling* and the Second Support Group.

Some weeks later, after analysis and examination of all the recorder tracks and the full records, the Commander-in-Chief sent the following signal, addressed to *Starling*: 'I wish to congratulate your Asdic team on the most outstanding performance of the war.'

Such praise was rare, deserved and welcome, but the C-in-C would have done better to omit the word 'Asdic'. A secret of Walker's success was his ability to involve a whole team of ships and all who sailed in them, as was to be proved very shortly when the Second Support Group moved on to the offensive and were to play a major part in re-establishing the Royal Navy's dominance in the Bay of Biscay.

The Monthly Anti-submarine Bulletin said:

'This hunt, lasting for 14 hours, of a U-boat employing every means to escape, is an outstanding operation. A perfect example of locating, hunting and destroying a U-boat.'

CHAPTER FIVE

THE BAY OF BISCAY OFFENSIVE

When the Second Support Group moved to the Bay of Biscay, a bitter struggle had been going on between the Germans and Coastal Command who not only had the task of dealing with the U-boats but also with the air cover that they enjoyed from the airfields around Bordeaux. By January, 1943, German Intelligence reckoned that Coastal Command were deploying thirty to forty aircraft in the Bay of Biscay, rising to fifty or sixty when a Gibraltar convoy was at sea. At least six JU-88s were thought by the Germans to be the minimum necessary to take on the Allied flying boats and four-engined aircraft.[1]

For many brave aircrew from the UK and the Dominions it was a fight to the death in its literal sense; not only were the chances of being shot out of the air very high, but also the chances of survival in the water were low. There was no friendly shipping in the Bay of Biscay. Aircrew who survived the destruction of their aircraft then faced the high probability of death from drowning or exhaustion and starvation in their dinghies.

Slowly Coastal Command turned the scales. In the month of May nine U-boats were sunk and seven so heavily damaged by aircraft that they had to put back. At the end of a long cruise in the Atlantic they faced ferocious attacks as they neared their home bases. When they put to sea after replenishing, they came under heavy attack before they reached the places where the convoys could be found, and too often had to return before sighting a target, to the dismay of their colleagues making ready for sea. Reports from Intelligence showed that the morale of the U-boat crews was beginning to crack.

On 20 May Dönitz ordered the conversion of ten U-boats to carry much heavier anti-aircraft armament; on 29 May, long before this order could have had any effect, he made one of his major errors; he ordered his commanders to cease their practice of crash diving whenever aircraft were detected. They were to remain on the surface and not to submerge if attacked, but fight their way through, travelling in groups to achieve maximum fire power against the aircraft. Coastal Command retaliated by grouping two or more aircraft before going in to attack simultaneously from different directions.

At the beginning of June the Admiralty had recovered from the shock of the heavy sinkings in March and April. They had seen through Dönitz's attempts to disguise his withdrawal from the Atlantic, and had now swung into a joint offensive with Coastal Command to endeavour to make it as difficult and slow as possible for the U-boats to travel to and from their bases in the Bay of Biscay. From 14 June the total effort of two Support Groups, supported by Beaufighters and Mosquitoes from Coastal Command, was devoted to harassment of U-boats in transit to or from the Biscay Ports.

By 14 July Dönitz had given up his efforts to fight his way through on the surface. Defeated by Coastal Command, the U-boats went back to the least effective alternative, traversing the Bay submerged, surfacing only when it was necessary to recharge their batteries, preferably only at night.

After a short stay in harbour to carry out routine maintenance, Walker was on his way down to carry this blockade a stage further. He sailed on 17 June, taking temporary command of *Woodpecker*, with *Kite*, *Wild Goose* and *Wren*, leaving Lieutenant-Commander Hugonin to bring on *Starling* when she had completed some minor repairs. This time the Group was leaving the Western Approaches Command to come under the Plymouth Command and to take the battle into the Bay of Biscay. The area in which the ships would be operating, code-named MUSKETRY, lay off Cape Finisterre and the north-west corner of Spain. The U-boats were now hugging the coast and using this route to get into the Atlantic.

In the ships of the Group there was a feeling of great optimism. The prolonged chase of *U-202* followed by its final spectacular destruction in a night action had had a powerful and exhilarating effect. Year after year many ships worked backwards and forwards across the Atlantic without ever seeing a U-boat, let alone a German prisoner. But not Walker's ships. The men had now seen in practice that his principle of offensive operations was successful. Even at this early stage under his command, they were developing the belief that they had a right to destroy U-boats without fear of retaliation.[2]

Starling followed two days later, but ran into delays. A summer gale on the way down was strong enough to bend the steel breakwater stretching across the foredeck of the ship. More time was lost on an Asdic echo which turned out to be a wreck; when depth-charged it gave a rich harvest of dead eels. In a deserted sea we found an abandoned landing craft floating by itself. It was a hazard to shipping and Commander Hugonin decided to destroy it by gunfire. I'm ashamed to admit that this unarmed target took one hour and thirty-one minutes to sink, an expensive and time-consuming bit of target practice. We then spent another day chasing after an aircraft sighting of a U-boat, at considerable danger to ourselves. Pilot's Log noted: 'I believe we crossed a minefield to do that, for we spotted several floating mines'.

The final delay was a long, unfruitful and sad search for airmen who had been shot down in our area, whose dinghy had been reported by an aircraft.

The rest of the Group had not done much better. This was the first large-scale attempt at cooperation between surface forces and Coastal Command aircraft, unencumbered by convoy protection duties, and it had its teething troubles. The area was full of U-boats travelling to and from their distant operating areas, but it was impossible to distinguish between the sighting report of an enthusiastic pilot directing the ships accurately onto an old oil barrel and a genuine report of an experienced pilot reporting an eddy in the water that might just have been the swirl left by a U-boat that had just crash-dived.

At 1930 on 23 June, after a week's absence, *Starling* welcomed her Captain back on board. He recorded: 'And so began an eventful 24 hours, of which I was to spend only 17 hours in my own ship'.

These seventeen hours started quietly; we spent the first peaceful night of the patrol. The almost continuous stream of aircraft spotting reports had died down. The normally grey Atlantic seas had been replaced by deep blue swells, and that night the wake and the bow wave sparkled with phosphorescence. Many of the people slept near their action stations on deck in the warm open air rather than in the airless messdecks. The tremble of the ship rushing from one false alarm to another no longer aroused interest. The men had become so hardened to the sound that they could even sleep through the noise of a depth-charge pattern.

After breakfast John Filleul grabbed his towel and went to take a bath. The Captain had gone down to his day cabin — a rare occurrence — to bring his paperwork up to date.

As the watch was changing, at exactly 0800 on 24 June, the Asdic operator reported an echo. By 0810 it had been identified as 'submarine' and the alarm rattlers were sending their wild clamour through the ship.

John Filleul, normally — even at sea — an immaculate and well-dressed officer, shot out of the passage-way clad in a bath towel and a duffel coat, flying down the deck to the depth charges on the quarterdeck. The gunnery officer climbed over the backs of the men swarming up the ladder to the bridge and on up to the director tower. Walker was behind the binnacle. The black flag broke out. We were going in for snap attack with a pattern of ten charges set to 150 and 350 feet, in the hope of catching the U-boat unawares and blowing it to the surface.

At 0822, the depth charges started to rumble down the rails and curled out in an arc on either quarter from the throwers; the long series of explosions started and the four forward four-inch guns swung round, waiting for *Starling* to alter course and head back towards the disturbed water. Kelly started his Asdic sweep astern and the difficult job of re-establishing contact with the U-boat which could now be expected to dive deep and to alter course in a burst of evasive action.

In the rush of activity, there was a sudden hush. Right astern, in the middle of the hills of water churned up by our pattern, there was the long grey shape of a U-boat. Water poured off its upper deck and conning tower as it shook itself clear to the surface. Not a soul was visible on deck and it started to charge ahead.

> 'For the enemy to surface in the exact spot where the eyes of the whole Group were concentrated, at the first conceivable moment after the pattern was fired, gave such a copybook result that one felt momentarily a sense of disbelief that this was happening.'

The pause was momentary. A few seconds later every ship in the Group opened up with all the guns that could be brought to bear, and the U-boat was enveloped in a forest of plumes of water. There were shells ricocheting in every direction as *Starling* picked up to full speed and came round on a parallel course. Still the U-boat ploughed on; through the director binoculars it looked like a ghost ship in a hurricane forging through the water with not a soul to be seen. The water surged over its foredeck as it started to dive. *Starling* turned hard a'starboard, with her guns still firing over the bow.

Walker hadn't moved from his place in the middle of the bridge on the platform behind the binnacle, sighting over the compass ring as the ship charged at her victim on collision course, her forward guns now firing at full depression.

'Coxswain, Steady as you go. Yeoman, Tell all ships to cease firing. Tell Number One to set a shallow pattern. I'm going to ram.'

A flash of red-yellow sparks flew up from *Starling*'s bow as a shell ricocheted off the bow and the bullring disappeared in a shower of sparks.

'A and B Guns won't bear, sir.'

'Cease Firing. STAND BY TO RAM. Going in now.'

A great cheer went up from the forward guns' crews as they peered round the sides of their gun shields, some still clutching the brass cylinders of their four-inch shells against their chests. There was a loud bellow from the Gunner's Mate, clear above the background of the surrounding activity: 'Stow those shells, you bloody fools and lie flat'.

Starling rose on a swell; her bows lifted clear of the water and came down fair and square at right-angles to *U-119*, hitting her with a horrid drawn-out tearing noise just abaft the conning tower. The ship slowed as if she had grounded and she bounced noisily on over her victim, her speed down to ten knots after the impact of the collision. The grey shape of the U-boat below the keel could be seen quite clearly, rolling over slowly as it scraped along the keel towards the stern and towards our too vulnerable propellers.

John Filleul watched his moment. His last order had been to set the depth charges, not to fire them. He assumed that, in the turmoil, the order hadn't reached him. As the U-boat came level with the quarterdeck, he fired the charges from the throwers. When he saw it rolling under the stern, he sent the rest of the pattern rumbling down the rails on top of it. Slowed by the collision, *Starling* did not have time to get clear before the depth charges exploded. Every light bulb in the ship was shattered. But Walker had already ordered *Woodpecker* in for a final attack and she was coming across our stern to put down yet another pattern.

Reports of flooding in *Starling*'s forward magazines started to come over the bridge telephones. The Asdic dome had been ripped out of the hull by the passage of the dying U-boat.[3] From the upper decks there were grandstand views of the climax of this brief and spectacular attack but it was very different down below in the engine and boiler rooms and the damage control stations. For the past fourteen and a half hours the teams in the engine rooms and the boiler rooms had been at their stations below. Their contact with the outside world had been limited to the running description of events passed down the telephone by Bill Johnson, Walker's secretary, punctuated by the telegraphs moving to 'Stand by for depth charges'. Stoker Petty Officer George Dyson wrote in his diary:

'Down below the stokers watch a madhouse of gauges, trying to keep feet downwards in the middle of the maze of smelly, demanding and noisy machinery. At one moment you are climbing up a steep gradient, and the next you are sliding down the same stretch ricocheting from side to side and swearing once again at the rim of the watertight door that catches the top of your head as you go through. Suddenly things start to happen. The Alarm bells go off. Both telegraphs spin to "Full Speed Ahead". The whole ship reverberates with the noise of heavy boots as the ship's company rush along the passage ways and up and down the ladders. The hull reverberates as the four-inch guns open fire. My stoker almost falls down the ladder, so fast does he move. Good kid — I sure was busy. The telegraphs ring again: they've found her. There's no rest down here and it's going to be nasty in a moment or two. We heel at full speed as the ship goes in to attack. Through the hull comes the dull thud of the depth charge throwers as ten charges arch out on either side and trundle down the rails for a full shallow pattern. Down below the series of explosions hit the hull like giant steel hammers swung by some monster from the deep. The ship shakes like a rag. You think that the plates you stand on have turned into a sea of crazy jelly. A cup on the bench has shattered, but everything else holds once again except for the paint which peels off the bulkhead in a thousand flakes like a fall of snow.

You can't shake off that feeling that this is it. Standing there, holding on for dear life, hoping that the pipes carrying the scalding steam will not burst or leak. Suddenly the valve that I am holding is torn from my hands and I'm thrown forward towards the boiler, then thrown back by an even bigger explosion. This one knocks all the senses out of my mind, but it's the last of that series and I just go on doing the jobs that are there to be done until at last the noises die down. It's still "Full Speed Ahead" and the message from up top is that we're going in to ram. The whole thing all over again and we hope for the umpteenth time that everything will hold. We feel very vulnerable because it only needs one fuel pipe to split or one steam pipe to burst and we could be the ones on the marble slab.'

Starling now went through a period of intense activity, during which the ship was involved in several almost separate actions at the same time.

Chiefie, John Filleul and the damage control teams were doing their best to shore up the bulkheads and decks around the damaged areas to stop any more flooding; we had two magazines and three other compartments flooded; it was four hundred miles to the nearest UK port; the ship was already three foot down by the bow. Chiefie had every reason to think that the propeller shafts might have been distorted or the propeller blades themselves chipped or shorn off as had happened to *Harvester* three months before.[4] Parties from the guns' crews were handing up ammunition from X magazine aft and passing it along the upper deck to the forward guns.

A signal from one of the Commanding Officers apologized for blowing our bullring off.[5] Walker was pleased with the day so far and replied: 'Quite all right. Just a friendly smack in the snout.'

A seaboat had been lowered and was pulling away to collect evidence of the kill.

'A determined-looking seagull succeeded in beating the outstretched grasping hand of one member of the whaler's crew for a small bloody mess, apparently of human origin.'

Walker himself was engaged on other, more important matters. A couple of miles away, *Wren* and *Wild Goose*, who had been carrying out a protective sweep around the disabled *Starling*, picked up the Asdic echo of the sunken U-boat's mate which was coming in to take revenge. While *Starling* lay helpless, dealing with her problems of flooding, each ship in the Group put in an attack without result and then went round for another try, again without success.

Walker gave them all two chances without any interference, but it was plain that things were going wrong. His patience, always in short supply when in action, ran out. He threw his cap on the deck, stamped on it, and signalled: 'Somebody is attacking SBTs. Keep contact while I transfer. *Wild Goose* to close and transfer Commanding Officers.'

Wild Goose came close alongside *Starling* while Walker explained his intentions over the loud hailer, addressing his remarks to 'Daddy' Wemyss, but aiming them mainly at the two ships companies at their action stations on the upper deck.

And so Walker's brief stay of seventeen hours in his own ship ended. In the Bay of Biscay, some four hundred miles from the nearest Allied airfield and the same distance from the enemy's airbase at Bordeaux, with one U-boat still on its way to the bottom and another under attack two miles away, the Chief Bosun's mate and his side party piped Captain Walker over the side into a whaler. As the boat's crew gave way and started to pull across to *Wild Goose*, all *Starling*'s men except those on watch manned the side and gave their Captain three hearty cheers, matched a few minutes later by the welcoming cheers from the men of *Wild Goose*.

At noon *Starling* received on board Commander Wemyss, who had now become Walker's tried, trusted and essential right-hand man in the Second Support Group.[6] He cannot have been delighted at this transfer from his command, *Wild Goose*, in the middle of an action, to a crippled ship trying to keep afloat and get home.

At 1230 on 24 June, Walker, his Asdic officer (Lieutenant L.C.H. Porter), his radar officer (Ceri Fisher), his secretary (Bill Johnson), his Chief Petty Officer Telegraphist (Tom Teece), his steward (Petty Officer Gardner) and of course his shadow, Yeoman of Signals Roland Keyworth, scrambled up the rope ladder to board *Wild Goose*.

> 'This somewhat unusual operation was carried out without trouble or incident in the middle of a further series of attacks on the U-boat now probably lurking very deep and manoeuvring at slow speed.'

It could equally well have been at periscope depth, watching for a chance to loose off a torpedo at its tormentors.

Starling had established another record by ramming and sinking a U-boat and having three Commanding Officers in seventeen hours. Walker was not satisfied with this. He advised the other ships in the Group that if another chance to ram came up, this would be the damaged *Starling*'s prerogative. Such was their confidence in Walker that all on board looked forward to this chance, although it would almost certainly have put paid to *Starling*'s hope of safe return to port.

In spite of Walker's previous misgivings, by the time he got on board *Wild Goose*, *Wren* was able to 'hand over, on a plate, a perfect U-boat echo'.

Walker and his team were now assuming that the enemy had dived as deep as possible and was using the 'blind period' to evade all attacks. The 'blind period' started when the attacking ship lost contact while coming in to drop her pattern, continued while she steamed up to the point where she started to drop her charges, continued while the charges sank under their own weight, and only ended when contact was regained after the explosions and disturbed water had died down. Building on his experience with *U-202*, Walker had now formalized for use in his own Group another original and unique method of attack to deal with this situation.

In the standard textbook attack taught by the Royal Navy, the U-boat knew the exact time to start evasive action. It could listen on its hydrophones for the sound of the attacking ship increasing speed to come in for the attack and for a decrease in the interval between the Asdic transmissions. After the attacker was committed to his course, the U-boat could take violent evasive action. This left the attacking ship guessing, in the same way that a goalkeeper tries to guess the direction of a penalty kick. Before the first charges exploded, a deep U-boat would have a good chance of being elsewhere.[7]

To avoid this long blind period, Walker had devised the 'creeping attack'. One ship (the directing ship) would lay back 1500 or 2000 yards from the U-boat, maintaining Asdic contact with the target. A second ship (the attacking ship) would then go ahead of the directing ship at slow speed, not transmitting on Asdics, on a course ordered by the directing ship. When about 500 yards clear ahead, the directing ship would guide the attacking ship right over the position of the U-boat and tell her when to drop her charges.

These new tactics were extremely simple. On the other hand they had to be carried out by several ships manoeuvring at low speeds (five knots in the case of the attacking ships and nearly stopped in the case of the directing ship), at very close quarters to each other, firing a great number of depth charges which potentially could do as much damage to friend as to foe. In open sea conditions, with wind and swell conditions blowing the ships about, this required a high degree of coordination and seamanship, with perfect communication and understanding between the Commanding Officers.

If this could be achieved, then the first thing that the U-boat commander would know about an attack would be the explosion of the depth charges around his ears, before he had any of the usual warning signals to enable him to take avoiding action.

Walker in *Wild Goose* directed *Wren*, as the attacking ship, into the first of these creeping attacks shortly after his arrival on board. The first variation was to send *Wren* straight down the course line of the U-boat to fire a pattern and then continue down the line dropping charges at five-second intervals. The second was to send in both *Kite* and *Woodpecker* in line abreast to fire a barrage of fifty charges once again directed from *Wild Goose* from about a mile away. Each of the attacks, once launched, took between five and ten minutes, but a much longer time was needed to station the ships on the right course in safe positions relative to each other, to *Wild Goose* and to the U-boat.

During the afternoon, the standard of drill in these new manoeuvres improved markedly, until a series of half-a-dozen curt orders were sufficient to line up the attacking ships, direct them in to the attack and tell them when to release their charges.

Finally a mass of wreckage floated to the surface and *U-449* had fired her last torpedo.

At 1700 the damaged *Starling* was detached. Butting her bent beak into the swells, she slowly and reluctantly turned and set course for Plymouth. She faced a journey straight across the paths of the U-boats which at this time were making the passage to and from their home bases in the Bay of Biscay in groups of three or more; in her damaged condition she would be a sitting duck if any determined U-boat commander spotted her. Lacking the ability to manoeuvre at speed, she would have a hard time defending herself against an air attack.

The hunting ships grew smaller and smaller on the horizon in the gathering darkness, and the noise of the depth charges became a distant rumble. A dimmed lamp flashed from *Wild Goose*.

No one who sailed in *Starling* on that patrol will ever forget the signal, which read:

'To *Starling* from Captain Walker:
"GOODBYE MY GALLANT *STARLING*. GOD BE WITH YOU." '

and shortly afterwards:

'To *Starling* from Captain (D) Second Support Group,
"Second U-boat destroyed. Splice the Mainbrace." '

Captain Walker had given this order verbally to celebrate the ramming before he left the ship, but *Starling*'s people didn't hesitate to take the second opportunity. There was a long way to go. In spite of a good day's work, the bulkheads over and alongside the flooded compartments were bumping and bulging like the sides of an old biscuit tin. All adjacent compartments had been battened down as a precaution. Another of the severe summer gales such as we had experienced less than a week before could result in a battle to save the ship. A couple of tots of Nelson's blood helped to keep up the flow of high good humour, and hands were dancing and skylarking while the work went on and the seas remained flat.

We had not been forgotten. As soon as the business with the second U-boat had been completed, Walker detached *Kite*. She came bustling over to give *Starling* support until she was relieved by a Hunt class destroyer sent out from Plymouth, releasing *Kite* to rejoin the Group at 1330 on 25 June.

Starling worked up to 12 knots, but did not steer very well with the stern cocked up in the air. Pilot, whose mind tended to run on predictable lines, came up on the bridge to report that there were no real problems. Although we had a gash in the hull and had lost our Asdic dome, his Chernikeef log, which stuck out three feet from the bottom, still worked perfectly, so he reckoned that we had nothing to worry about.

He was right. The weather remained perfect; early on the morning of 26 June we spotted the Bishop Rock lighthouse sticking up like a lamp post and Chiefie managed to work the speed up to 14 knots on the chance of getting us home for a pint before the pubs in Devonport closed.

At 1930 on that fine summer's evening we passed the breakwater into Plymouth Sound; the shouts and laughter of children bathing in front of The Hoe came clearly across to the sailors on deck at stations for entering harbour. Some of the bathers must have looked curiously at this odd-looking ship as she steamed past with her damaged bow buried deep in the water and her stern tilted grotesquely in the air with the propellers visible as they thrashed up the wake. We turned to starboard past Devil's Point, gave the Commander-in-Chief the marks of respect which were his due and came up to the Devonport South Yard to make fast. The jetty was crowded with dockyard men who had mustered all the big pumps on the dockside in case the ship decided to take a last-minute dive. Wemyss's last job, before taking over the command of *Wild Goose*, had been ashore in the dockyard and he was welcomed with a big cheer from his old friends as he brought the battered *Starling* alongside to add to their impossible work load.

At 2030 leave was piped. Nobody who was not required on board was too tired to join the mad rush for a pint of draught beer ashore; Doc Fraser, acknowledging the salute of the naval patrol and the dockyard police at the gate, fell flat on his face over an eyebolt. On that trip he was our only casualty.

When *Starling* was dry-docked, a wide gash twenty-five feet long came into view, where some part of the sinking U-boat had caught in the ship's bottom and ripped it open like a tin opener. The stem was turned back to starboard like an old cardboard box and leered in a dissipated fashion at the dock wall. Both the forward magazines − formerly the Gunner's pride − were filled with a slimy mass of soaking disintegrated cordite and shells rolling around the decks. Before work could be started on repairs to the hull, all this mess had to be manhandled out of the ship into waiting railway trucks which would carry it to the armament depot for destruction. At the bottom of the enclosed dock the stink was overpowering; the hard and unpleasant work was made no more enjoyable by the Very Important

Dockyard Officer who objected to the music that we played on the loudspeakers to cheer up the men as they worked stripped to the waist on one of the hottest days of the year.

Walker was still operating with the Group off Lorient. By 28 June he was running low on fuel and turned for Plymouth, passing through the boom at 0640 on the 30th, with *Wild Goose, Wren, Woodpecker* and *Kite*.

He had returned from a historic patrol. In a period of twenty-four hours he had sunk two U-boats. For the first time since the fall of France and the occupation of the French ports by the Germans, Walker had led the Royal Navy back to the close blockade of waters that they had known and dominated for so many generations. A new type of warfare had proved successful; Coastal Command blasted the U-boats under the surface of the water where they could be destroyed by the ships' depth charges. The ramming of *U-119* and the successful sinking of *U-449*, using various types of creeping attack, was the beginning of yet another dark phase in the history of the U-boats' fight against the combination of air power and support groups.

Although Walker had only three days in port before he returned to sea, he was wanted at the Admiralty to make a first-hand report. He had different priorities. As soon as he stepped ashore he set about getting all available dockyard resources on to the repairs to *Starling* and sorting out the problems of communication with Coastal Command. On the first evening he came down to the wardroom with a bulky brown envelope.

'Is anybody going up to London tonight on leave?'

'I'm going up tomorrow morning, sir.'

'I'd like you to get on the night sleeper, Alan, and drop off this Report of Proceedings at the Admiralty. You are to deliver it to the Director of Anti-Submarine Warfare personally. You'll get an extra day's leave, a free travel warrant and a first-class sleeper to yourself. A car and driver will meet you at Paddington, take you to the Admiralty and drive you home to Kingston when you've delivered the documents. Can you make it?'

This was a rhetorical question. Two hours later, I was walking unsteadily along the platform in Plymouth station, where the night sleeper was waiting in a siding. Two Captains RN were hovering around the ticket inspector, who was peering at a piece of paper clutched in his hand.

'Are you Sub-Lieutenant Burn, sir? I have an order for you to take over a first-class sleeper with official documents. That'll be number five sir.'

I slipped quickly into number five and locked the door as instructed, while an animated discussion took place between the two Captains, who had been thrown out of their carriage, and the ticket inspector.

In the morning I was delivered to the Admiralty, ushered into a small waiting room and asked to hand over the parcel of papers, which I could not do as I had been ordered to deliver them personally. With remarkable speed the D.A/S.W. appeared and signed for the parcel.

'Are you one of *Starling*'s officers?'

'Yes, sir.'

'Were you on board when she rammed that U-boat?'

'Yes, sir.'

'Stay there, Sub.'

I sat down, full of misgivings. There were plenty of better things to do on a summer's morning in London, on the first morning of leave, than to sit in an Admiralty waiting room. I consoled myself with the thought that maybe this was the very seat on which Nelson had sat, seeking Their Lordships' approval to send him to sea. The furniture seemed to be of that vintage.

The D.A/S.W. reappeared: 'Follow me. Someone wants to see you. What's your name again?'

We went at speed along the dark rabbit warren of Admiralty passages, and into a great room where a mass of gold braid sat round a long oval table. When I had time to count, I totted up one Vice-Admiral, three Rear-Admirals and three Captains.

'This is Sub-Lieutenant Burn, sir. One of *Starling*'s officers who was on board.'

Apart from one or two curious sidelooks as I took a seat at the table, there was no break in the quick-fire discussion of Walker's report. There were one or two tentative smiles when they read that 'There was no Lebensraum for Herrenfolk on the U-boat's upper deck'. An occasional question of clarification came my way. At the end, the Admiral at the head of the table addressed me and said that his colleagues thought that we were putting in too much sea time and needed more leave.[8]

I was amazed, our life was sea time and leave was an added bonus if it came. We did not *need* leave, and morale was sky-high. I was trying to explain this, but was interrupted before there was time to complete my mumbled reply. The Admiral leapt on the interrupter.

'Let him speak.'

My ideas about the brass hats in the Admiralty changed that day for the better.

After a series of conferences and intensive lobbying in Plymouth, Walker took the Group back to sea for its second patrol in the Bay of Biscay on 3 July, still retaining temporary command of *Wild Goose*. He left Wemyss to supervise and keep up the pressure on the repairs to *Starling*. After the successes in the month of June the offensive in the Bay was further intensified. B5 Group and the Second Support Group continued to work with Coastal Command to block the U-boats' passage along the north coast of Spain. The MUSKETRY area was still full of reports of U-boats on the surface trying to get to or from their bases but the blockade operations were once again plagued by difficulties of air-sea communication. This joint operation of support groups and land-based aircraft was an unexplored type of anti-submarine warfare. The speed with which this offensive had been mounted had left no time for joint training of surface and air forces and it was not surprising that there were difficulties and inefficiencies in both services.

Aircraft, not very sure of their exact positions, were trying to report the position of U-boat sightings, some real, some imagined, by geographical coordinates. These could be very inaccurate, particularly in bad visibility. When the surface forces arrived, there was nothing there, because, after several days at sea, their positions could be equally inaccurate.

Walker pressed very strongly for a better method. Aircraft should attach themselves to the Group and circle at a range of about thirty miles, thus greatly increasing the effective visual cover of the surface forces. When a U-boat was sighted and dived after an attack, its position should be identified by dropping markers in the sea. Aircraft should remain over the markers and lead in the surface forces by direction finding, or, if close enough, by visual signals.

The level of activity during this patrol was very high and the strain on Walker and his commanding officers correspondingly heavy. Every step was taken to close with the enemy, and much of the patrolling was only about ten miles from the coast of Spain off Cape Ortegal. *Wren* picked up some survivors from *U-607*, sunk by a Liberator which had dropped a life-boat alongside the German survivors swimming in the water. Otherwise the ships had no contact with the Germans, returning to Plymouth on 16 July, frustrated and very tired.

The third patrol started on 23 July, with the Group strengthened by *Woodcock*, another of the modern sloops. Walker took command of *Kite*, leaving Lieutenant-Commander Willie Segrave to take over the supervision of the completion of *Starling*'s repairs while Wemyss came back to sea and resumed command of *Wild Goose*. In five weeks Walker had been to sea in four of the ships of his Group in action conditions; it is not surprising that the communications in his command were becoming outstandingly efficient. He always took his tiny staff of specialists with him and was personally aware of all the problems that could affect the efficiency of the Group's operations.

He had no intention of allowing the short gap in the run of his successes to lead to apathy or boredom in his command. When he arrived back in the Bay he signalled the Group:

'The Boche... must be made to realize that the Royal Navy considers the Bay of Biscay a happy hunting ground and will stamp out any attempt to restrict the free and rightful passage of Allied shipping. When we meet him we will destroy him.'

That evening, came the first of a series of incidents with Spanish trawlers. Before the close blockade of the Bay started, the Admiralty had declared the areas in which Allied forces would be operating to be prohibited and gave notice that any neutral ships entering these areas would be 'sunk at sight'. This order was directed specifically at the Spanish boats which fished in large numbers in the areas that were now being used by the U-boats as their route to and from their bases. Their presence made radar detection of the Germans extremely difficult, and there was always the possibility that German agents could be forcibly planted in their crews with instructions to report any sightings of Allied activity.

The first Spanish trawler was sighted on the evening of 25 July. Her crew was taken on board *Wren* and the trawler was sunk; two days later more appeared, until on the 28th, 'from 1200 onwards the sea seemed to fill streadily with fishing craft'.

So much for the Admiralty's stern warning. The numbers enjoying the hospitality of His Majesty's Ships became an embarrassment. The Spanish fishermen were so pleasant and got on so well with the British Tars that volunteers started coming forward to join the Royal Navy as additional Hostilities Only seamen. Walker reported:

'The Spaniards seemed to be enjoying themselves hugely. Several had applied vociferously... to be allowed to join the R.N. and shrilly expressed their disappointment when their applications were turned down.'

One of their skippers, when asked how he felt when his boat was sunk, replied: 'I should worry. My trawler belongs to Franco.'

The sloops by now were overcrowded with the friendly Spaniards, and Walker decided that he must call a halt to their entertainment. All the crews were transferred to one of the trawlers, *H. de Valterra*, and after promising that they would go straight home and not do it again, set off home cheering their hosts. As soon as they had been despatched, another three appeared, but no more hospitality or free transport could be offered because there were two more U-boat sightings to be followed up.

On 30 July a Liberator spotted a group of three U-boats on the surface travelling in company; the position that it reported was eighty miles in error, but fortunately first a Sunderland and then the Catalina attached to the Group (as suggested by Walker) made a further sighting and at 0714 *Wild Goose* picked up an HF/DF bearing of a U-boat transmitting a long signal.

The Group closed the position at speed. There was much coming and going in the clear sky above; the two aircraft had been joined by an American Liberator and two more Halifaxes, and at 0947 the sound of depth charges could at last be heard and the aircraft were seen circling overhead.

The ships went to action stations, increased speed to eighteen and a half knots and at 1005 three conning towers could be seen from their crow's nests. Walker hoisted the signal 'General Chase'[9] and each ship was then free to make its best speed towards the action ahead.

The U-boats, when first sighted, were in line abreast with *U- 461* in the centre and *U- 462* and *U-504* on either side. With their combined fire power they had beaten off the first un-coordinated attacks from the aircraft. The Germans had then called for air support, but the nine JU-88s on patrol had insufficient fuel to enable them to come to their help.

The first Coastal Command success came from an attack by a Halifax from No.502 Squadron; her attack, with anti-submarine bombs, damaged *U- 462* so badly that it could not dive. As the U-boats turned into line ahead, the American Liberator, 0-53, went in very low to attack the leader, *U-504*, thus drawing the concentrated fire from all three boats. 0-53 was badly shot up in this attack, but managed to make the safety of the coast of Portugal.

At the same time, taking advantage of the diversion created by the Liberator, Sunderland aircraft number 461 from U squadron, came in from astern and blew a great hole in *U- 461* which sank very quickly with few survivors.

The determined attacks by the aircraft enabled the sloops to close until *U- 462* was just within range of their forward gun mountings. All four ships opened fire at a range of about six and a half miles and the U-boat was soon surrounded by shell splashes. 121 rounds were fired, 37 from *Wren*, 16 from *Wild Goose*, and 12 from *Woodcock*. But most were fired by *Kite*, urged on no doubt by Walker. She fired 56 rounds and in a remarkably accurate display of gunnery, registered a hit on her tiny target at 13050 yards. Shortly afterwards the Halifax signalled: 'Congratulations. U-boat is no more.'

According to her Commander, after the initial damage from aircraft attack, *U- 462* had been hit by the Group's gunfire and had given up hope of diving or of escaping on the surface. He therefore set his scuttling charges and abandoned ship.[10]

U- 462 had tried twice before to get out of Bordeaux to take up its station as a milch cow off the coast of Africa, but had been driven back on both occasions. Severe damage had forced it to return on the first occasion and caused a delay of several weeks; its second attempt also failed when it had to return again after damage by air attack on 2 July. It was badly needed to provide fuel for the U-boats which were waiting for its arrival off the Azores so that they could fill their fuel tanks and leave for an attack to be launched in the Indian Ocean. This was the third attempt.[11]

U-504 had dived when shells from the sloops started to fall around it and had gone deep in the hope of escaping detection among the wreckage and disturbed water from the destruction of *U- 461*. When Walker came up to the diving position, he deployed *Woodpecker*, *Wild Goose* and *Woodcock* in a square search round the area, ordering *Wren* to join him.

By 1034 he was in firm Asdic contact. The sea was littered with German survivors from the two U-boats that had been sunk who were crowded into dinghies quite close to the position of the submerged *U-504*. Able Seaman Clem Bray was one of the port side heavy depth-charge thrower's crew. As *Kite* came in to attack he said a silent prayer that he would not be ordered to fire the thrower as it would have landed right in the middle of the Germans in their dinghies. It was a close thing. Asdic conditions were bad and there could be no question of giving the surviving U-boat any chance of escaping, but Walker deliberately took his time to prepare while the U-boat drew slowly away from the position of the German survivors, stationary in their dinghies on the surface.

When Walker launched his attack and the depth charges started to explode, he was: 'still close enough to see the whites of their eyes... but after the attack the Boches in their dinghies were still seen to be rocking gently on the bosom of the ocean.'

The first attack was not successful but contact was regained almost immediately and *Wren* went in with a second attack six minutes later. Neither *Kite*'s nor *Wren*'s attacks produced any evidence of destruction, but they had established that the U-boat had gone deep and that it was one of the smaller U-boats (500 tons) able to take quick evasive action. Asdic conditions were very poor; one mistake and *U-504* could slip away.[12] Walker set about a methodical elimination by means of creeping attacks.

These attacks took a little time to set up because everything was done at the slowest possible speed so that the U-boat would get the least possible warning from listening to the noise of the attackers' propellers. The final attacks were made by *Woodpecker* not operating her own Asdic, directed by Walker in *Kite*. She fired a pattern of twenty-two charges set to 500 and 750 feet and was followed by *Wild Goose* firing a similar pattern.

The echo on the Asdic faded and patches of oil and wreckage started to well up to the surface. The ships lowered their sea boats to pick up trophies for identifications by the surgeon, which were accurately and colourfully described by Walker in his Report of Proceedings.

When *U-504* had been dealt with, the Group went back to pick up the two U-boats' commanders and the survivors who had been able to abandon ship before their boats went down. They must have wondered whether their luck had run out, because it was four and a half hours since they had abandoned their boats after the aircraft attacks. The first to be picked up was the engineer officer of *U- 462*. He had tried to clear a blockage on the U-boat's gun, opened the breach and been hit in the face by the empty cartridge. The commander of *U- 462* was Oberleutnant Bruno Vowe: 'He looked the part. He was dressed in a sea green leather suit, black shoes, brown gloves, cap with plenty of scrambled egg and a Van Dyck beard,' exactly as Clem Bray had always imagined a German commander would look. He was met by Lieutenant F.L. Boyer, resplendent in belt and gaiters, accompanied by an able seaman carrying a .303 rifle with five rounds of ammunition.

Vowe: 'I want to speak to the Captain.'

Boyer: 'You will speak to me.'

Vowe: 'No − I wish to speak to the Captain'.

Boyer: 'I am responsible for the discipline in this ship and you will speak to me.'

Vowe: 'I wish to speak to the Captain.'

Boyer: 'If you don't speak to me, I'll bloody well throw you overboard'.

This combined air and surface attack on the U-boats' route along the coast of Spain was a severe blow to the Dönitz offensive. It finally convinced him that even a group of U-boats well-armed against aircraft attack could not stand up to coordinated attacks from the air. They had no alternative but to dive. Once driven down, they faced depth charges from marauding surface support forces which could be directed on to their diving positions.

The Germans suffered particularly badly on this day. Dönitz pinned great hopes on his large Mark IX supply boats, or milch-cows, whose main function was to refuel and replenish U-boats in their operating areas, in this way at least doubling their time on offensive patrol, and reducing the number of times that they had to face the hazardous passage through the Allied air and sea patrols in the vicinity of their Biscay bases. In one day, in less than four hours, he had lost three of his U-boat fleet, two of which were milch-cows. With accurate information from Ultra, the Royal Navy had located and destroyed his surface supply and refuelling ships. In a week he had lost nine U-boats trying to get through the blockade of the Bay, of which four were milch cows.[13]

His options were running out. He had now to abandon his plans for attacks in the Indian Ocean.

The Second Support Group had no rest. On the following day they picked up the crew of a Focke-Wulf 200 that had been drifting around the Bay for four days and at 0900 on 1 August they were making their way into heavy seas at seventeen knots in pursuit of an aircraft sighting. The communications problem had still to be solved. This aircraft had to return to base for fuel before the ships came within visual contact, but at 1246 a Catalina took over and started to direct the Group to the spot by dropping smoke floats. The ships came up to find a Sunderland bombing the U-boat, but just as they were coming within range the aircraft made its final fatal attack during which it was itself shot down by its victim. The two pilots were lost, but six of the crew survived to be picked up by *Wren*, and in their turn *Kite* picked up thirteen of the crew of *U-454*, including the commander.

Kite was now in the unique position of holding on board as prisoners the commanders of three U-boats — *U-461*, *U-462* and *U-454*. The commander of *U-454* was reluctant to give the number of his U-boat before coming on board, but gave in quickly when he saw two of his fellow U-boat commanders who had been paraded on *Kite*'s deck to meet him. Walker noted that:

> 'The morale of the German survivors did not appear to be very high.... There was a tremendous amount of howling and squealing amongst them and members of the "master race" cried out continuously for twenty minutes before their turn came to be hauled aboard. They were uninjured but in an advanced state of panic.'

One of the survivors was shouting his head off. Walker picked up his megaphone and told the coxswain of the whaler, 'If he doesn't stop shouting, hit him over the head with a bloody oar.'

On 2 August it seemed that the great success of the Allied offensive by air and sea had finally goaded Dönitz into making an attempt to get back the fast passage of his fleet across the Bay by driving out the Allied surface patrols. There were aircraft reports that the Narvik Class destroyers were at sea and hopes ran high that the Second Support Group would be able to make a new and better kill. Battle ensigns were bent on to the signal halyards as the sloops headed at full speed on a course to intercept the enemy that night.

At 1815 the masts of three, and then four ships were sighted and wrongly reported to be Germans. (They were in fact the masts of the 40th Escort Group.) Night dispositions were made to cut them off from their bases. Even with a cruiser lurking in support over the horizon, these powerful German ships with their heavier guns and great speed advantage could have done a lot of damage to the little escort ships in a short time had they been handled aggressively, but during the hours of darkness they slipped through the radar screen and disappeared at high speed to the east and the safety of their home ports. This finally convinced the ship's companies that Walker could take on any odds and win.[14]

On 2 August Dönitz suspended all sailings from the Atlantic bases.

Two days later the Group set course to return to Plymouth. On the way back it was reported that one of the German prisoners had lost his Iron Cross. Lower deck was cleared and the ship's company was told that there would be no leave until the medal was returned. The Coxswain found the medal lying on his desk when he returned to his office. The five ships made fast to No 2 Jetty in Devonport's South Yard at 0730 on 8 August. A signal was flying from the C-in-C's flagstaff: 'Well Done Again Second Support Group.'

In his Report Walker commented on this two week's patrol in which the Group had been involved in sinking four U-boats, six Spanish trawlers, rescuing six R.A.F. men, repatriating a hundred Spaniards, and in capturing three U-boat commanders and ninety-five other ranks. He criticized strongly the orders for dealing with unidentified craft (which included Spanish fishermen) in the prohibited area, saying:

'The Spanish fishermen collected by the Group appeared harmless, ignorant, cheerful and pro-British: it is unlikely that the order to "Attack at Sight" would ever be carried out by a British Naval Officer who was aware of this.'

Walker asked for the order to be modified but his suggestion was not accepted, although his assumption was, I'm sure, correct. British naval officers, not only in the Second Support Group, were still issued with blind eyes and telescopes to use on such occasions, albeit at their own risk.

In the Bay of Biscay, in July, 1194 aircraft sorties were made: nearly all the eighty-six boats that attempted to cross the Bay in July came under attack by aircraft. From the beginning of June to 2 August twenty U-boats were sunk, seventeen by aircraft and three by the Second Support Group.[15]

The Group went to sea again at the beginning of August with Walker back in his own ship, *Starling*. The Devonport dockyard, working day and night, had repaired her stem and the gash in the hull and she was itching to get back into the fray. With their recent successes and sorties within sight of the coastline of Europe, the morale of all the ships was higher than ever. The increase in tempo and continuous operation with aircraft patrols had eliminated all possibility of boredom and they were looking for more close action.

There were still sightings from aircraft but the surface of the sea off the Spanish coast was empty now except for the odd fishermen who were still chancing their luck. The weather was perfect and the sea smooth. After the busy days of July there was a feeling of unreality. Where had the Germans got to and why were they not coming out to continue with the next round? Something unusual was in the air.

The first sign of trouble came with the appearance of groups of eight or more JU-88s, flying low on the horizon. This seemed like a new challenge; it appeared that the Germans had abandoned hope of getting their U-boats through the air and sea patrols and were now going to try to drive us out by aircraft attacks. Down went the semi-armour-piercing shells for use against the U-boats' hulls and up came the high-explosive shells with their proximity fuses for use against aircraft. The guns' crews waited for the JU-88s to come in to the attack; the time had come to try out the guns against German aircraft.

It would also be interesting to see whether the proximity fuses worked. In theory, the wizards ashore had eliminated one of the unknowns in gunnery; we no longer had to bother too much about fuse settings. The shell was fired and it exploded when it passed close enough to the aircraft to bring it down. For the gunnery officer, this was like playing darts on a special board where the dart disappeared if it didn't hit double top. During practice shoots, which we carried out each time we left harbour, the drogue target usually came fluttering down, but this event was always accompanied by a string of scathing remarks from Pilot, who reckoned we had hit the towing wire half-way along its length and that it was time that we stopped shattering the lights in his chart room. It would be interesting to see how these fuses worked in action. We'd show him.

The guns followed the JU-88s around as we zigzagged at full speed and waited for the attack. After half an hour of this the aircraft ceased their circling and disappeared over the horizon. This routine was carried out several times, which was very frustrating because it meant that the ship's company had to stay at action stations instead of acquiring a tan lying in the sun.

At last the attack came. Quite suddenly a swarm of black hornets appeared low on the horizon, broad on the starboard bow, coming straight for us. Within seconds the nearest ship had opened fire. A great firework display of green Verey lights shot out from the aircraft. A bellow, from the Yeoman as usual.

'Mosquitoes, sir!'

'Cease Firing.'

'Check! Check! Check!'

'Secure from action stations.'

An anonymous voice came from one of the voice pipes, muffled and unrecognizable, but quite audible on the silent bridge as people pulled off their tin hats once again.

"Hands to dance and bloody skylark."

These visits from enemy aircraft, interspersed with alarms, sightings and exercises, became part of the daily routine. Something was going to happen but there was no indication what the Germans had up their sleeves; the U-boats had disappeared and nothing had taken their place.

At the end of this patrol the Group returned to Liverpool. As *Starling* passed through the lock gates at the entrance to Gladstone Dock and before the gangway was ashore, a staff officer leapt on board and reported to Captain Walker that, on 10 August, 1943, His Majesty's Submarine *Parthian* was sunk by a mine on passage from Malta to Alexandria. Among her officers was Sub-Lieutenant John Timothy Ryder Walker RNVR, Captain Walker's eldest son, reported missing.

Eilleen Walker arrived just after the ship made fast alongside. The gathering of people with urgent business to discuss with Captain (D) found a solid block of ship's officers between themselves and their target.

The officers and their wives had invited Captain Walker and Eilleen to dinner in the wardroom the following evening. These were very special events, much valued as occasions when it was possible to forget for a while the discomforts and lack of social life at sea. Our suggestion to postpone the date was rejected and the dinner party took place as planned, but it was quieter than usual and Johnnie Walker didn't do his usual trick of standing on his head and drinking a pint of beer. The war had never been closer to *Starling* and her crew than it was that night.

When the Group returned for the final patrols in the Bay in August and September, Dönitz was ready to try to drive them out. These sinister aircraft appearances were the final reconnaissance and training of the aircraft which were to launch his next secret weapon.

On 27 August *Egret*, with the First Support Group, was joined by the Canadian destroyers *Grenville* and *Athabascan*. They were shadowed by a large group of eighteen enemy aircraft. Five of them split off. As they came abeam, a black puff of smoke suddenly appeared below each aircraft, detached itself and hurtled towards the ships at great speed. As they came nearer these puffs resolved themselves into powered gliders with a wingspan of about eleven feet. Two of them plunged straight into the sea; three of them came straight on towards *Athabascan*; two of these failed; but the third hit her at right-angles on the port side between B gun and the wheelhouse. It went straight through the Chief Petty Officers' mess and exploded 20/30 feet clear on the starboard side. All the officers and men working on the A.R.L. plot were casualties. As *Athabascan* was trying to recover from the shock of the explosion, *Egret* disappeared completely in a column of smoke about 200 feet high, leaving only a few bits of wreckage behind.

When *Athabascan* had steam on she went to pick up *Egret*'s survivors, before limping back to Plymouth.

Two days earlier a similar attack had been made on *Bideford* and

Landguard. Eight glider bombs were released of which four were complete failures and four were described as 'astonishingly accurate'.

One or two of these glider bombs could be carried under the wings of the German bombers. They were armed with a charge of 1,100 lbs and were guided on to their target at 300-400 knots by radio control from the parent aircraft.

Nearly all our anti-submarine escorts, including the frigates and British destroyer escorts coming over from Canada and the United States, had been designed and pushed into the water to beat the U-boats, but not aircraft and U-boats simultaneously. These ships had no way of disturbing the aircraft that fired and controlled the glider bombs as they circled outside range. The ships were too far from base to call up fighter protection at short notice and their only defence was to try to shoot down the bombs themselves when they came within reach of their close-range armament. Exceptions were the sloops of the Second Support Group, designed as anti-aircraft ships and fitted with strong main anti-aircraft armament — better than many classes of destroyers. Even so, the fire-control clocks in the sloops could not be set to deal with targets capable of the speed of the glider bomber; nor was it pleasant to know that these powerful missiles would be steered to follow their targets' evasive action.

Had this new weapon been fully developed and tested, and its operators fully trained, with adequate fighter protection, it would have been an even greater threat. But Dönitz had been forced by the major and successful onslaught and the disasters that he had just suffered in the Bay to use these weapons before they were fully operational.

Starling, on her return to Plymouth, was boarded by a group of officers and men, distinguished by their gleaming new gold braid, their spanking new uniforms and smart regulation caps. These additions to our already over-crowded ship brought with them arrays of aerials and electronic equipment. When we took them to sea they showed an unusual susceptibility to sea-sickness and also an unhealthy enthusiasm whenever enemy aircraft appeared. The buzz went round the ship that their most sophisticated and successful technique was to hold an electric razor close to a microphone and transmit through all likely wavelengths. It was said that, when they found the right frequency, even the most determined glider bomb would give up the ghost and plunge into the sea. It was hoped that the Second Support Group would attract further attacks, perhaps shoot down and recover one or two of the glider bombs, and so provide valuable information to our intelligence services for the development of counter-measures. However, no ships in the Group were able to oblige by attracting close misses.

At this time we had some changes in the wardroom. After a trip in *Wren,* Lieutenant Bill Johnson RNVR had taken over from Lieutenant-

Commander Ingram Poole as Walker's secretary; he was a great addition to the small staff and without doubt lightened some of the administrative burdens which came with Walker's appointment as Captain (D). He also brought a great talent for amateur dramatics which he used to alleviate the tedium of long patrols. Regular shows, in which much talent was revealed among the ship's company, were masterminded by him, often using very valuable material borrowed from his friends in the theatrical world. These were broadcast over the internal system during the dog watches. In addition to his other duties, which included much exacting encyphering and decyphering of long signals, some of which were boring in the extreme, he came to do duty as an Officer of the Watch, which was a rare honour for an officer in the paymaster branch and an indication of Walker's confidence in him. His action station at sea was on the bridge in the middle of the activity, where he kept the record of events and also, very important, kept up a running commentary on the telephone to the engine room.

There was also a change in the all-important Asdic team. The formidable Lieutenant Michael Elijah Impey R.N. who had been Walker's First Lieutenant and Asdic officer from *Stork* days and had been awarded a DSO and DSC needed to go ashore for medical reasons. He had been replaced by Lieutenant L.C.H. Porter RNVR as Asdic officer.

In his selection of a new First Lieutenant, Walker enjoyed almost unlimited choice. He had all the officers in the Group to choose from. He could go outside the ship or the Group for the pick of the experienced lieutenants, any of whom would have jumped at the opportunity of taking on this key job. A signal from him to the Commander-in-Chief would have had any officer of appropriate rank hurrying up the gangway. He chose to take on John Filleul, whom we have already heard of in *Stork* as the gunnery officer and as the officer in charge of the depth-charge crews in *Starling*'s actions. John was a very junior officer; he had been made up to Lieutenant just before *Starling* was commissioned. His birthday was 30 October, 1920. He was thus not yet twenty-three when chosen by Walker.

The job of First Lieutenant in any ship is extremely important. In this case, because *Starling* was Captain Walker's ship, it carried a lot of additional responsibilities. John had to be certain that Walker was happy in his own mind that the standard of efficiency in every part of the ship was impeccable — just a little bit better than any other ship in sight. Because of Walker's many other duties as Captain (D) much of the work which would normally have fallen to the Commanding Officer of the ship fell on John's shoulders. As we have seen, Walker frequently transferred to other ships of the Group; during *Starling*'s commission John had to work for no less than seven other Commanding Officers when Walker swopped ships. John was now the only other commissioned regular Royal Navy officer in the ship. All the others were RNVR, several of them older than he, and not always an easy bunch to deal with, since they did not have the ingrained discipline and career ambitions of the regulars.

These changes in key roles had no adverse effect on the ship. Walker was still there. The superb technical efficiency of the Asdic team was continued by Petty Officer Darby Kelly and his team, and John's appointment was welcomed, because he was well liked, well respected and everyone knew that it would have been very difficult for anyone else to take over this key role.

As soon as the technical equipment had been installed the Group set course for the patrol areas to carry out the dual role of tempting out the glider bombers, shooting down one of their missiles to take home as a specimen, and of continuing the blockade.

Unfortunately, although the Group patrolled brazenly on the Germans' doorstep, the sloops of the Second Support Group not only greatly resembled little cruisers but they were also handled in such an aggressive fashion that the German aircraft showed no signs whatsoever of wanting to take them on. They continued to circle in the clouds, occasionally peering out cautiously but seldom coming within range. When they did there were six four-inch guns in each ship which immediately opened up on them.

The Group now had a personal Catalina attached for reconnaissance purposes, for which we developed a motherly concern. On one occasion it lumbered out of the clouds pursued by eight Junkers and sought refuge under the guns of the sloops, patrolling backwards and forwards only a few hundred yards away on the disengaged side, while the sloops drove off its pursuers.

But the Germans never fired at us and none of the special gear rigged over the side to pick up a specimen to take home was ever used to pick up a glider bomb. The days went past with many false alarms but no useful contacts with the enemy. Towards the end of the patrol we cruised by night just outside the three-mile limit off the north-west coast of Spain, so close that we could smell the land and see the lights ashore as the darkened sloops slunk along, not far from the gaily lighted fleets of our friends, the Spanish fishing boats, home and snug in their own waters for once.

Aided by information from Ultra, which gave vital and quite fresh information based on the U-boats' own reports of their positions, courses and speeds, Coastal Command had established a very remarkable record in the month of July by sighting fifty-five of the eighty-six U-boats that attempted to cross the Bay, sinking sixteen of them, badly damaging another and turning back six.[16] The Germans had now lost seven of their ten milch-cows, and with them the chance of effective operations in distant waters. There were several U-boats now lying off the Azores, now so short of fuel that they could not get home. The U-boats no longer tried to gain time by travelling on the surface and attempting to fight their way through in groups. They took the longer route round, hugging the coast of Spain. The few that tried to cross the Bay had given up their efforts to take a fast passage and had been ordered to submerge by day and to surface by night and only if it was essential to charge their batteries.

The activity of the Group was as high as ever, but there were no sightings of U-boats. The main task now was to continue to discourage the Spanish fishermen from coming out of their territorial waters and entering the prohibited zones. The radar echoes from their vessels, and the high cliffs behind, made it difficult for the radar operators to detect U-boats creeping along the coast. Later the Group had similar problems with the French tunnymen. Walker did not like this task. He described the sinking of one French boat, after taking off their crew as: 'the nearest the Second Support Group ever came to shooting an albatross.... She went down with her mainsail still set, and her outsize fishing rods waving plaintively against the sky.'

The ships were able to come to the aid of a number of aircrew shot down and drifting in dinghies with little other hope of survival. To establish and to maintain this blockade, Coastal Command had made 2,549 sorties in the months of July and August. There was no other friendly shipping to come to their help if they were shot down. But we were not always in time. There were nine in the crew of the Liberator P/224. Two were killed as they pressed home their attack on a surfaced U-boat. Of the seven in the dinghy, two died having been refused water by a U-boat that came alongside and spoke to them. After eight days, the five survivors were brought on board *Wild Goose* in a very bad state. Two of them died on board after making their reports.[17]

Bitterness crept into the attitude of the ships' companies.

The Group returned to Plymouth. At sea neither the Captain nor the officers nor the crew wore anything that resembled uniform. But it was our custom to enter harbour in style with the ships in line ahead, the hands on deck in their Number Ones, the guns trained fore and aft with their crested brass tampions in place, the ensigns flying and our signature tune, "A'Hunting We Will Go" blaring out over the loudspeakers as we passed in front of the Hoe. The Captain was in full uniform, standing up behind the binnacle. When we came up to the lighthouse on the breakwater, a small coaster appeared, plodding along clear of the ships and to port of the main channel; there were three grey-haired men and one white-haired man to be seen on the bridge, watching us. Why not? The Second Support Group was a fine sight to see on a summer's evening.

As we came up from astern, the white-haired man raised his hand and

waved. I picked up my binoculars; there was the little ship's name on her stern, "ENOS". No! It couldn't be true!

'Captain, sir. What do you think of that fine ship? That's my father waving.'

'What's he doing there, Alan?'

'He goes to sea to deliver these little ships sometimes, so that he can see how the other half lives. He told me in his last letter that he would be bringing one down from Glasgow, arriving about now.'

'Yeoman, hoist "Disregard my movements." Ask Petty Officer Gardner to bring up a bottle of gin, Number One. I'm going alongside to pass over that bottle. Port fifteen.'

Starling pulled gracefully out of her position at the head of line, and slowed down. Leading Seaman Smith appeared below the bridge, alongside B gun, with his heaving line. He was a big heavy man and no one could throw a line as far as he could. The bottle went across. The other ships steamed majestically past. Scores of binoculars watched every move.

'What's the Old Man up to now?'

The Yeoman was leaning over the edge of the bridge; just his hands moved as he semaphored a private message across to his opposite numbers in the other ships. Within two minutes the story had passed right throughout every ship and down into the engine rooms.

'Get me back in station, Pilot. We must be there before we get to the Melampus buoy, or I shall be in trouble.'

There was a half-smile on Walker's face. It was quite clear that that bit of fun had made his day. Now Pilot could do a bit of ship-handling to drop us back into place at the head of the line, without leaving the swept channel or running aground.

In September *Starling* had problems with her gyro compass, bad leaks and, worst of all, managed to entangle a wire round her port propeller. Walker transferred for a short patrol to *Wren*, and *Starling* had Commander Aubrey as her Commanding Officer while the repairs were effected. Commander Aubrey was an eccentric character. He was a cheerful veteran of the convoy battles with a most distinguished career that went back to the start of the conflict. He loved his ship, *Wren*, but he fought shy of women, even WRNS; indeed when the Wrens came aboard to see their ship and friends in harbour he had been known to lock himself away. He succumbed at last. When I met him long after the war, he had married and was the bursar at a girls' school in Windsor. A late starter.

When *Starling* was in the floating dock in Belfast, Chiefie walked round below the hull and tapped out row after row of defective rivets with a toffee hammer.

While *Starling's* defects were repaired, the Group went off to Tobermory to prepare themselves for the renewal of the battle. *Starling* with the holes patched up, the gyro compass working and no wires round the screw, returned to Liverpool with Captain Walker.

13. 'The Greatest Cruise.' Walker's ships sink six U-boats in one patrol. The Second Support Group is cheered into Gladstone Dock, Liverpool (see p.141).

14. Captain Walker sees the First Sea Lord and the Commander-in-Chief, Admiral Sir Max Horton, ashore while the side party pipes the side led by the coxswain, Chief Petty Officer Unsworth.

15. One of the sloops closes for orders.

16. The escort carrier, HMS *Nairana*, in North Atlantic seas. 'Nothing could be as terrifying as watching an aircraft carrier caught on her beam ends and lying farther over with each sea.' (see pp. 110, 192) HMS *Tracker* recorded rolls up to 52 degrees, and was often invisible below the wave crests.

17. HMS *Magpie* was one of the early ships to be fitted with Hedgehog, accounting for the destruction of one of the U-boats on 8/9 February 1944. As this picture shows, the weather was often the worst enemy on Arctic conveys (see p. 126).

18. HMS *Starling* digs in. The whole of her bow right up to A gun mounting disappears under green water and spray. Picture taken from HMS *Wren* as she closes for orders.

19. After ramming *U-119* in *Starling*, Walker and his key men were rowed across to *Wild Goose* in a sea boat, to continue against *U-449*. 'This somewhat unusual operation was carried out without trouble or incident in the middle of a further series of attacks on the U-boat'(see p.88).

20. The view from the Director Tower. In the foreground is the bridge showing its formidable array of voice pipes. Invisible in the dark shadow along the forward side is a solid mass of alarm pushes, switches and telephones connecting with all parts of the ship. The chart table is in the port corner and the Asdic team are tucked under the front in the closest possible contact with the Commanding Officer and his team clustered round the binnacle. Further forward is B mounting with its twin four-inch guns and, beyond that again, A mounting, protected from the seas by a steel breakwater, which was torn away from the deck by big seas during the Atlantic hurricanes of the winter of 1943/44. Hands are at action stations after dropping a depth charge pattern, as the ship turns back onto the U-boat's bearing. No one is wearing a tin helmet, because these were usually not donned until the last moment, and few of the guns' crews ever wore the anti-flash gear provided.

21. A frayed battle ensign was hoisted aboard the destroyer HMS *Hesperus* and half-masted when she carried Captain Walker's coffin to its last resting place below the waves beyond the Bar Light Vessel.

22. After the service in the Anglican Cathedral the gun carriage bearing Walker's body, escorted by eight Captains, Royal Navy, was hauled through the streets of Liverpool by a team of bluejackets.

23. The coffin is laid on board *Hesperus'* quarterdeck, guarded by four seamen with arms reversed.

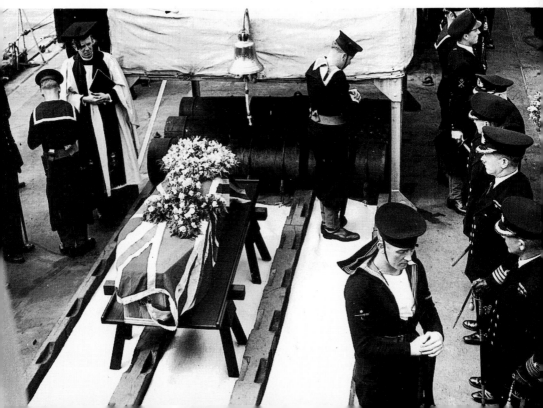

FREDERIC JOHN WALKER
C.B., D.S.O. & THREE BARS,
CAPTAIN, ROYAL NAVY.

✝

IN MEMORY OF THEIR COMMANDING OFFICER,
FROM THE OFFICERS AND MEN OF
H.M.S. "STARLING",
JULY, 1944.

24. This Memorial Tablet was designed by men who served in Walker's Second Support Group. The ship's crest of an angry starling plucking a U-boat from the water was their idea and bore little resemblance to the more formal and correct version approved by the Admiralty.

CHAPTER SIX

NORTH ATLANTIC
HURRICANE CONDITIONS

There were many awards to the officers and men of the Second Support Group following the operations in the Bay of Biscay. These included a second DSO (in July) and a CB to Walker: in *Starling* Michael Impey received a DSO, John Filleul, in addition to his appointment as First Lieutenant, a second DSC, Roland Keyworth and Tommy Teece both received second DSMs.

By 14 October the rest of the Group had finished their retraining at Tobermory and rejoined Walker in *Starling* to sail from Gladstone Dock in thick fog. Walker gave full support to the working-up training at Tobermory, but once again had avoided taking part himself.

To add to our strength, and to the complications of Walker's command, we were to operate with the escort carrier *Tracker*. We met her for the first time off the north coast of Ireland on a dark but clear night with no moon. She stood out like a block of flats.

The sloops *Starling*, *Wild Goose*, *Woodcock*, *Magpie* and *Kite* were in line abreast, with *Starling* in the centre and *Tracker* one or two miles astern, all ships zigzagging independently.[1] At night the sloops increased their distance ahead to two and a half miles. When the carrier was launching or landing aircraft all ships turned into the wind together, with one ahead and another astern to carry out rescue duties if needed.

After a lifetime of study, four years of war experience and sinking nine U-boats, Walker said:

'I am no believer in the formal Asdic screen 1500 yards apart, for *Asdic is an uncertain weapon of defence.*'[2]

When we had cleared the Irish Channel and the north coast of Ireland had disappeared astern, all hands not on watch were piped to lay aft on the quarterdeck for a short talk by the Captain. He told of the Germans' new horrors and of the work that had been going on for many months to develop counter-measures. He explained his plan to lure the enemy to the attack by pretending to be the outside screening force protecting a non-existent convoy. He explained his personal plans for retaining the initiative against the U-boats and emphasized again the need for even more practice for the ships as a Group.

However, for the next few days, the priority was to survive the war against the weather, which was quite abominable, rather than the war against the Germans. The little ships battened down, battling continually with the great rolling walls of green seas. Salt spray whipped across the decks and the bridge in cutting, stinging sheets. Somehow it always penetrated to sore necks and trickled in icy streams down shivering backs. Watchkeeping, particularly during the long nights, was very trying, but it was even worse down below. After several days of being thrown about, small things assumed an exaggerated importance and it became hard to retain a sense of humour. Meals became a test of strength and endurance.

Clem Bray remembers being so seasick on board *Kite* for three successive days that he wished he had been torpedoed, particularly when he saw one of his colleagues being sick into the mess jug. The Royal Navy did not provide sick bags.

Handling the sloops and the aircraft carrier when hove to was a major problem of seamanship. On the third day of one storm, in a really vicious force ten, *Tracker* was having a particularly bad time, and all ships were hove to. *Starling*'s propellers were turning fast enough for eight or ten knots, but she was making good only three knots through the water, just fast enough to keep her bows up to the fifty foot seas and the 500-yard-long swells[3] in spite of fierce pounding. With less power the wind would catch the bow as the ship came up to the top of the swell and throw her broadside on. Any more power and there was a serious risk of structural damage from the frequent green seas that swept over A and B gun mountings. In the half-light as dusk came down, *Tracker* and *Starling* slowly but inexorably started to converge. *Tracker* tried to alter course, but as she came round the wind and sea caught her and threw her beam on, and she hung over at an awful angle. Down below a couple of Swordfish had broken adrift and were crashing from side to side like mad stallions, on a hangar deck that was awash with oil and sea water, pursued by a gang of matelots who had to secure them before they smashed up the rest of the planes. Using bursts of power in the trough of the swell, *Starling* worked clear. Ernie Green in *Tracker* remembers that he wondered 'how you survived on those little boats of yours', but nothing could be as terrifying as watching an aircraft carrier caught on her beam ends and lying farther over with each sea.[4]

When *Tracker* had recovered, Walker made a signal. (Yeoman in full oilskins, hanging on with one hand and working the shutter of the signal lantern with the other, red face streaming with salt water, peering out from below his black sou'wester.)

'Do not attempt to turn again. We have no room for survivors.'

When the wind eased and the sea and swell slowly levelled out, *Tracker* got her own back. The Spitfires that she carried were rarely used, as they were too fragile for Atlantic conditions. As it had been some time since the guns had been fired Ernie Green asked for permission to test them on the flight deck.

'We got a couple of planes on deck facing outboard, tails secured and the guns (20mm cannons and .303 machine guns) armed. We had a bit of a roll on but the sea wasn't too bad, so we let off a couple of bursts. Everything seemed to be going fine until someone came tearing down from the bridge. There was a signal from *Starling*: "We are used to being fired on and it doesn't worry us, but it's usually the enemy, so turn those X!X!X guns the other way".'

This change from the comparative quiet of the patrols further south aggravated many unsuspected leaks in the hulls and decks. From the time the ship left Liverpool until she arrived at Argentia, a period of four weeks with two short breaks in the weather, a bailing party worked for twenty-four hours a day with buckets to keep pace with the two inches of water swishing to and fro across the deck of the after flat; not a single officer's cabin was dry.

'The messdecks are near impassable: they have our hammocks, our fag ends and a goodly share of our food on the deck as we search for a place to snatch sleep.'[5]

Twice at night spectacular electrical fires broke out in the director tower, the highest inhabitable place in the ship, way up above the bridge. Green water found its way down one of the ventilator shafts amidships on the forecastle deck level on to the dynamos. Depth charges, their securing eyebolts torn out of the deck, rumbled and chased each other around the quarterdeck.

The Group was patrolling right in the middle of the U-boat concentration, but the U-boats were no more able than we to continue the battle. They were never good observation or gun platforms, due to their low freeboard. The Biscay blockade had caused Dönitz to add a great deal of anti-aircraft armament and to protect the bridges with armour. These additions not only made them more difficult to handle when submerged but caused them to roll heavily when surfaced in Atlantic weather. The rolls averaged thirty degrees and reached a maximum of sixty degrees.[6] If they stayed deep enough the U-boats could avoid some of the discomfort of such weather, but on the surface they ceased to be effective fighting units.

When working with convoy ON 207, Walker was ordered to take command of three Support Groups, (his own, 7th EG and B.7) and two aircraft carriers, *Biter* and *Tracker*,[7] but the weather remained so bad that by the end of October he was getting fed up as he could find no U-boats in the Atlantic ready to do battle.

Suddenly, during the middle watch of 6 November, the wind dropped and died down to a murmur. There was still a long high swell, but, through breaks in the clouds still hanging ragged and low over the sea, there were occasional glimpses of stars against a blue-black sky. It was a little quieter below as the ship ceased to pound and fell into a more rhythmic roll: the lucky men off watch fell at last into deep sleep. On the bridge the crackle of the T.B.S. started again as the ships reformed ahead of the escort carrier and settled at twelve knots to their long weaving search. The report came back from the last ship, 'Am in Station'.

Young Jack Moss was learning fast. The seasickness had gone and he was defrosting his backside by sitting on the galley stove and drinking kye. Luxury!

Far away to port, flickering lights hovered momentarily over the low clouds like slow lightning.

'Starshell to port, sir.'

Up the voice pipe, shattering the peace of the bridge, came a roar from Tommy Teece in the W/T office: 'From *Kite*. U-boat has dived'.

'Action stations! Port Twenty! Signalman, tell that bloody carrier to get out of the way. Captain, Sir, *Kite* has a U-boat.'

There was the sound of gunfire as *Kite* opened up. *Starling* swung away to port as men came pouring up the companion ways, pelted down the black upper deck to the depth charges and swung up the ladders to the guns. As *Starling* crossed *Tracker*'s bows − too close − her huge bulk loomed up out of the darkness and seemed to rush towards us as we took the shortest route to join *Kite*.

To *Tracker* from *Starling*: 'Keep Clear. Attacking.'

The carrier heeled as she passed under our stern and sought shelter behind *Wild Goose* and *Magpie* as they escorted her away from the danger area.

Amplifying reports streamed through from *Kite* as *Starling* closed the diving position. The lights were *Kite*'s starshell falling through the low clouds. She had picked up a radar echo at 3,800 yards, and her lookout had first spotted the U-boat as it came clear of a patch of fog some 500 yards ahead, trimmed down but still on the surface, on a reciprocal course which would have put it nicely in a position to have a shot at *Tracker*.[8] In the darkness and patchy fog, if the U-boat and *Kite* had continued without alteration of course they would probably have collided a minute later. However, the U-boat dived immediately, firing a torpedo as she went, helped on her way by *Kite*, who dropped a few charges fired by eye.

This immediate action and her turn away saved *Tracker*'s skin.

It was pitch black on *Starling*'s bridge as she swept in to join *Kite*. Ahead it was just possible to see the black outline of the forward gun muzzles against the white of a breaking wave; closer, the bulkhead carried an array of bells, switches, alarm pushes and voicepipes; to the right and left, recording instruments and invisible batteries of telephones and buzzers. Behind the binnacle a quiet strong voice floated up the voicepipe from the wheelhouse, 'Coxswain on the wheel, Sir.'

Chief Petty Officer Unsworth on the wheel. It might be the middle of the night, but he would be wearing his cap and a spotless white polo-necked sweater – and his lifebelt.

In the eerie darkness, the bridge messengers flitted to and fro and an able seaman reported back the states of armament readiness as the guns and throwers were made ready for attack. Outside and around all this was such complete blackness that it would have been easy to turn 360 degrees without knowing it.

Over the T.B.S. Walker and Segrave spoke in short terse phrases to each other as the two ships, manoeuvring at close quarters, passed the contact from one to the other and *Kite* went in for another attack. No time to have Foxers trailing over the stern: not the sort of situation that any sane person would include in exercises at Tobermory.

The attack went without a hitch, but the only result was to provoke the U-boat into loosing off S.B.Ts.

With *Starling*, *Kite* and *Woodcock* stalking their prey in firm Asdic contact, Walker decided that there was no point in risking further hazardous operations in the pitchy black and that the next attacks could well wait until daylight. He ordered the two ships to keep clear, and for four hours jogged along behind the U-boat on one engine. At dawn he ordered *Woodcock*, under Commander Clive Gwinner to close so that he could pass instructions to him over the loud hailer. While *Starling* continued to track the U-boat, scarcely moving through the water, *Woodcock* crept in at five knots with her Asdics switched off, to deliver a creeping attack with charges set deep, directed by Walker.

The centre of the pattern fired was reckoned to be within two degrees of bearing and a few yards of range, covering an area 400 yards long by 100 yards wide. As the charges started to explode, many hundreds of feet below the surface, there was a terrific roar and a column of water shot high up into the air. At 0719 the Asdic operators reported breaking-up noises. At 0733 there were two explosions of which the second was near the surface and audible to all on deck. At 0747 the remains of *U-226* started to float to the surface. These included a torpedo which we hoisted on board – with some misgivings – to take back for the experts to examine.

Kite reported that this had been a very large U-boat, either a milch cow or a 1200-ton supply boat which was shown by their plot to have a turning circle of 340 yards.

This was another successful creeping attack.

Walker signalled "Splice the Mainbrace", a most welcome break in the grey, cold monotony of this patrol. The Group reformed ahead of *Tracker* and resumed their sweep, and the hands set about preparing for Captain's rounds.

It might seem strange that such formal inspections continued remorselessly during long, unpleasant and protracted periods of sea time. They were another way of marking the passage of the days and breaking up the monotony. Nutty was issued once a week. Some ate the whole ration immediately: some made it last until the next issue. The wardroom bar operated normal hours at sea, but it was not used by the watchkeeping officers except for a weekly drink to celebrate the arrival of another Sunday, and when the signal "Splice the Mainbrace" was made. However, U-boats weren't sunk every day, so, to celebrate this occasion, Bill Johnson set about shanghai-ing volunteers from every part of the ship to put on one of his more ribald shows over the loudspeaker system.

Captain's rounds had just been completed. The wind was down to force two and even the swell had flattened out. The whole ship's company were really enjoying the luxury of the break in the weather, when, at 1303, Archie Pitt's team picked up an HF/DF bearing of another U-boat transmitting on the surface about twenty miles away.[9]

This time it was the turn of *Woodcock* and *Kite* to look after *Tracker*. *Tracker* flew off an aircraft and a Liberator appeared from Newfoundland. Had the U-boat been able to remain on the surface it could now be a long way away, but this aircraft support kept it submerged, so cutting its ability to move away from the position where it had transmitted its message. Walker and Pilot huddled together over the A.R.L. Plot working out the most likely course. An hour and forty-five minutes later speed was reduced to fourteen knots and the three ships started a systematic Asdic search. Nobody was very optimistic, since the Group had just spent several weeks in the Bay unsuccessfully following up scores of similar alarms. There is a lot more empty space in the Atlantic Ocean than there is in the Bay of Biscay.

There was no contact after the Group had been steaming for two and a half hours; it had covered forty-five miles since the original HF/DF bearing, in which time the U-boat, submerged, could have gone ten or more miles in any direction.

Hope faded. Walker won many of his gambles, but it seemed that he had lost this one. Down on the depth charges and round the gun mountings, there was some subdued murmuring from men longing for the warmth of their bunks.

Suddenly *Wild Goose*, one mile away on *Starling*'s port beam, reported an Asdic contact at 1800 yards, a couple of minutes later classified by her H.S.D. as 'submarine', and then confirmed by *Starling*, who went in for the first attack, while *Magpie* started a square search outside the area. Walker said of this attack: 'This attack will bear no analysis and was in fact shocking'.

He had anticipated that the U-boat would take evasive action, both by a burst of speed and a violent alteration of course. It did neither. He missed by miles. (Even the best striker can miss the odd penalty.)

But *Wild Goose* had retained a firm grip on the contact, which was just as well because *Starling*'s gyro compass had been thrown out of action by a shallow depth-charge explosion. When this had been repaired Walker directed *Wild Goose* in another creeping attack to fire twenty-six charges. Something went wrong and she only fired ten. Walker was in a fury, first at his own mistake and then because his most trusted ship had let him down, and last because in the middle of the attack he was told that his gyro compass was not two degrees out but nine. He threw his cap on the deck and jumped on it.[10] This was most unusual. The circle round him on the crowded bridge grew wider, as people found important things to do in the far corners. In his Report he said: 'I would have staked my last penny that the attack was bum (and I should have lost my money) .... I could have stamped with rage when both ships reported "Lost Contact".'

He started to send a stinker to *Wild Goose*.

He was interrupted by a loud underwater explosion, relayed over the bridge speakers, followed by reports from the Asdic operators of unmistakable breaking-up noises. Then oil started to come to the surface and, finally, up popped another headless and tailless torpedo. A seaboat was lowered and came back with the necessary evidence of destruction.[11] That was the end of U-842.

The signal changed to 'Splice the Mainbrace'.

Several important things had been achieved in this short period. A single HF/DF fix had led three ships straight to a U-boat forty-five miles away. The creeping attack had proved lethal for the fourth consecutive time. Once again it had been shown how very inadequate the standard Asdic attack could be, even in the most experienced hands. Finally Walker made the point in his Report that once again a great tradition of the Royal Navy had been upheld. When Lieutenant-Commander Segrave sighted *U-226* he decided on his own initiative not to 'step-aside' as recommended in A.C.I. 138 para 16d. He accepted the risk of a Gnat and had he not done so he could have lost the U-boat and presented himself as a broadside target to its attack. Instead he turned towards at full speed, opened fire and went straight in with a depth-charge attack fired by eye.

This was the second occasion on which two U-boats were sunk by the Group in twenty-four hours – in the one available break in the weather.

Even as the Group reformed ahead of *Tracker* the weather started to break and we saw the last of the sky and the sun for many days. In the rising sea, while the crew were fully employed in putting out a fire that had broken out in the carrier, a torpedo exploded off her port quarter. The Group turned back to locate the U-boat but sea conditions were now making Asdic operation very erratic and no contact was made. During the search *Starling*'s radar went out of action. A moderate gale was now blowing, but Ceri Fisher, clutching his small bag of tools, crawled up the wildly gyrating mast like a fly in a wind tunnel to repair the defect.

For the rest of that night and the whole of the following day the Group was once again experiencing dreadful seas, running at right-angles to the huge swells. This particular spell was described by Walker: 'The Group was hove to on course 320 degrees in quite the fullest gale I have yet met.'

The course ordered could better be described as the course hoped for. Much of the time the sloops could not see each other. Their small outlines were obscured by the driving spray, appearing occasionally on the crest of a wave and then disappearing behind the crest as they sank down into the trough. In these conditions, radar was of limited assistance. The only method of keeping in touch without the need for chattering on the radio or flashing lights was to endeavour to keep *Tracker* in sight, since she was the most visible and least manoeuvrable of the ships. She appeared from time to time through the spray, heaving and twisting in her agony.

For the second time on that patrol the majesty and ferocity of the Atlantic seas had become our chief adversary. It blew, and continued to blow, so hard that if a U-boat had surfaced fifty yards away, neither side could have done more than exchange small-arms fire. In the sloops any major alterations of course required carefully judged bursts of full power on the main engines to avoid the certainty of sustaining extensive damage to the structure and the armaments while butting into the solid walls of water. On the other hand the upper deck of a U-boat would have been uninhabitable and the chance of a successful snap shot would have been nil.

Since our patrols covered the danger areas outside the reach of land-based aircraft from Iceland, Newfoundland and the United Kingdom, the Support Group was only withdrawn when the weather made all forms of action impossible. At times such as these the Group retired into less ferocious waters where one or two of the sloops refuelled from *Tracker*. This entailed steaming on the same course, close to the carrier while the fuel lines were passed across and fuel was pumped over. A small error in seamanship, a mistake in the engine room or any lapse in steering were sources of potential disaster, since the operations were carried out in conditions where the wind seldom fell below force six. The whole operation could take six hours steaming at eight knots in close company. Both *Tracker*'s and *Starling*'s steering gear had already given cause for alarm, having broken down on that patrol on more than one occasion.

As soon as there was any sign of the seas moderating the ships usually returned to the patrol area, but on this occasion they had been at sea for nearly six weeks in the worst weather imaginable. Food and ammunition were now running low, and all the ships were beginning to show serious signs of structural damage brought on by frequent exposure to explosions from charges released at slow speeds, a great deal of sea time and the recent vile conditions.

Extra depth-charge racks had been installed on the quarterdeck and every available square inch of space above and below decks in the after end of the ship had been used to accommodate more charges. The decks started to crack right across the stern from side to side. In *Starling* the crack was so pronounced that daylight (and sea water) came straight through. This split might have been patched, but the propeller shafts were in danger of distortion and day by day the fault was growing visibly more pronounced.

In August Walker had reported these defects: structural strengthening to the sloops had been approved 'By Command of Their Lordships' on 28 August, 1943.[12] The extent of Walker's influence and the importance that was now attached to his recommendations can now be seen. On 12 November a signal from Captain Donald Macintyre (for the Commander-in-Chief) confirmed that: 'all Modified Black Swan Class Sloops need structural stiffening. Arrangements being made to take *Starling*, *Kite*, *Wild Goose* and *Magpie* in hand on return'.

Meanwhile in mid-Atlantic the winds blew, and the sterns 'waggled like those of angry ducks', and the water poured in.

As the Group set course for Argentia in Newfoundland, it was clear from the amount of wireless activity and the HF/DF bearings that there were still at least four U-boats in the vicinity. One final torpedo was fired at *Tracker* before the Group was swallowed up in the worst gale of all on 9 November. Although keen to get into harbour, the ships had to butt into the howling wind, making good a speed of only two knots along their course line. All the sloops had a bad time, but *Woodcock* suffered most. Seas had forced her forward guns to full elevation and jammed them there, tearing her steel ready-use ammunition lockers from their welded fittings in the deck and tossing them over the side.

When the Group neared the coast the wind moderated, to be replaced first by dense fog and then by normal Newfoundland Banks mist. Pilot looked strangely confident, considering that the Group had been weaving around the Atlantic for too long to give him much chance of knowing where he was.

Today he had a good plan. He could rely on a bearing from a beacon that would give him a position line, and the echo-sounder, which would tell him when he crossed the hundred-fathom line. These would give him a nice fix and he would do his usual magician's act, staying in the charthouse until an excited lookout reported land. He would then remain down below until the O.O.W. asked him in exasperation where he thought we were, and whether any alteration of course was necessary. He would then amble on deck, not even look at the land and announce the new course and the time when we would be alongside.

The bosun's mate stuck his head round the chart room door. 'Captain would like to see you, sir, in his day cabin.'

Captain Walker and Bill Johnson were putting the finishing touches to the Report of Proceedings, and wanted to confirm a few things from the Pilot's plot. Half-an-hour later he was back in the charthouse, gazing at the echo-sounder and realizing that he had missed the exact time of crossing the hundred-fathom line.

'Signalman, ask *Woodcock*'s navigator the exact time that we crossed the hundred-fathom line.'

'Reply, sir, "Sorry I missed it too".'

Pilot took his binoculars and joined the row of searchers sweeping the horizon. Down in the radar cabin, Ceri Fisher and his team watched the outline of the coast on their screen with amusement. 'One day those navigators'll put a bit of trust in radar, maybe.'

The weather-beaten, rust-marked sloops that entered Argentia, the base in Newfoundland leased to the United States' Navy, could scarcely have been recognizable as the trim ships that had steamed past the Hoe in Plymouth only a few weeks before. Everything from the top of the ensign to the Captain's last socks was soaking wet and caked in salt. But the morale of the men was sky-high and their reputation had gone before them. The Americans' welcome to these tired men, used to the war-scarred dockside at Liverpool, was quite overwhelming. A brass band played their signature tune and a crowd of press photographers climbed aboard as the ships came alongside to a jetty lined with cheering American crewmen.

Walker said of this patrol: 'Perpetual paddling, snatches only of sleep (in wet blankets), no radiator for drying and warming, a succession of long faces reporting one dynamo flooded out, gyro, director and radar out of action, three depth charges chasing each other round the quarterdeck; but what are such things compared with the satisfaction of having given the Boche another mouthful of dust to bite?'

The Americans' hospitality was endless. All their clubs, their transport and sports facilities were laid open to all ranks. The paperwork from the UK had not caught up with the ships which enabled everybody to relax: we relaxed so much that the contrast lay between the wild abandoned behaviour of the Limeys and the restrained strictly correct attitude of the Yanks. A dear old Stringbag from the carrier was said to have been zooming and stunting over the airfield at midnight. Two engineer officers turned right instead of left when going ashore and paddled pathetically round the very cold harbour. Commanding Officers' motorboats raced each other for large stakes. We went for walks, played football, boxed, drank and slept. We drove out in magnificent American cars, the like of which we had never seen before, to the tiny wooden villages of Newfoundland. Fergie, our wild bearded Australian, celebrated by crawling around playing crap and betting heavily. In the officers' club, John Filleul did an exhibition rhumba on the first night and followed it on the second night by doing the same dance while playing a borrowed trombone. He was asked by the polite American owner to desist 'Because it was not hygienic'. Joe Foster, a more serious-minded and thoughtful officer, who analysed his own emotions and reactions, declared that a large number of rye highballs produced 'a delightful condition between nausea and intoxication'.

But Captain Walker was invited to give a series of lectures to the U.S. Navy before leaving by train and plane for Halifax, at the invitation of the C-in-C North Atlantic, to give the Commanding Officers of the new Canadian escorts whatever help he could from his own experience. For him alone there was no relaxation. More and more work and responsibility was falling on his shoulders. Almost invariably now, he was the Senior Officer of any force of convoy escorts at sea in the North Atlantic, which meant that he had not only his half-a-dozen sloops to think about but also the disposition and tactics of any other groups that were in the vicinity. His command at sea should have been that of a Rear Admiral, supported by the appropriate staff and with adequate accommodation. Instead he had to make do with his leaking sea cabin and his indomitable communications team, headed by Tom Teece and Roland Keyworth, both now promoted to Chief Petty Officer, who coded their signals in their tiny compartments with sea water swirling over the decks, clambered over each other, cursed, swore and grumbled while they got on with the job.

Apart from the weakness in the structures of *Starling*'s stern, other major defects had started to show up. The brickwork had started to fall down. The steering gear had failed for the third time, this time for several hours, which could have been disastrous in the weather conditions, or in the middle of an attack, or when steaming alongside an oiler.[13]

At the end of the boiler clean, with the worst defects patched up, there were twelve hours to spare before we were due to take up our next patrol. Since it was on the way to our operational area, Walker seized the chance of taking *Starling* and *Wild Goose* round to St John's, Newfoundland, for a shopping spree, since it seemed that one patrol would just get us home for Christmas if we were lucky. As the ship was still securing to the buoys, the motor boat, packed to the gunwales with liberty men, towing the whaler, also packed, started to take the sailors ashore for a shopping expedition, with no coupons needed in well-stocked shops such as they had not seen since the beginning of the war.

This was a pleasant end to a much-needed break. The Newfoundlanders were helpful, friendly and cooperative. Large bales of Red Cross comforts came on board as free gifts, including a many-coloured patchwork leather waistcoat which became Captain Walker's favourite rig at sea.

Starling, *Wild Goose*, *Magpie* and *Kite* came out from this short interlude in harbour well rested and ready to resume the fray. *Woodcock* had already set off with another convoy bound for the UK and repairs to her severe weather damage. *Tracker* had been detached. The Group steamed at economical speed to meet a convoy that was just entering the area where the U-boats were known to be concentrating.

Scarcely out of sight of land, the urgency of the battle surrounded us. We were diverted at full speed to the support of east-bound convoy SL 140 which was under threat twelve hundred miles away, between the coast of Portugal and the Azores. For nearly three days we rushed towards this convoy in moderate seas, while its close escort and the Fourth Support Group held off the mounting waves of U-boats. Ultra intelligence indicated that pack attacks could be expected from the night of 27 November and it was touch and go whether we could get there in time to help the convoy through the crucial stage.

In a fairly rough sea with overcast sky and intermittent rain squalls, we came out of the loneliness of the chase across the apparently empty ocean and into the company and warmth of the great merchant ships.

The accuracy of the intelligence reports was immediately confirmed. While we were taking up our stations in the deep field around the convoy, HF/DF interceptions indicated that there were at least nine U-boats shadowing the convoy. Walker stationed the Fourth Support Group on the starboard bow and took over the port side.

There were in fact fourteen U-boats stalking convoys MKS 31 and SL 140 which had been sighted by German aircraft on the 26th. Dönitz had moved Group Weddigen into attacking positions, travelling submerged by day and at speed on the surface by night. From 2030 to 0130 on the following night the convoy was shadowed by German aircraft transmitting homing signals.

Wild Goose and *Magpie*, operating as a pair, lost no time before they made off after one promising sighting. This first chase came to nothing, but as they returned to their station they became aware of a U-boat on the surface following them: *Wild Goose* illuminated it by star-shell and opened fire, whereupon it dived, not far ahead of the sloops, but no Asdic contact could be made. After an hour of searching, *Wild Goose* left to rejoin, leaving *Magpie* to continue the search by herself and hold off any other prowlers trying to break through the screen on the surface.

Meanwhile *Starling* and *Kite* had sighted a searchlight about eight miles away, but had assumed that this was one of two American Task forces known to be operating with aircraft carriers not far away. Shortly after she set off, *Wild Goose* picked up a firm Asdic echo, rapidly identified by her navigator as the original target.

At midnight, just before *Starling* joined her old partner, the U-boat surfaced for no apparent reason not far from *Wild Goose* and was once again forced to dive by gunfire. The two veterans settled down to finish off their victim. A start was made with three plaster attacks, without result. Meanwhile the convoy was drawing away and an Admiralty signal gave warning of a probable air attack at first light on the next day, when the convoy would need the anti-aircraft protection of the sloops. Time was running out: starshell and snowflake firework displays were appearing at all points of the compass and it looked as if the main battle was starting to develop on the other side of the convoy. Walker put in three more careful attacks, still without result, and the two ships reluctantly hurried back to their stations round the convoy.

During the night *U-262* passed right under the convoy, surfaced in the middle and carried out an attack, claiming four ships. There were in fact no merchant ships sunk and Wellington L/179 sank *U-542*. No aircraft attack took place the following morning. No further attempt was made to attack the convoy and the Group Weddigen was dissolved. The expected glider bombs did not show: the U-boats had once more disappeared. The Germans put down their failure to harassment by aircraft and escorts which misled and delayed the wolf pack, and to the large number of starshells, 'which, it was obvious to us, the enemy deliberately used to create a diversion.'[14]

The rest of the passage was uneventful. The Group broke off for Liverpool for fuel, boiler clean and the two months' paperwork that had now caught up. This was the first occasion on which the Second Support Group had abandoned the hunt before making absolutely sure that any known U-boat had been finally dealt with.

As *Starling* made fast in Gladstone Dock the buzz went round that the Commander-in-Chief was on his way down from Derby House to look at the structural damage and see if the leaks were as bad as Walker had reported. John Filleul and Chiefie came charging out of the Captain's day cabin issuing strings of orders. All normal activities came to an abrupt halt. C.P.O. Unsworth appeared in his Number Ones and started inspecting and rehearsing his side party. Gangs of stokers and seamen appeared, lugging high-pressure hoses down the starboard side of the ship. All access from the port side of the ship to the starboard side was unobtrusively obstructed or blocked off. Once in position, the hoses were camouflaged, and the men resumed their normal activities.

The signalman posted as a lookout at the dockyard gate gave warning that the Admiral's car had been sighted. (He might not have recognized the Admiral but he wouldn't make a mistake about his Wren driver.) Walker appeared at the gangway, welcomed the Admiral and his retinue on board and introduced Chief E.R.A. Eddie Freestone, who was almost unrecognizable, having changed out of his normal greasy working overalls into his Number One uniform, resplendent with all its gold badges and medals.

Admiral Horton was not a man to waste time and set off at once along the upper deck, down the ladder onto the quarterdeck, and down again into the after flat, followed by his experts. As the last head disappeared, the working parties reappeared, driven by petty officers whispering their instructions. The hoses were pulled out of hiding and hauled into position with their nozzles pointing at the more vulnerable places on the crack across the deck. When the inspection party down below were nicely positioned, all the hoses were switched on at full power. There was shouting down below and the grinning head of a messenger appeared at the top of the ladder: 'Captain says to switch off those damned hoses.'

The hoses were switched off and disappeared. By the time the Admiral reappeared, the upper deck had gone back to normal, with men washing down the paintwork and going about their duties, and not a stoker in sight. Admiral Horton's uniform was very wet but his face showed neither anger nor amusement. The water jets seemed to have missed Walker. The pair went off as planned up the port side of the upper deck, crossed over to the day cabin, talking without a break and apparently oblivious to everything else.

The deed was done. All ships of the Group were dispersed for repairs in docks around the coast. On 17 December *Starling* went over to Wallasey to dry dock in Bidston, right up at the head of the port complex, surrounded by green fields, almost in the country.

This was an indication of the importance which was attached to these ships and to Walker's recommendations. Every port and every dock was now cluttered with preparations for D-day, as troops and supplies poured over from the United States, but the date of the landings depended on keeping the sea-lanes open and, once the landings started, the U-boats must be kept away from the invasion armada. The ships of the Second Support Group would be needed at full strength in both these vital tasks.

All leave, except local leave, had been stopped. Captain Walker tried to have this ruling waived, on the grounds that the ship was in dry dock and could not possibly go to sea, and that it seemed unreasonable to keep men on board when most of the accommodation was stripped and uninhabitable, but he had no success. The best he could do was to interpret the term 'local leave' in its most liberal sense. For the locals among the ship's company, and there suddenly seemed to be many of them, this meant a little time and even the chance of Christmas at home. For Walker, with his house on the outskirts of Liverpool, it meant that he could for the first time in many months get away from the sea and the war for a short while.

Once again the ship resounded to the clatter of riveting, and the filth and dirt of a winter refit cloaked her from truck to keel. Christmas and the New Year came and passed in a haze. These were not happy times for the men separated from their families, who had to spend the Christmas period on board. They all did their best to work up enthusiasm by decorating the mess decks, which were full of good food. But it was all a cloak to hide homesickness and the lack of family life that the sailor so often feels and so gallantly tries to hide in a whirl of parties and celebrations.

There is a pleasant memory of the hospitality of Captain Lawford and his base ship HMS *Irwell*. Just before Christmas Day he learnt that the Walkers were short of a turkey. He would have raided every shop in Birkenhead rather than fail to find one. He didn't fail; indeed he came up with several. The dockside seemed to be full of naval pairs, one carrying a turkey and the other riding shotgun. There is another impression of the Yeoman, who had just downed his tot, swaying precariously at the masthead, securing a Christmas tree to the highest point of the mast.

By the middle of January many rivets had been replaced and four new longitudinal beams put in to prevent the working of the stern. Steps had been taken to stop the leaks in the deck heads of the messes[15] and the officers' quarters aft, but the dampness from the condensation, which resulted from so many living in such crowded conditions, inevitably remained.

Starling was warped out of the dry dock and towed down the docks. The traffic was held up and the bridge rolled back for her to cross the main road and through the lock gates which controlled the access into the muddy Mersey. This ship, which seemed so tiny against the majesty of the Atlantic rollers, towered so high above the streets that she dominated the whole road and the pygmy cars and lorries that waited for her to pass.

CHAPTER SEVEN

THE ROUT OF THE U-BOATS

By the end of 1943 Dönitz accepted that convoys were so heavily covered from the air that it would continue to be very difficult to locate them and even more difficult to gather groups together for pack attacks. U-boats could risk surfacing only by night, so cutting down the distance that they could travel in Atlantic weather to 100 miles or less per day.[1] It was now taking them as long as twenty days to get to and from their bases. They could no longer replenish food, fuel, torpedoes and essential stores at sea from the milch-cows and supply U-boats, because most of them had been sunk.

The U-boats were allocated areas west of the British Isles where unproductive travel time would be minimized and they might expect help from the JU-290 heavy bombers now equipped for the first time with radar. They were no longer transmitting regular daily reports, because they believed that the Allied string of HF/DF stations was fixing the position of each boat as it made its report. In fact it was Ultra that was now regularly decoding the German traffic and so making it much easier to route the convoys in mid-ocean clear of the U-boats. They were still obstinately convinced that the signals used by their U-boats could not be deciphered, and that, logically, a bee cannot fly.

Consequently Dönitz no longer knew exactly where they were, what they were doing, or their fuel and torpedo status. When they did report, they were sometimes wildly optimistic: one group reported hitting nine destroyers with their acoustic torpedoes and sinking five: in fact no Allied destroyers were sunk at this time.[2]

The additional bridge armour and heavier A/A armament had made the boats unstable. Their newly fitted anti-aircraft guns were unreliable and subject to rust, but they did not dare carry out trial firings when in transit for fear of attracting attention to themselves.

Nevertheless, the Germans now had 424 U-boats in commission, of which 159 were operational. It was still a formidable fleet, of which the largest concentration of fifteen to twenty-five boats was marauding some three or four hundred miles to the south-west of the coast of Ireland.[3]

Starling, *Wild Goose*, *Magpie* and *Wren* put to sea again at the end of January, 1944, with their sterns strengthened and some of the leaks repaired, to be joined by *Kite* who would be catching up a couple of days later. The Group was operating with two escort carriers, *Nairana* and *Activity*. This was unexpected because, after the previous patrol with *Tracker*, both Walker and the Commanding Officer of *Tracker* had reported that there were serious drawbacks to escort carriers and Support Groups operating together in North Atlantic weather. Although the Group had sunk two U-boats during the one lull in the weather, for the rest of the time the need to detail two or even three of the sloops to screen the carrier halved the offensive power of the Support Group. The carrier had been able to do little flying in the filthy weather experienced in one of the stormiest parts of the Atlantic. The winter was the worst endured during the five war years: the number of storms recorded was double the 1939 figure. Gale-force winds were recorded on seventy-two days in three months. In December there were twenty-eight gales, six of which were force ten storms.

Nevertheless, the Group was ordered to meet the two carriers on 29 January off Oversay and to come under the command of the senior officer in *Nairana*, Captain R. M. T. Taylor, RN. That night the half-moon was semi-obscured by cloud, but both the big ships were clearly visible to the naked eye at five miles and it was obvious that they would present a tempting bait.

At the beginning of February three groups of U-boats, with strong air reconnaissance and support, were planning an attack aimed at convoys in the area in which the Second Support Group and the two carriers were operating. Their attack on the convoy was planned to take place on the 18th: two groups of U-boats were drawn up across the expected line of advance of the convoy, relying on full air support and reconnaissance.

On the morning of 31 January the sloops were sweeping ahead of the carriers at twelve knots one mile apart in the order from port to starboard, *Wild Goose*, *Magpie*, *Starling*, *Wren*, *Woodpecker*. The two carriers were zig-zagging seven and a half cables apart and two miles astern. At 1015 the carriers were taking advantage of a break in the weather to operate their aircraft: *Nairana* was heading out towards *Wild Goose* as she turned into the wind. *Kite* had just caught up with the Group and was closing from astern.

During their time in dock a fierce rivalry had built up between the depth-charge crews in *Starling* and *Woodpecker*. A dummy rig had been set up in the dockside sheds and there was a daily competition between the crews. Now the ships had been at sea for two days. In *Starling* the guns' crews and depth-charge crews were practising their drills, this time competing to beat their own ship's record times achieved before the refit. The prize was a bar of nutty for each member of the winning crew. It was a cold, sunny, bright winter's day: the upper decks were alive with men: the shouts of their Petty Officers urging them on to better results and the cheers of the winning crews were clearly heard on the bridge. The ships were eager to return to real action.

At 1015 Wemyss was below in the chart house with his navigator when his Asdic operator picked up a doubtful echo at the end of one of his sweeps, on his starboard beam, half-way between *Wild Goose* and *Magpie*.

If this was a U-boat, it had nearly slipped through the sloops' line and was already in position to loose off a torpedo at *Nairana*.

Before Wemyss had reached the bridge, the echo had been classified as 'Submarine' and *Wild Goose* was turning to starboard under full wheel: the Officer of the Watch had immediately dropped her speed to seven knots to avoid attracting a Gnat while she was beam on and had warned off the carriers by R/T.

Wemyss had a few seconds in which to make up his mind. As soon as he was bows on to the bearing of the U-boat, he increased to full speed and went straight in for an immediate attack. As the black flag broke out at *Wild Goose's* crosstrees, the carrier started to alter course away to starboard. Walker detailed *Kite, Wren* and *Woodpecker* to shepherd them away, while *Magpie* and *Starling* came in to join *Wild Goose* who was already dropping a pattern of charges to drive the U-boat down.

It was touch and go. The carriers and the sloops in the attack were all fine targets and within range of a Gnat, but *Wild Goose's* immediate reaction and attack might just have put the U-boat off its aim or delayed the firing for long enough for the carrier's alteration of course to take effect.

Six minutes later, *Magpie* came in with another attack, using her Hedgehog.

Neither of these attacks were successful, but the immediate danger to *Nairana* was past, and she had survived by the narrowest of margins.

Walker said in his Report: 'Unquestionably *Nairana* was saved by *Wild Goose's* exemplary speed and decision. Another minute or two and she would have been a sitter . . . *Wild Goose* handed me Asdic contact with the Boche on a plate. I could ask nothing better than to take the field again partnered by this doughty well-trained warrior.'

Conditions for Asdics were good, but the wind was rising and the sea was beginning to get up. This would not affect the U-boat, which had dived deep, but in these conditions time was on the side of the Germans. Walker called *Wild Goose* alongside. Communication between these two veteran ships was so good that by 1040, nineteen minutes later, the two ships had stationed themselves astern of the U-boat and *Starling* went into attack.

She lost contact at 700 yards, which indicated that the U-boat had gone deep, but retained touch with her Q attachment[4] up to 150 yards. The attack was unsuccessful, but Walker now knew that the U-boat had gone deep and he settled down to a systematic and long hunt, hoping that the weather on the surface would not make it impossible to handle the ships at low speed.

Starling now tried out yet another variation of the creeping attack. She adjusted her course by use of the Q attachment, and *Wild Goose* gave her the range taken from her range-finder. The long series of detonations started and continued at five-second intervals as the charges rumbled down the rails over the stern and curved out from the throwers on either quarter.

A few seconds after the fourteenth charge disappeared over the stern, there were two almost simultaneous explosions: the first was part of the normal pattern, set to explode seven hundred feet down and not very dramatic. The second was far more frightening, heavy, inexplicable and totally unexpected, throwing up a huge hill of water, ten yards from *Starling's* starboard quarter.[5]

The great mass of water climbed higher than the ship's masthead and seemed to hang for seconds over the quarterdeck. The ship jerked unnaturally as if she had come up all standing on a rock. A fully primed depth charge was hurled over the side and another fell five feet on to the steel deck. Neither exploded. All the electrical switches were thrown in the power room. Tons of solid green water began to descend on top of the depth-charge crews. As the water cascaded over the side, they emerged, soaked, shaken, some badly bruised, but still pushing out the remainder of the pattern.

Starling shook herself. The quarterdeck emerged from the water. Depth charges continued to leave the ship in the strict pattern of the creeping attack. There was no hitch or delay in the drill.

At 1132½ John Filleul was able to report that the pattern had been fired. He didn't sound excited or upset, but at that time he didn't know that the explosion had shattered the contents of the wardroom wine store (a repetition of *Deptford's* escapade with *Stork*).

This was a remarkable effort by the depth-charge crews carrying out their drills amidst feet of swirling water thrown on board by the explosion. But the successful completion of the attack was only made possible by the gallantry of Stoker Wilfred Mockridge, battened down below in the bowels of the ship in the power room with the watertight doors shut all round him. The shock knocked him off his feet: when he got up he saw by the dim emergency lighting that the main electrical switches had been thrown open by the shock. On his own initiative he immediately put them all back and so restored the ship to normal in a few seconds.[6]

Three minutes later the Asdic team reported a heavy underwater explosion, just before *Wild Goose's* follow-up pattern started to explode.

There were tapping and banging noises and two more explosions. Oil, wood, coats, books, clothes and human remains came up to the surface, to be collected by *Wild Goose*. The Asdic echo faded as the remains of *U-592* and its crew went on its long journey to the ocean bed 2500 fathoms below.

Two hours later, having made sure that the job was done and having collected evidence, both ships set off to rejoin the carriers and continue the patrol, going south to avoid the heavy swell and strong winds which were making flying conditions difficult. The ships of the Group took it in turn to top up their fuel from *Activity* on 3, 4 and 5 February, before setting off to support Convoy SL 147/ MKS-38 which was being escorted by B3 Group under the command of *Towey*. During this time the U-boats were still endeavouring to intercept convoys in this area, but were slowly withdrawn to the south-west as the Germans decrypted signals that indicated that support groups were covering this area.

On 7 February the carriers entered the convoy in an endeavour to hide themselves from the U-boats. They wanted to intensify their efforts without frightening away the U-boats by revealing their presence. Walker took up station in the deep screen and once again became his own boss, with freedom to handle his ships as he saw fit, without the responsibility for the close protection of the carriers. During the day he brought his ships in closer to provide protection to the convoy from the thirty four-inch guns that the Group could bring to bear against aircraft attack.

They were back in their stations on the deep screen the following night, which was fine and moonlit but with deceptive patches of mist lying on the surface. Creepy weather for the escorts, sometimes in the fog and sometimes silhouetted against the bright path of the moon reflecting from the smooth swells. The air was saturated with fine droplets which settled on duffle coats and collected on exposed surfaces like a white frost; the sea and sky joined in a vague haze so that the ship seemed to be flying through low-lying clouds. As it grew dark, a hush settled on the sea and over the ship; the stars were blotted out and the ship moved in a white world of its own containing just the swish of the water and the slight roll of the decks.

The first sign of danger came from *Wild Goose*, who was covering her port bow sector of the convoy about eight miles out. Able-Seaman J. G. Wall, her port look-out, reported a 'black object' on the bow and simultaneously the signalman on watch identified it as a submarine diving about a mile away. Wemyss immediately reduced speed to seven knots in case of Gnats and pointed his ship at the U-boat as he reported to Walker by R/T. The Asdic team had picked up the echo, but the U-boat let off an SBT and came straight on. Wemyss, who had been ordered to hang on until Walker could bring up more support, kept very quiet, manoeuvring at slow speed.

The submerged U-boat made no attempt to alter course and seemed to be unaware of *Wild Goose's* presence. The range closed steadily until it became obvious that it must either hit *Wild Goose* head-on or pass right underneath her. As the tension built up on the bridge, the ever-alert lookout let out a yell: he had spotted its periscope as it came up to have a look around. It was just 20 yards away as it went past on a reciprocal course, so close that *Wild Goose* had time only to empty a magazine of oerlikon shells into the periscope before it disappeared astern.

Woodpecker then came up to join *Wild Goose*, while *Kite* moved in to fill the gap in the screen round the convoy. The two ships went in for a plaster attack, during which *Woodpecker* dropped twenty-two charges, just before *Starling* arrived on the scene, running through the area covered by the attack. Clearly over the hydrophones came the sounds of the U-boat trying to blow tanks, and then an unmistakable series of five underwater explosions. *Starling* was just in time to summon *Woodpecker* back. By the light of the searchlight her seaboat was able to pick up wreckage, tins, paper, clothing and more human remains. Walker signalled to Commander Pryse in *Woodpecker*: 'Come over here and look at the mess you have made.'

By 0134 on 9 February the ships were on their way back to their stations with their second victim on its way to join *U-592*. During the night the convoy had altered course to avoid the hunt, and proceeded on its way, disturbed only during the middle watch by aircraft that flew around reporting its position.

As *Starling* slid back into her normal station astern of the convoy during the early morning of 9 February a burst of radio activity was picked up by the ships of the Group. An HF/DF fix placed one U-boat nine miles away on the surface ahead of *Kite*. Twenty-five minutes later *Kite*, searching ahead in visibility of only half a mile, nearly ran straight into a long grey shape as a U-boat emerged from a patch of mist at full speed on the surface, heading straight for the convoy. At this time the radar was searching for *Magpie* and detected the U-boat no earlier than the lookout, giving no advance warning.[7]

Walker ordered *Magpie* to join *Kite* at full speed. We must leave this pair for a few hours, because three minutes later *Starling* was off in the opposite direction to join *Wild Goose* who had detected yet another U-boat by radar at a range of three thousand yards, trying to get through the gap left in the deep screen on the port beam of the convoy while the previous attack was going on.

Wemyss read the mind of the U-boat commander: his first action was to reduce speed to seven knots because of the danger of Gnats and open fire with star-shell in the hope of making the U-boat take refuge below the surface. Sure enough the echo faded at 2,400 yards, which meant that the U-boat had submerged. It was picked up immediately by Asdic. As it went down it let off an S.B.T. and at 0732 there was an explosion as a Gnat blew up at the end of its run.

Starling would take a couple of hours to catch up with *Wild Goose* and Wemyss decided to carry out Walker's standing orders to put in an attack to keep the U-boat submerged and give it something to think about. This had no apparent effect and it continued on its way making no effort to shake off its pursuer.

The main onslaught started immediately after *Starling* arrived. Walker took over the contact, directing *Wild Goose* in yet another variation of the creeping attack, followed up with a pattern fired by eye on the position indicated by *Wild Goose* by flares.

The full effects of the attacks were not apparent for some time. The first heavy underwater explosion came twenty-five minutes after the creeping attack, followed by cracking and breaking-up noises. After an hour another creeper followed, during which the U-boat 'let off a couple of loud farts suggestive of firing torpedoes' and fired another Gnat which exploded in *Starling's* wake. The next attack was fired while the U-boat was altering course, but it completed the job. The final very heavy explosion, followed by the usual debris floating to the surface, took place one and a half hours after the first charge had been dropped.

This was the end of Number Three,[8] but *Kite* and *Magpie* had not yet got rid of their target. When he saw the U-boat emerging from the fog, Lieutenant-Commander W. Segrave altered course immediately towards and dropped his speed to seven knots, firing a single depth charge set shallow. He had got off a single round from his four-inch gun before the U-boat dived. Seconds after his charge exploded there was a thunderous roar and *Kite* disappeared completely from view behind a pyramid of foam and water several times higher than her masthead.[9] To the dismayed crew of *Magpie*, it was quite obvious that *Kite* had been hit in the stern by a Gnat. For several long seconds nothing was visible except the spray mounting slowly into the air, mushrooming out and then slowly drifting down.

A cheer went up! *Kite's* mast appeared out of the spray and then the familiar grey hull: the hill of water settled back to the surface revealing *Kite* plodding methodically along, undamaged except for badly shaken members at their action stations on the quarterdeck, some buckled plates and the depth-charge rails a bit distorted.

The German had fired at sight before submerging, but his Gnat had been counter-mined by *Kite's* single depth charge. Segrave reckoned that 'the chances of a stone-cold kill at so close range are not very good and the risk of running into a Gnat or other infernal device was not high.'

Segrave was a dashing character with much charm, but he was now aggravated. He increased to full speed and ran straight in with a shallow pattern fired by eye; then, to keep the target busy and in the hope of finishing the business off before the Asdic contact disappeared in the very poor conditions, he put in three more ten-charge attacks at half-hourly intervals until *Magpie* came up to take part in a creeper.

The two ships then set about the task with great verve, attacking once with a creeper and follow-up, once with a Hedgehog attack and twice with ten charge patterns, before Walker arrived on the scene at 1245.

At this time another Petty Officer, Kelly, the HSD in *Kite*, and the anti-submarine officer had held contact for five hours with the 'toughest and wiliest U-boat' yet encountered by *Kite*, in very poor Asdic conditions in which echoes came and went unpredictably.

After a night at action stations, with a brief rest on the way from one job to the next, *Starling's* ship's company was in no mood to appreciate a grey Atlantic morning with the visibility down to half a mile, but the chase was not over yet. Walker reported that: 'This Boche went slow downwind and sea, at considerable depth, making it difficult in the prevailing weather conditions to hold the directing ship long enough in position to direct the creeping attacks.'

There were only seventeen depth charges left on board *Kite* and she went to join *Wild Goose* in the patrol round the scene of action while *Starling* and *Magpie* took over the attacks. Walker was perplexed; a very large number of charges had been expended on this target without any results. Stocks were getting low. On the other hand, *Magpie* was the only ship in the Group fitted with Hedgehog, and Walker had thought up a new way of using this more modern weapon.

He directed *Magpie* at slow speed until she was just short of the U-boat's position and pointing in the right direction, whereupon she was ordered to fire her Hedgehog at a range calculated by *Starling's* navigator. This caused a lot of laughter on the bridge — imagine any one of twenty-four bombs dropping seven hundred feet through the water and getting a direct hit on the twenty-foot diameter hull of an invisible U-boat! The laughter was cut short by two sharp underwater explosions as two bombs found their target twenty-one seconds after the Hedgehog fired. Not content with this result, he directed *Magpie* to carry on without interruption with a creeper, firing old-fashioned charges, followed up by *Starling* four minutes later. To everyone's surprise and to the amazement of Walker and his specialist anti-submarine team, this makeshift attack produced all the usual evidence of destruction as oil-soaked wreckage came to the surface in quantities. Walker wrote: 'I was highly tickled by this hedge-hoggery. Complicated instruments are normally deemed essential to score even occasional hits with this weapon; to get two bull's eyes first shot with someone else's Hedgehog 1000 yards away was of course a ghastly fluke.'

This was Walker at his most ruthless. The chase had gone on for eight hours with fifteen depth-charge attacks (252 charges) and two Hedgehog attacks (48 bombs). *Starling* had expended all her depth charges. If this last attack had not succeeded, there was no doubt that he would have continued to stalk the U-boat until it surfaced for air, when it would have been destroyed by gunfire, or rammed as a last resort.

The Second Support Group had sunk three U-boats in the past 15 hours.[10] But nerves were ragged; there were two many of these Gnats and maybe other devices exploding too close. In a signal timed 092030A to C-in-C Western Approaches, Walker reported, among other events: 'Several "Gnats" fired during operations but all avoided by use of low speed.'

The convoy of fifty-seven ships and twenty-four landing craft proceeded unharmed on its way, guided neatly between these two battles without casualties. It had been shadowed by aircraft all night but was not attacked. On the evening of 9 February, the two aircraft carriers were ordered to return home while the Group continued the patrol. They went off in ones and twos to refuel from an oiler in the nearest convoy and to replenish with depth charges. *Starling* had none left out of her usual armoury of 160 charges, *Magpie* seventeeen and the remainder about sixty-six each.

Transferring depth charges at sea was a long and trying operation. With the coxswain, Chief Petty Officer Unsworth, on the wheel for several hours, the sloop steered parallel with the munitions ship at a distance of twenty-five to fifty yards while the charges were hauled over by hand. If the depth charge hit the water the line was liable to part; if the line parted the charge was swept in to the side of the ship in the vicinity of the propellers. This happened twice. The officer in charge did not escape adverse impromptu comment from the bridge.

Signals came in with doleful tales of steadying lines wound round propellers and parted fuel hoses. Two men were lost over the side during these operations and could not be recovered by the ships astern. This caused great grief. The men of the Group considered themselves invulnerable and these were the only casualties that the Group or the merchant ships under its protection had suffered. Everyone was tired and bad-tempered.

Starling and *Wren* were the last ships to replenish their stocks. *Kite* was ordered home suffering from condenseritis. Walker sent off Commander Pryse'in *Woodpecker* with *Wild Goose* and *Magpie* to sweep back over the previous day's battlefields.

During the night of 11 February these three were sweeping along in their usual formation in a calm sea with visibility of two miles. Asdic conditions were poor, confused by fish echoes. In the middle watch *Wild*

Goose picked up a contact on her Asdic. The ships were in no sort of formation, caught in the middle of an Easy Item turn, altering course in succession, 90 degrees to port from south to east. *Wild Goose*, quite undeterred, attacked immediately. She had to alter course to starboard to attack her contact (instead of to port as planned) and ran straight across the rest of the line coming in on the new course. To avoid collision, or blowing up one of her own, she had to break off her attack and restart when she was only four hundred yards short of the U-boat. She didn't have enough time to build up much speed. Wemyss says: 'I went through a hair-raising time as I had to break off and stop the ship . . . and then re-start the attack from only four hundred yards' range. The explosion lifted the stern of the ship, but she still held together and the instruments still worked, so the battle could proceed.'[11]

Asdic conditions were bad, with many false echoes from fish and from the barrage of S.B.T.s which the U-boat had let off as a screen behind which it was making frequent course alterations. Neither *Woodpecker* nor *Wild Goose* were able to keep continuous contact, and a plaster attack of twenty-two charges by *Woodpecker* on a doubtful contact produced no results. Both ships lost touch altogether; things were looking hopeless until *Wild Goose* picked up an echo right astern at maximum range. Wemyss at first was pessimistic, but was persuaded by his Asdic team to go back to investigate. As they got closer the contact became better and the enthusiasm grew; the echo then faded entirely in the middle of the attack, Wemyss was 'fed up with this dot-and-carry business . . . [and was] determined to have a bang',[12] realizing that it would be a long time before Walker could get to the scene and fearful that the conditions would allow the enemy to escape.

After the charges had been dropped, Asdic contact was lost by both ships, but thirteen explosions were heard clearly through the hydrophones and a mess of oil and wreckage started to come up to the surface. The three ships patrolled round the area until dawn, hoping either to gain more positive evidence of destruction or to pick up the U-boat again on Asdic if it had survived the rather inconclusive action of the night. Walker joined during the morning, but there was nothing convincing to be found and he decided to continue the patrol and come back in the evening before dark. Wemyss managed to snatch a few hours' well-earned rest and came up to the bridge in the afternoon to find the ships surrounded by an enormous pool of oil spreading for six miles. Walker accepted this as final evidence of destruction as the result of *Wild Goose's* and *Woodpecker's* three attacks, and gave permission to splice the mainbrace.

At first light the Group went back over the sea covered during the night, in an effort to locate the two U-boats that had attacked, before they had time to recover from the pasting that they had just received.

Walker signalled his intentions to the C-in-C Western Approaches and set off to cover the previous night's battlefield. He could not know that Dönitz had ordered a regrouping of the U-boats ahead of the convoy, any more than Dönitz could know that seven of them had already been sunk, five by Walker's Group and two by aircraft.

A signal arrived ordering the Group back to the convoy, but it was too late. While Walker was pondering how to react to this order, *Woodpecker* had picked up an Asdic echo and dropped a flare on the position. Walker ordered her to hold the contact but to take no other action for fifteen minutes while any Gnats could run their course and blow up.

At 1016 *Starling* confirmed the contact and dropped a ten-charge pattern while the other three ships started Operation Observant. The U-boat was wriggling behind many SBTs and Asdic conditions were very bad. Contact was only held on poor and faint echoes. The many alterations of course and sea conditions were making it difficult to keep station astern of the target while the creeping attack was set up. Contact was lost for twenty minutes by both ships. It was nearly an hour later that the first attack was launched by *Woodpecker*, directed by *Starling* who followed up with a twenty-six charge pattern. After this attack the U-boat did a full 360 degree turn, exercising the seamanship of Walker and Pryse who were trying to keep astern and line up for another attack.

This time the Asdic contact was broken for an agonizing forty-seven minutes during which neither ship was in contact; it was difficult to know at this stage who was the hunter and who was the hunted. There was a nasty feeling that the U-boat commander might be gazing at us through his periscope to launch a torpedo from the beam while we wallowed around at slow speed.

A poor and intermittent contact was regained after the U-boat had had an hour's respite. In the next attack *Woodpecker* fired the creeper, steering by the use of her Q attachment while *Starling* gave her the range. She lost contact at the crucial moment but still dropped her charges. *Starling* did not follow up because she was once again down to only sixteen charges. Contact was then lost again in the turmoil created by the exploding charges. A despairing team then searched by running back over the last known course and going up to windward to allow for the drift of the sloops as they crept around at slow speed in the dirty sea and wind conditions. The contact was renewed in time for another ten-charge pattern to be launched by *Woodpecker* at 1400. The first sign of success came ten minutes later when a loud underwater explosion was picked up on the hydrophones.

For two hours the two ships then trailed behind the U-boat, sometimes in contact and sometimes not. At no time was the echo good enough for a co-ordinated attack until 1617, when Walker sent in *Woodpecker* for a final fling, following up with his last sixteen charges. None of the usual noises of destruction were heard and once again contact was lost. It looked as if a long test of endurance was developing.

There were murmurings around the ship. The hands who had kept the morning watch had now been on watch or at action stations for twelve hours with only just enough time to grab their breakfast. The depth-charge crews had nothing left to fire and, for want of anything better to do, had gone to their gunnery stations, clustered round X turret.

It was beginning to get dark; the convoy had been steaming away over the horizon, for seven hours at nine knots. The three ships patrolling round the area had detected no sign of the U-boat trying to break out of the ring of ships. It could be anywhere by now.

Walker came up on the bridge from a long and dispirited study of the plot with Pilot. He climbed into his chair and sat there, silent. He had never lost a U-boat in this way before and had no intention of giving up now, signals or no signals. He kept the ships slowly weaving round the area, only moving occasionally to hang over the side of the bridge and look at the water, giving an uncanny impression that he was somehow in touch with his adversary.

U-264's bow broke the surface with no warning 1700 yards away on *Starling's* port quarter, water cascading off the grey plating as she shook herself free.

The text-book move (Walker's written orders to his Officers of the Watch) was to present the smallest target to the U-boat, simultaneously reducing to 7 knots, to reduce the danger of attracting a Gnat by the noise of the propellers. This meant turning away from the U-boat and presenting *Starling's* stern to the enemy. All very sensible and logical, but Walker gave no evidence to anyone around him on the bridge, or in his subsequent report, that he had even considered this alternative. As the bow broke the surface he was out of his chair shouting down the voice-pipe: '*Full ahead together! Hard a'port! Open fire!*'

Starling rolled to starboard and heeled further as she dug her bows in and started to turn sluggishly as she gained speed. Tracer centred on the target as the first broadside roared out from the four-inch guns. More tracer crossed her bows as the other ships opened up. A dull red glow at the base of the conning tower showed the first hit. Showers of sparks as the U-boat's gun mounting went over the side.

Walker stood on top of the bridge throughout the action waving his cap and cheering on the crew of B gun below him to further efforts. He reported: 'The U-boat surfaced at 1659 and gave the guns' crews some compensation for many tiresome hours of waiting for U-boats that never surfaced. Firing was a bit wild at first with the ship under full wheel but soon settled down to score five four-inch hits and many oerlikons.'

Puppet figures started dropping over the side from the decks and the conning tower into the water. Through the shell splashes and smoke, little yellow dinghies could be seen floating towards us, crammed with bodies paddling frantically to get clear.

U-264 hung for a while stationary, almost invisible in the shell splashes and the hail of fire now pouring into her from all angles. Then the stern dropped, the bow rose into the air and the hull slid stern-first under the waves.

Looks, her commander, had been chased through the convoy by *Forester* the night before, and then pounced on by the Second Support Group the following morning. The day's attacks had put his steering out of action and caused great damage down below.

When he surfaced and found himself surrounded, he ordered 'Abandon Ship', saw all his men out of the boat and then set the scuttling charges to make sure that there was no danger of his top-secret Schnorkel falling into enemy hands. Only then did he follow his crew over the side.

It says something for the discipline and efficiency of the Group's gunners that, with every gun blazing and the U-boat's hull plastered with gunfire, the Germans in the water were not shot to bits. *Starling*, *Woodpecker* and *Wild Goose* hauled the whole crew of *U-264* out of the water, seven officers, nine petty officers and thirty-five men, and stuffed them down below under guard. Once again Archie Pitt lost his cabin to officer prisoners.

U-264 was the first of the only two boats then at sea with a Schnorkel; it was sunk before making any report on the operation of this latest important equipment under action conditions.[13]

The score was now six-nil with no casualties in the convoys. So far at least twelve Gnats had been fired at the ships of the Second Support Group. *Starling* and *Kite* had survived near misses by the skin of their teeth; all ships had replenished their stocks of fuel and depth charges on one or more occasions. The Commander-in-Chief had run out of his stock of standard complimentary signals.

On this grey February evening, the Atlantic Ocean was cold and menacing. It could not go on like this.

By the start of the first watch at 2000, the prisoners had been sorted out and the ships reformed to carry on their patrol. By now all on board had had a basinful; those not on watch made for their bunks and normal cruising watch routine was resumed. Some optimists even thought that we might soon be setting off for a couple of days ashore in Liverpool.

Two hours later Archie Pitt, with sadistic glee, was announcing that he had an excellent HF/DF fix on a U-boat transmitting on the surface fifteen miles away, and the ships once again were bashing through a moderate sea at seventeen knots in pursuit.

'Roll on my bloody twelve'.[14]

The ships' companies were back at action stations by 2200. At 2216 there was a distant explosion and some flares flickered in the water on the port beam where *Woodpecker* should have been. The radar operator reported an echo close by her position. Tom Teece's voice with a note of urgency in it came up the voice-pipe: *'Ware Gnats!'* And a minute later: 'From *Woodpecker*. I have been torpedoed.'

We closed the scene at seven knots: *Woodpecker* reported that she had obtained an Asdic echo ten seconds before being hit, range 600 yards on her starboard quarter between her and *Starling*, but had not had time to alter course or put in an attack. The radar echo on *Starling's* screen had disappeared, hidden behind the wreck. Walker immediately sent the other ships on a protective patrol, but there was not a man in the Group who didn't know that there was a U-boat inside this wall.

A strong wind was blowing as we came up: our forecastle, the boat deck and quarterdeck were crowded with men going about the task of getting out and laying down the tow wires in the darkness. Walker's plan was to pass the line across from our starboard side as he ranged slowly down *Woodpecker's* port side. *Woodpecker* fortunately had turned out her port seaboat, which hung from the davits between the two ships. In the sea and swell both ships were rolling heavily. Walker misjudged the distance and the two ships crashed together beam to beam; we scraped noisily along her side, buckling our depth charge traps on the quarterdeck (not that this mattered much; we had no depth charges left). Pieces of timber and gear from the shattered seaboat, which had taken much of the force of the impact, cascaded down on to the boat deck by Chippy's workshop.

As we passed, we saw the damage that *Woodpecker* had sustained; the after fifty feet of the quarterdeck had been blown in the air and folded back on top of X gun, so that the underside of the deck was now facing up to the sky; forty feet of the stern had vanished and the gallant *Woodpecker* that had so lately rejoined us from her refit now looked like a sad tailless duck.

Working with shielded torches the heavy tow ropes were laid out on the quarter-deck and eased across. As I belted along the upper deck, I ran into Chippy, outside his workshop, struggling along with a big lump of timber.

'What's that you've got there, Chippy?'

'Nothing important, sir, really.'

'Come on Chippy. What is it?'

'Just a spare rudder, sir. I found it on the deck. Might come in handy sometime.'

As the ships rolled together, *Starling's* shipwright, an old hand, had taken the opportunity of wrenching the rudder and tiller from the smashed boat, to add to his secret horde of spares.

The first attempts to get the tow under way failed. The wreckage below the water, and the windage of the blown-up stern, caused *Woodpecker* to fly up into the wind as soon as she started to move.

This pulled *Starling's* stern to starboard until the two ships lay at right angles to each other and the hawser parted.

It was exhausting work; the cables and towing lines had to be dealt with manually by gangs of men, because the sloops had only one capstan and that was in the bows of the ship. After several attempts, the job was abandoned until the morning.

There was no sign of the U-boat; this one and the other one HF/DF'ed earlier in the day got away. All through the night we expected that they would take advantage of the darkness and have a shot at the lights of the two ships stopped and helpless, lying alongside each other for several hours, busy on other matters.

Next morning a sea was still running and a wind blowing. The task of transferring some of *Woodpecker's* men was under way, as the seaboats were pulled from ship to ship. Another light line was rowed across preparatory to passing yet another tow. As the sea-boat crept nearer to *Woodpecker*, dragging the line behind, *Woodpecker's* bow rose and fell like a giant meat cleaver; at one moment we could see right under the forward thirty feet of the hull as it rose on a sea; the next, the ships rolled together, the strain came off the rope and the seaboat hurtled down the face of the wave as the bow came crashing down.

With many curses and prayers, the tow was passed and the procession got under way, pointing in the general direction of home and making good about one and a half knots.

On 20 February at 1030, *Woodpecker* had transferred the eleven German U-boat prisoners to *Magpie*. By a stroke of good fortune they had not suffered the same fate as their countrymen when *Deptford* rammed *Stork* in December, 1941.

The following day in a rising sea a procession of seaboats transferred four officers, seventy nine ratings and six prisoners to *Magpie* and *Wren*. Just after 1300 *Storm King*, an ocean-going tug, arrived, escorted by the trawler *Lady Madeleine;* she passed her great towing cable and set off in style at four and a half knots in the right direction, with Commander Pryse and his skeleton crew still on board.

The ships of the Group were now on their last legs. Fuel was once again running low. We had not tasted bread for days; even ship's biscuits were in short supply. The thousand men still at sea in the sloops, officers and ratings alike, were haggard and jumpy from lack of sleep and too much exposure to the weather on deck at action stations and the threat of Gnats.

It was an enormous relief to turn over the care and protection of the damaged *Woodpecker* to her tug and escort, properly equipped for the task of towing, and to set course finally for Liverpool. As we left her a signal was received on board the ships of the Group:

> 'The War Cabinet wish to convey to you and Escort Group under your command their congratulations on the excellent work performed by your Group in recent destruction of U-boats.'

We entered the Irish Sea: the long swells of the Atlantic gave way to the shorter steep waves of coastal waters. A spirited private exchange of signals between Officers of the Watch took the place of the all-out effort against the U-boats. With the scent of land in their nostrils, the ships of the Group went into close line ahead at maximum economical speed, and signal lamps blinked messages from ship to ship:

From OOW *Starling* to OOW *Wild Goose* – 'You are astern of station'.

From OOW *Wild Goose* to OOW *Starling* – 'Why don't you keep a steady speed?'

From Navigator *Wild Goose* to Navigator *Starling* – 'We seem a bit close to a minefield.'

Pilot shot into the chart house, shot out again, took a couple of swift bearings and shot back inside. A few moments elapsed; then he came back at a dignified speed, went over to the Yeoman and said:

'Tell him not to worry.'

Captain Walker paced the starboard side of the bridge: these were internal matters between the officers in the Group and officially he knew nothing about them.

While the ships were still some way out of Liverpool, Doc Fraser transferred to *Wren* to help with an urgent operation for appendicitis. It was successful. Both doctors would try anything once.

Early on the morning of 25 February, the ships fetched the Bar Light Vessel at the mouth of the Mersey. In the previous twenty-four hours the sailors had found their second wind and had turned to with a will to remove some of the signs of weather from the paint and brasswork at upper deck level. John Filleul did his best, but not much improvement could be made to the ship's sides which were battered by the sea and carried scars along the starboard quarter, where bent guardrails and distorted depth-charge racks gave proof of close contact with *Woodpecker*. John had short words for a group of able seamen who were scrubbing away while singing the old song:

> 'Side, side, *Starling's* ship's side,
> Jimmy looks on it with pride.
> He'd have a blue fit

If he saw any dirt
On the side of the *Starling's* ship side'.

Pilot had been given a signal the evening before requiring the Group to enter the lock at 0900 the next morning, when the ships would be cheered into harbour and welcomed by the First Lord of the Admiralty and the Commander-in-Chief. There was a panic. The bugler was tipped out of his hammock and locked in a remote place to practise his calls and to polish up his instrument. John Filleul put a party to work on the paintwork on the port side of the upper deck, which would be the only section that would be visible to our distinguished visitors as they came over the gangway.

As the ships steamed past the yacht *Philante*, the buzz spread round the ship that the duty signalman had spotted the First Lord peering out of a scuttle at the ships as they trod majestically along, one and a half cables apart, dressed in a rigid line, new white ensigns flying. The buzz gathered momentum; by the time it had reached the boiler room, the news was that the First Lord had not shaved, was dressed in pyjamas and a dressing gown and had put on his cap for appearance's sake to look through the scuttle.

Pilot's log records proudly that we arrived thirteen seconds late, to be greeted by a tremendous volume of cheering as *Starling* led the line into Gladstone Dock, the ships' loudspeakers blasting out the Group's signature tune, 'A Hunting We Will Go', with all hands lined up on the upper deck. Walker stood on the flat deck at the front of the bridge as the ships came through the lock gates.

This was a proud moment for all on board, but especially for Pilot. He had brought us back safely after over 7,000 miles, steaming without sight of land. Coming through the lock gates, he remembered that the last time he had seen a cheering party was when he was ordinary Seaman Ayers, one of the party manning the side when Force 'H' returned from Gibraltar after dealing with *Bismarck*.

On the dock side two bands played and every inch of space was crowded by people of all sorts gathered to welcome us back. A long string of signal flags spelt out a message of congratulation: 'Johnnie Walker still going strong'.

The aircraft carrier *Victorious* manned her flight deck and took up the cheering, but the largest numbers, the most important, the noisiest contribution came from the WRNS who seemed to be there in their thousands, including Wren Gillian Walker (now known throughout the Liverpool docks as the Demon Driver from the dashing way that she drove her Bedford van) in the forefront and Eileen Walker waiting to be first on board, with Nicolas on leave from *Woodcock*.

The German prisoners were marched ashore and handed over to the Army.

The ships' companies lined up for inspection; a small but very distinguished party in the ranks, dressed in borrowed uniforms and overalls, represented the survivors from *Woodpecker*.

The First Lord made his ninety-second speech, in which he referred to the achievement of Walker and his men as: 'One of the greatest cruises — the greatest cruise perhaps — ever undertaken in this war by an Escort Group.'

He said of Walker that he had 'established for himself, by reason of the help that you (the assembled ships' companies) have given, the position of our leading submarine ace.'

The newspapers took up this phrase: the front pages were covered with pictures of the ships and of Captain Walker, who said in a public speech in Bootle: 'Please don't call me the Ace U-boat killer. That formidable character is a Thousand British Tars.'

At noon these thousand British tars piped down and made for their hammocks to catch up with their sleep before sampling the blessings of the land. In the ships alongside the jetty there were no watches on deck, except for the Officers of the Day, the Quartermasters and the Bosun's Mates on the gangway. No one had yet gone ashore on leave and as a result the hands were packed like sardines down below: there were not enough hammock slinging spaces and there were men sleeping on the decks of the messes, on the tables and on the locker tops; even the passageways were cluttered with bodies enjoying the luxury of their first safe and undisturbed sleep for a month.

There was no movement, no noise of machinery, none of the creaks and groans of the ship working in a seaway, just the hum of the fans and the moan of the foghorn at the end of Gladstone Dock. A hush spread over the ship as she lay safe in her home port.

One shadow lay over the celebrations. We had left *Woodpecker* under tow on course for Falmouth five days before. By 25 February the weather had started to deteriorate further. Commander Pryse reduced his complement by another officer and fifty-one ratings who were rowed across to *Rother*. Before this they had rigged hawsers from X gun to the bridge and over the bridge to the forecastle to relieve the strain on the after end of the ship. The Admiralty weather forecast of 26 February gave winds force eight to nine. In the afternoon, Commander Pryse, having been ordered by the Commander-in-Chief to take no risks with the crew, decided to clear lower deck and abandon ship.

He veered to four shackles (fifty fathoms) of cable on the tow line, pumped the ship dry, made certain that all watertight doors and deadlights were properly secured and at 1830 abandoned ship, transferring the remaining seven officers and ratings to *Azalea* and *Chilliwack*, with the wind blowing force six to seven and a nasty sea with heavy rain.

He had judged it exactly: on the morning of 27 February *Storm King* cast off the tow; six minutes later *Woodpecker* capsized. She was sunk by gunfire 60 miles to the south-west of the Bishop Rock Light and 120 miles from the safety of Falmouth docks.

Woodpecker had played a major part in this great patrol and in the successes of the Group. All ships made vital contributions to the overall result, but *Woodpecker* in her short life of eleven months, was directly involved in the sinking of *U-449, 504, 762, 424* and *264*. By superb seamanship and judgement, aided by good luck, she suffered no casualties.

'No Commanding Officer could wish for a more gallant and efficient company of officers and men, and on each occasion of reducing complement many of the volunteers to stay behind had to go. Signed H. L. Pryse, Commander R.N.R.'

A great deal had to be packed into the few days before the Group went back to sea. Walker was put through the hoop on the many points made in his Report of Proceedings. He recommended that Senior Officers of escort carriers and escort groups should be given a chance to get together before operations. (14 months after the sinking of *Audacity*!) In the last patrol both had suffered from not knowing what was in the mind of the other, not helped by the fact that *Nairana's* T.B.S. had not been working.

He repeated his conviction that defence of hunting (support) groups must lie in tactics and not Foxers, which greatly reduced the chance of killing U-boats, especially in vile Asdic conditions when echoes were poor and faint. He considered that occasional casualties must be accepted, but emphasized that Gnats could not home on sloops at low speed. The Commander-in-Chief agreed − in the case of experienced groups.[15]

The specialists in the Anti-U-boat Division got hold of the report and unanimously condemned Walker's habit of putting in a first attack to drive the U-boat deep. The comments are interesting in that they give a strong indication that, in the Admiralty, many were still not convinced that the creeping attack was the best method of making certain of the destruction of the U-boat.

The original copy of this report in the Public Records Office is heavily annotated but bears a clear authenticating stamp on the front cover from a standard Admiralty coffee cup. It contains the classic comment: 'The only reason to support this (procedure) is that it has been successful. It seems a waste of depth charges and Hedgehogs'. The comments also note that 'S.O. EG2 [Walker] would be hard to persuade' and that influence could best be brought to bear on other officers through the Captain in command of the training yacht *Philante*.[16]

Walker concluded that 'The chief credit for this sock in the jaw for Dönitz should undoubtedly go to HMS *Wild Goose*, Lieutenant-Commander D.E.G.

Wemyss DSC RN. Of 6 killed, 4 were detected by *Wild Goose* and her prompt action saved *Nairana.*'

The ships were in harbour in time for the Walkers' wedding anniversary, 27 February, and the Walkers found time to dine on board in the wardroom and host a dinner party for some of the officers and their wives back at the White House, where Johnnie Walker, in his private capacity for once, did an excellent job as butler and wine steward.

CHAPTER EIGHT

TRIUMPH OF SEA POWER

A week later, refuelled, reammunitioned and with full stores, the ships were back at sea. *Whimbrel* had joined the Group to fill the gap in the ranks left by *Woodpecker*, and we were to work with the escort carrier *Vindex*.

Before sailing, Walker learnt that he had been awarded his third DSO. This was itself remarkable, but it was not considered enough. The Honours and Awards Committee had a problem. On principle the Royal Navy did not reward exceptional service in action by promotion in rank. The matter of Walker's awards had been given a lot of thought. The decision, in which the Lords of the Admiralty themselves were personally and individually involved, was to back-date his seniority as a Captain by two years, effective from 30 June, 1940, thus restoring him to the position that he had been denied when he was passed over for promotion to Captain in the interwar years.[1]

The Germans suffered badly from lack of weather information. The Allies had thousands of ships and the American shore stations in the west to pass readings from the areas whence all the big systems come. The Germans had a dearth of such facilities. The impact was important and wide-ranging: it affected such things as the timing of Allied and German air raids, the movement of major naval units, and the programming of the Russian convoys; it was an absolutely vital factor in deciding the exact date when the Normandy landings would start. For these reasons, there were always several U-boats stationed in remote parts of the Atlantic whose main function was to send out regular weather reports.

These U-boats were at a grave disadvantage: they had to surface to transmit their messages; the format of their reports was difficult to disguise; the Allied HF/DF stations gave broad indications of their positions; they could subsequently be accurately located by ship-borne fixing and finally pin-pointed by the Asdics of support groups in their vicinity.

This sequence was now followed, culminating in aircraft from *Vindex* locating the U-boat on the surface only ten miles away from the Group. Once again it was *Wild Goose* who made the first contact, passing it to Walker in *Starling*, who attacked immediately. As *Starling* (flying the black flag), swept close by *Wild Goose*, there was a very loud hail from one of

Wild Goose's depth-charge party: 'Why don't you go and find one of your own!'

In contrast to the protracted chase and destruction of *U-264* only three weeks earlier, this single ten-charge pattern was all that was necessary for the destruction of *U-653*. Walker apologized to *Wild Goose* for his 'unwarrantable intrusion', and gave the Anti-U-boat Department in the Admiralty fresh proof that he didn't always waste depth charges and that his armoury was not restricted to just one sort of creeping attack.

The Group returned to Liverpool. *Starling* had completed her first year in commission. Pilot's log records that:

> *Starling* had steamed 47,369 miles. The screws had turned 40,000,000 times. The ship's company had been paid £16,000. Twenty-five per cent of this was spent in the canteen. 2,940,000 cigarettes had been smoked (averaging about 35 per man per day). £1,016.13s.3d. changed hands at Tombola. The Officers and men had received 13 decorations: 12 Mentions in Despatches, 11 C-in-C's Commendations. 747 gallons of rum had been drunk. There was a lot of wear and tear on the mainbrace! It was spliced 9 times! *Starling* had used 3919 tons of oil fuel. The Officers of the Watch had drunk 4,320 cups of cocoa.

Multiply this by five (and sometimes six) and the picture emerges of the enormous logistical problem of keeping just the Second Support Group at sea. But we never seemed to be short of anything for long.

Arthur Ayers' comment on a very uncomfortable time at sea, tired, often in action and frequently in danger, sums up the attitude of Walker's Thousand British Tars. He says: 'And now we are off to Scapa, and I don't know what is going to happen. I expect it will be fun anyhow.'

Captain Walker's ships in the 36th Escort Group and the Second Support Group, were rarely involved in routine tasks: most of their operations were reactions to Dönitz's redeployment of his fleet. (The Bay of Biscay offensive was an exception.) From 1943 onwards, the movement of the ships was much better targeted, because, unknown to us, Bletchley Park was reading the Germans' intentions regularly and with little delay. The information may well have turned the balance of the Battle of the Atlantic, but by the time it was filtered through to the ships at sea it could never be absolutely reliable and was usually not sufficiently up to date to be of positive, immediate, tactical use. It put the Group in the right area but it was aircraft sightings, radar at night and HF/DF bearings that pinpointed the targets within striking range of the ships. To know the location and strength of the enemy was very useful but it did not give victory in the fight.

While the production of a new type of U-boat was put in hand, Dönitz's large fleet had to be kept employed in the area in which they could do most harm. They could not be left in their bases because there were not enough safe bunkers and their morale would deteriorate further if they did not put to sea. He shifted his attention to the wastes of the Norwegian Sea.

Hitler still believed that the invasion might well start on the coast of Norway and insisted that about fifty U-boats should be stationed to cover this area. Here they could perform the three functions of providing defence against such an invasion, screening the heavy ships if they ever came out and attacking the Allied convoys to Murmansk, carrying the vital arms that Stalin had been demanding and needed so desperately on the Russian front.

In the autumn of 1942 priority was given to the African landings and a stop was made to the Russian, Gibraltar and Sierra Leone convoys. The Russian convoys were resumed in November, 1943, at irregular intervals, and since then 220 ships had made the passage with the loss of only three merchant ships.[2]

The Atlantic convoys never had an easy time, but the Arctic convoys faced even greater risks and worse conditions. Most of the convoy route, particularly the northern end, was close enough to the German air bases in Norway to be under aircraft surveillance and the threat of attack from the air. As the convoys got closer to their destination, so they got further away from Allied land-based fighter protection and closer to the enemy-held Norwegian coast. At the same time the opportunities for evasive routeing away from the U-boats or surface forces, were limited by the narrowness of the navigable waters from the southern edge of the ice to the coast of Norway, where the remnants of the German High Seas Fleet was holed up in the fjords. The weather in the North Atlantic was appalling, but it was much more difficult to bear on the Arctic run where the temperatures fell to fifteen degrees below freezing, and in mid-winter the sun never climbed above the horizon.

For these reasons, exceptionally powerful forces were mustered for the passage of each of these convoys. Released by the withdrawal of the U-boats from the attack on the Atlantic convoys, the Second Support Group, *Starling*, *Wild Goose*, *Wren*, *Magpie* and *Whimbrel*, was sent up to Scapa Flow, to reinforce the large escort already waiting.

The news of the Group's record trip in the Atlantic had just been released and a great deal of inaccurate nonsense written about it by the more sensational daily papers. The First Lord of the Admiralty was reported in some papers to have compared that patrol with the Battle of Trafalgar, scarcely an apt comparison and not well liked by those who were involved. The newsreels had just released the films of the Group's arrival in Liverpool, with the cheering crowds and the bands playing. The B.B.C. had broadcast a long description of the patrol, which included contributions made under duress by several members of the ship's company.

When all this publicity hit Scapa Flow, the ships of the Home Fleet had been lying in the bleak cold anchorage since their magnificent victory at Christmas,[3] with very little home leave, their entertainment limited to the fleet canteens. The only variation in their routine since then had been the provision of support for a Russian convoy, which they might never see, or sorties into the North Sea, a horrible place, to tempt out an enemy, the *Tirpitz*, that would or could not fight.

The ships of the Second Support Group did not make themselves popular by coming into this remote Fleet anchorage in their usual style with loudspeakers blaring out cheerful music, which the destroyer flotillas considered to be undignified. We dug out our bugler to sound the "Still" when going alongside the depot ship, *Tyne*, wearing Vice-Admiral (D)'s flag. (Neither the destroyers' nor the sloops' complements included a bugler, but *Starling* had found one on board who could put up a very fine performance.) A frigate was sent up on a special mission to Scapa Flow loaded with Arctic clothing for the Second Support Group. Captain Walker's ships by this time had sunk eighteen U-boats; his recent award of two years' additional seniority made him senior to most of the Big Ships in the anchorage, which had to turn out the guard to salute as the little *Starling* went by.

The depot ship was extremely efficient but the Group did not feel at home as they did in the happy family atmosphere of Liverpool. The ships would be going into yet another different type of battle, and Walker, for the first time, would not be Senior Officer, but under the command of a Rear-Admiral (Dalrymple-Hamilton) in the cruiser *Diadem*. The maintenance crews and armourers in the destroyer depot ship threw themselves into preparing the sloops for the extreme cold conditions, but there was a distinctly edgy feeling about, and it was a relief when the whole force put to sea on 25 March to rendezvous with Convoy JW 58.

It was a big convoy with thirty-two ships in the escort force, including our old friends the aircraft carriers *Activity* and *Tracker* right in the centre, and the old cruiser U.S.S. *Milwaukee*, on her way out to be handed over by the Americans as a gift to the Russians. Among the escorts were two flotillas of Fleet destroyers, *Saumarez* leading D.23 and *Onslow* leading D.17. They were immensely impressive, steaming effortlessly with great grace and style to take up station at a speed that the sloops could never approach even with both engines at full ahead. They had so many signal flags flying that it looked as if they were dressed overall for a Fleet Review. In *Starling* we began to feel rather proud to belong to such a smart Fleet, a feeling that was almost immediately dispelled by a signal from our new boss's large staff with all sorts of information about turning circles and other administrative detail, and shortly afterwards another signal refusing permission to carry out a short gunnery exercise, firing live rounds, which was part of our normal routine on putting to sea and particularly desirable in view of the cold weather modifications that had been carried out on our guns. Walker tried for twenty minutes to get a favourable reply, slowly getting redder and redder in the face. Eventually he turned to me and said, 'I'm sorry. You can stand down the guns' crews. I can get nothing out of that ship.'

The first night was worse, spent in a tight anti-submarine screen around the larger ships. It had long been one of Walker's principles, based on many years' experience as a Fleet Anti-Submarine Officer, that many escorts packed into a close screen reduced their own and each other's efficiency. The Officers of the Watch became too intent on station keeping and avoiding collision. Their objectives became less clear, whereas he never forgot his own — to seek out and destroy U-boats.

The escorting force met the convoy at 1100 on 29 March. There were forty-nine merchant ships and four naval vessels in the convoy, making good 9.12 knots in twelve columns, five cables apart with three cables between each ship and her next ahead.

With patient signals Walker extricated himself from this great body of ships. Before the short night came down, (there were only five hours of darkness), the two Western Approach Support Groups came under Walker's command. He immediately deployed *Keppel* and her group in the outfield on the port side, just within visibility of the convoy's mastheads, with a free hand to work his own group.[4]

Starling's station was astern of the convoy at visibility range, or at extreme radar range in the snow squalls. The Officer of the Watch kept within a sector of a circle many miles deep and covering forty-five degrees of arc. As long as he kept within this sector, he had complete freedom of action; he made up his own zigzag and could turn through 360 degrees if he so wished; his course was thus totally unpredictable, and the ship was never on a steady course. There was no danger of collision and anything in his patch could be attacked and sunk without fear of confusion.

Joe Foster had the first watch. To fill in the time he had evolved a game which was to remain in his allotted sector and to weave and zigzag as ordered, but to adjust his courses so that he never suffered the inconvenience of going through one of the unpleasant snow squalls. It was becoming more difficult now because the short night was upon him and the edges of the squalls were not so well defined. He decided to move in closer to the convoy so that he could be sure of keeping radar contact in the darkness.

At 2208 the Asdic operator reported an echo at 1900 yards. He immediately dropped speed to seven knots, pressed the Alarm rattlers and turned towards. Four minutes later, with the ship at action stations, Kelly and his team on the Asdics and Walker on the bridge, it was classified as 'submarine' and *Magpie* was called in to join the hunt.

Starling attacked first with a ten-charge pattern set to explode at 150 and 300 feet, followed fourteen minutes later by another similar attack, both of which were extremely accurate attacks with the primary objective of sinking the U-boat and the secondary objective of keeping it down and giving it some damage repairs to think about, while *Magpie* took station for the execution of a creeping attack.

Kelly reported noises of tanks blowing. The loaded guns came round onto the bearing. There were further noises of knocking and breaking up and ten minutes later at 2301 a very heavy explosion which shook *Starling* from truck to keel, followed by a patch of disturbed water. This was probably a torpedo exploding as the U-boat broke up or a Gnat self-destructing at the end of its run. Shortly afterwards, in the light of the ten-inch signal lamps, the familiar mass of wreckage started to float up to the surface in a spreading patch of oil.

By the time *Magpie* arrived it was all over.

This was the sudden end of another U-boat, probably minding its own business on passage and unaware either of this convoy or its heavy escort. It was unfortunate for *U-961* that Walker, as he reported; 'had the good fortune to stub my toe on her'.

Seventy-five minutes after the first Asdic contact, *Starling* and *Magpie* were on their way back to rejoin the convoy which meanwhile had moved on another dozen miles towards its destination.

The whole armada of ships had been maintaining strict radio silence until then, but it was a great satisfaction to be the first ship to break this silence with a signal reporting sighting and sinking an enemy unit.

This was another copy book exercise, which made it look only too easy to locate and sink U-boats. 100% opportunities taken − 100% success. One brief signal: 'U-boat sunk in position 64° 31′ North, 03° 19′ West.'

The start of the next day, 30 March, was crystal clear, so clear that there was no limit to the visibility. Many miles away the topmasts of the merchant ships projected above the horizon like little stakes and needles. When we came closer, the hulls rose out of the sea, grew bigger and took shape, until the white foam could be seen where the bow waves curled away from the stem posts. Like little terriers, the close escorts weaved and scurried round their charges. Sometimes in the freak conditions the merchant ships appeared to be flying above the surface of the water in a glassy mirage haze; sometimes they glided along upside down on the tips of their masts looking like crude wooden images of surrealistic water hounds. The convoy did not appear to advance over the flat sea surface, but the sea and clouds seemed to pass it by. It was very beautiful, but extremely cold and the great, heavy, full-length sheepskin watch coat hung like a fetter from a carbuncle which had developed on the back of my neck. The scar is still there − my only war wound.

White blankets of snow appeared with greater and greater frequency hanging below big black clouds which were gliding slowly and inexorably towards the convoy. The circle of sea containing the body of ships waited for the first gun.

This atmosphere did not suit the good ship *Wild Goose*. She had vainly sought permission to exercise her guns' crews by firing a few rounds. This had been refused on the grounds that one gun fired anywhere within sight or sound of the tense convoy would be welcomed by all the dozens of cold and bored gunners as an excuse to loose off a magazine or two to break the monotony.

But no sooner had permission been refused than her guns began to bark, and little puffs from exploding shells showed low along the horizon. Shortly afterwards the misty gremlin shape of an aircraft could be made out, dancing along just above the surface of the sea many miles away. This was the first visible sign that the convoy had been located by the Germans and was being shadowed. The wheels would now begin to turn in Norway to prevent the continuation of its peaceful passage. The aircraft buzzed around, pursued by *Wild Goose*'s anti-aircraft fire and eventually dissolved into the watery haze, pursued by fighters launched from one of the carriers. *Wild Goose* signalled back gleefully to Captain (D) in *Starling*: 'Practice shoot completed.'

At intervals, more planes appeared and aircraft from the carriers circled overhead. Occasionally one or a pair of them would rocket off over the horizon in pursuit of a German. The weather started to deteriorate until the white blanket of snowstorms formed a solid line across the sea and sky ahead. Big painful hailstones whipped the faces of the signalmen and the lookouts until it was impossible on the open bridge to look into the teeth of the wind. The best way to protect the eyes was to look through the wrong end of a megaphone.

The Fleet Air Arm pilots from *Activity* and *Tracker* swung on their patrols, taking off and landing while the decks of their mother ships canted, twisted and dipped with growing ferocity. In *Starling* their calm voices could be heard over our wireless receivers and were broadcast back over the loudspeakers to the ship's company at their action stations. Quiet voices discussed with exaggerated calm the position of the enemy planes: 'Bogey in the cloud behind you.'

Sometimes the long blind chases through the snow frayed the pilots' calm and they forgot to switch off their microphones while using violent language about the Fighter Direction Officer as he steered them on to the enemy from the warmth of the carrier. As the loudspeakers described the second-by-second progress of these grim struggles, we in the ships down below remembered that to ditch in the icy water meant certain, swift death.

Three times while we listened, the personal note broke through with a triumphant shout of 'Tally Ho!' as a pilot spotted and made for his opponent. On one occasion we heard the Fighter Direction Officer guide a plane onto a bogey, heard the pilot spot him, and then watched the German crashing into the sea a mile from us, followed by the voice, once again calm and impersonal: 'I have bogey's aerial wrapped round my starboard wing.'

And so back to base — a dipping swaying flight deck — to be lifted half-frozen from the cockpit.

Harassed and intimidated by the watchful aircraft and the size of the surface patrols, the U-boats stayed submerged until the long day merged into a short bright night, with the rising full moon on one side vying with the watery setting sun on the other. With darkness, the wireless traffic between the U-boats started up as they surfaced to report the convoy's course and speed, exchange notes and plan their attacks. The main activity was on the starboard bow of the convoy in the sector patrolled by *Wren* and *Whimbrel* acting as a pair. In the next sector, forward of the starboard beam, *Wild Goose* and *Magpie* kept guard while *Starling* brought up the rear on the starboard quarter.

There were so many HF/DF bearings and they were so unreliable that Walker decided not to chase any of them. With the aircraft cover the U-boats would have little chance to surface and take up good attacking positions. In any case they lay ahead and to starboard of our course line, indicating that the convoy would pass by well to port of their position and that they would fall behind on the starboard beam and astern before they had time to attack.

Sure enough at 0228 *Starling* picked up a radar contact two thousand yards away on the starboard beam and shortly afterwards sighted a U-boat at speed on the surface. The Officer of the Watch immediately reduced speed to seven knots and turned hard a'starboard to point bows on to the U-boat which fired a torpedo as it dived. The track could be clearly seen in the moonlight as our bows swung round towards the U-boat's diving position. It passed across our bows much too close for comfort. Saved by the bell again.

Fifteen minutes later there was another underwater explosion, probably a Gnat blowing up at the end of its run; two minutes later the wake of another passed down the port side as *Starling* picked up an Asdic contact and attacked with a ten-charge pattern set to explode at 150 and 300 feet, calling in the Group for a search for the other U-boats that appeared to abound in her immediate vicinity.

The Asdic conditions were very bad. No further contact was made by any of the ships, although the U-boats were clearly quite close. This was an area where layering[5] could be expected, making it impossible even for the most skilled and experienced Asdic operators to pick up an echo. In these conditions the escorts were operating blind, but the U-boats could hear them on their hydrophones and sometimes risked a quick look through their periscopes. Armed as they were with Gnats, the odds in these conditions favoured the U-boats.

The Group searched for two hours without finding any trace of the U-boat or U-boats that had fired torpedoes at *Starling*. While this attack and the subsequent two-hour search had been going on, the convoy had been drawing ahead at nine knots. A more menacing HF/DF bearing was picked up shortly after 0500 and the Group reformed to follow this up with support from Swordfish aircraft from *Activity*. Once again there was no trace of the U-boat that had been making the signal, but the air was still full of W/T transmissions indicating that the convoy was still being shadowed by several U-boats, and at 0930 on the 3rd we were off again to join *Magpie* and *Whimbrel* who were chasing a sighting of a U-boat on the surface only eighteen miles away. This was confirmed by both ships' Asdic contacts (at last), as *Starling* came to join them.

Asdic conditions were described by Walker throughout this patrol as 'exceedingly bad'. Nevertheless the three ships were able to maintain contact for 2½ hours and put in three creeping attacks. The level of proficiency in the ships of the Group now permitted each of the three ships to direct these attacks in succession, but none of them produced results. While these attacks were going on, Walker had ordered *Wild Goose* and *Magpie* to follow up another aircraft sighting six miles astern.

At 1430 the sloops were ordered to rejoin the convoy, leaving reluctantly with the knowledge that at least one U-boat had survived, although it was under attack.

It was apparent from the bearings of the U-boats' radio chatter that a number of them had now fallen behind the convoy. They would have difficulty in rejoining the battle owing to the aircraft patrols, which kept them submerged, and the deep cover from the Support Groups operating some distance from the centre. Before taking up the long chase to rejoin the convoy the sloops swept astern, hoping to pick up any of these U-boats which might be attempting to catch up on the surface during the night. At 0700 on 3 April this sweep was abandoned and the ships rejoined, arriving in their stations in the deep field on the starboard side at 2300.

During the previous night, *Keppel*, from her position in the deep field on the port side of the convoy picked up and sank *U-360* single-handed, which was another feather in their cap for the Western Approaches ships.

The night passed with little activity. It had not proved easy to reconcile our navigation with the Senior Officer's, and it became a bit trying when his appreciation of the situation put an imaginary U-boat in *Magpie*'s sector and another in the exact spot in the Norwegian Sea then occupied by *Starling*. But he got his own back when he pointed out that Pilot had given him one of his reciprocal bearing problems to solve when reporting the sinking of *U-961*.[6]

Some half-hearted depth-charging was heard closer to the convoy and sightings outside the Group's sector, but dawn on 3 April found *Starling* and *Magpie* going hell for leather after a U-boat on the surface, hull down on the horizon but just out of gun range. At 0520 we saw in the distance a large explosion as a violent concerted attack by aircraft from *Tracker* and *Activity* put paid to this one, *U-288*. When we passed through the position, all that remained was a spreading pool of oil, a few bits of clothing, some books and a fine U-boat captain's cap complete with an oily white cap cover. Only U-boat commanders wore white cap covers. We picked up some of the evidence for the benefit of the aircraft pilots who had made the attack and set course to rejoin the convoy.

No sooner were we on our way when a torpedo exploded midway between the two ships; both turned back and made a search but no trace could be found of the unfriendly type that had fired at us. He had at least given us another dramatic reminder that there were still U-boats lurking around and that our Asdics were not picking them up.

As we came up with the convoy from astern a thick mist reduced the visibility to a couple of hundred yards. Between the two sloops and the rearmost ships, there were two radar echoes, close together following behind the convoy where no merchant ship or escort should have been. At action stations and the guns trained on the radar bearing, we charged along at full speed. The range came down; one mile to go; the semi-armour-piercing shells were rammed home; scores of eyes and a dozen pairs of binoculars tried to pierce the mist; half a mile to go and still nothing; four hundred yards; the radar became useless.

Quite suddenly, up above the mist a mast appeared right ahead, then the bulk of a merchant ship's topsides. With her wheel hard over and guns trained on a safe bearing, *Starling* turned clear. We had been chasing a straggler, with steering trouble, escorted by a corvette.

'Did you ever hear the story about *Deptford* and *Stork*?' asked John Filleul. 'Once bitten, twice shy.'

The convoy arrived off Murmansk without loss. We did not learn until later that an even more important operation by the Home Fleet had been timed to coincide with the passage of Convoy RW 58. The sailing of this large and important convoy had been used as a diversion while operations were mounted against the one remaining German capital ship, the battleship *Tirpitz*, sister ship of *Bismarck*, said to be the most powerful warship in the world.[7]

Intelligence reports had shown that the repairs to *Tirpitz*, holed up in Altenfjord, were complete and she was about to put to sea. A strong strike by the Fleet Air Arm from the aircraft carriers *Victorious* and *Furious* was planned. Encouraged by the convoy's progress, Admiral Fraser decided on 1 April that it no longer needed his support and brought forward by twenty-four hours his air attack on *Tirpitz*, launching forty-two Barracudas and forty fighters on 3 April at 0415 and 0525.

It was as well that he took this opportunity. When the second wave took off from *Victorious*, *Tirpitz*' escorting destroyers were already moving out to sea, the anti-torpedo gate had been opened to let out the battleship which was about to leave harbour, and, conveniently, it also let in the torpedo bombers. The strike put *Tirpitz* out of action for another three months, starting from the day that she finished her repairs to previous damage.

These operations demonstrated the meaning of the words sea power. JW 58, a convoy of forty-nine merchant ships that the German U-boat Command had decreed 'must not be allowed to get through unscathed', passed safely along one of the most hazardous convoy routes and arrived intact at its destination. The escorting warships and carrier-borne aircraft fought off sixteen U-boats and sank four of them.[8] Aircraft from the carriers kept the attackers submerged, polished off one themselves and shot down six long-range aircraft. The enemy claimed the sinking of nine of the escorting destroyers and four probably sunk, but in fact there were no losses to the merchant ships or to the warships. Simultaneously, a few hundred miles away, aircraft flying from aircraft carriers of the Home Fleet off the enemy-occupied coast of Norway put out of action the last remaining German battleship as it endeavoured to put to sea.[9]

The Group wended its way slowly up the long inlet behind the procession of merchant ships, under the nominal guidance of a taciturn Russian pilot who had boarded *Starling*. He did not speak a word of English and we did not speak a word of Russian. When we were safely at anchor, Captain Walker endeavoured to break the ice by filling the Russian's drink with a variety of our best spirits, which were downed without comment or enthusiasm. John Filleul then took over the job of host with equal lack of success. By the time we had settled down to dinner the problems of language difficulties had almost disappeared. Incoherence reigned and everybody, except our guest, was happy. Arthur Ayers took over the job. Clutching a stanchion to steady himself against the imagined roll of the ship, he hauled himself to his feet, swayed gently and said loudly and clearly, 'Bring our guest a bottle of that half-crown cooking port,' and sat down.

The Russian took the bottle. In twenty minutes he had finished it with no assistance. Then, this time with some assistance, he made his way to his bunk in the Captain's sea cabin and nothing more was heard of him until late the next day.

The high spot of our stay was a concert to which we were invited by the

Russian Naval Theatrical Party, with magnificent singing and dancing. But there was nothing else for the distraction of Jack ashore. The most depressing aspect of our stay was the suspicion shown if any attempt was made to make friends or establish personal contact. The Russian sailors would not even accept the offer of a cigarette.

A few walks over the hills, some snow-balling, and one or two pleasant evenings spent in other ships of the Group, and the whole Fleet sailed to join RA 58, a convoy of thirty-six merchant ships homeward bound, which sailed out from the Kola Inlet on 7 April, two days later. In the morning it was clear and fine with the sun shining brightly on the five sloops as they tramped in line ahead down the fjord towards the sea.

Sixteen U-boats were spread across the convoy's route home to Loch Ewe.[10] There were sightings on 9, 10 and 13 April which were followed up by the Group, but not once was Asdic contact established, even though the whole Group swept right through the position of a marker dropped by *Tracker*'s aircraft half an hour after it had forced a U-boat to dive. Aircraft from the carriers sighted one or two trying to skirt round the edge of the deep screen to get into position for an attack and forced them to dive.

This seven-day period provided complete proof of the spasmodic performance of Asdics: in certain water conditions it proved completely useless. The failure of the U-boats to take advantage of these circumstances was a sure sign of their poor morale and lack of fighting spirit at this stage of the war.

When the convoy was clear of all danger the fleet destroyers peeled off to Scapa Flow and turned over the duty of close escort, for the first and last time, to the sloops. Two days later in shirt-sleeves we enjoyed the beauty of a glorious sunset on a warm early spring evening as we went down through the Minches on our way home to Liverpool.

In Liverpool we were distressed to find that only local leave was authorized. Dennis Logan was a signalman in *Starling*. His mail contained bad news. His house in London had been bombed and his parents taken off to hospital. He went straight to Walker, who waived the rule and gave him a rail pass for compassionate leave, with the admonition that he must, whatever happened, be back in forty-eight hours, because the ship was sailing and he had no authority to give leave. Dennis boarded the next train and made his way to his house. It was a heap of rubble and it took him some time to find out to which hospital his mother and father had been taken. His father had been badly hurt by flying glass, but they were overjoyed to see him, even though they understood that he had to get back to the ship almost immediately.

He boarded a bus to Liverpool Street station. The bus drove into a bomb crater and overturned. When they hauled him out and carried him to the ambulance, he was unconscious and the first thing he remembers is waking up in the hospital having lost his suitcase in which he had put the travel warrant for the return journey. His cap had gone and his uniform was filthy. He discharged himself from the hospital and made straight for the Naval Transport Office at the station. They treated with great suspicion this dirty scarecrow with no papers to show that he had special leave, and an unlikely story similar to that of any man who had over-stayed his leave. Eventually he managed to get them to put him on the next train to Liverpool. He was frantic. The forty-eight hours had passed, and ship would have gone.

When he got to Gladstone Dock he couldn't see the familiar funnel with the broad black band[11] amongst the ships alongside and he knew that the worst had happened. *Starling* had sailed without him and he had broken his trust.

He looked further down the dock. The gates on the seaward side were opening, and there she was, just starting to move slowly through the gates. One of his mates on the bridge spotted and recognized the lonely figure, scarf flying, no cap, dirty uniform, belting down the dockside. A cheer broke out: 'Come on, Bunts. What's the matter? London beer?' He jumped, and hands grabbed him and pulled him on board.

Walker, standing on the top of the Asdic compartment, ahead and on top of the bridge, was busy conning the ship out of the lock into the fast stream of the River Mersey. He didn't seem to have noticed. *Starling's* record was still unbroken. She never went to sea with a man adrift.

Starling, *Wild Goose* and *Wren* went back to sea with our old friend the escort carrier *Tracker*. Before sailing, Walker had at last got agreement that his solution to acoustic torpedoes − reducing speed so that they could not hear the propellers − was more effective than trailing a lot of wire over the stern, and had ordered that the Foxer gear be put ashore. We were once more searching for a U-boat on weather-reporting duties.

We searched diligently until 3 May, when *U-473* unwisely popped up and torpedoed U.S.S. *Donnell*, two hundred miles from our position. The Group was immediately ordered to the area. We set off at eighteen knots on a course of 209 degrees, but altered later to due west as a result of a strong hint, based no doubt on information from Ultra. Now the Atlantic weather started to interfere. The wind blew up from the north-west, forcing the ships to reduce speed to fifteen knots. By midnight it was blowing a full gale. *Magpie* and *Whimbrel* were detached to escort the damaged *Donnell*.

The search continued throughout the next two days. There had been times when the whole fleet of U-boats had tried for weeks to find sprawling convoys of fifty or more ships without success. It had been said that Walker and his team, aided by the wizards in the Submarine Tracking Room, could often read the minds of the U-boat commanders, but on this occasion the task was obviously hopeless. The chances of finding a single U-boat in the Atlantic Ocean after forty-eight hours of unrestricted movement were comparable to identifying an individual eel in the Sargasso Sea. On the surface the U-boat could be anywhere in a radius of 700 miles and even if it remained submerged it could have moved 200 miles from its last known position.

The sloops, now joined by *Bentley* and *Gore*, continued the search, encouraged by an HF/DF bearing at 2319 on the 3rd, putting the U-boat only thirty miles away. Walker guessed that it was going west and played his hunch, taking the Group well beyond the probable position and at first light he deployed the five ships to start a north/south sweep across the course that he thought the U-boat might be taking.

On the morning of the third day, at 0859, the ships were in the middle of a course alteration when one of them (guess which), ran up the black flag. She made an immediate ten-charge attack.

Tracker was detached and sent clear of the area while the three sloops settled down to a very long and exasperating chase. After several attacks the U-boat set off to the north-west, harried by a deluge of depth charges from the deadly trio, *Starling*, *Wild Goose* and *Wren*, positioned close together in line abreast about a mile astern and using every ruse to upset their adversary in poor weather conditions.

In addition to no less than twenty attacks, when 345 depth charges were dropped, the sloops made seven dummy attacks, to which the U-boat responded, using up its air and battery reserves. *Wren* made five attacks (114 charges), *Wild Goose* seven attacks (107 charges) and *Starling* eight attacks (124 charges). Walker was convinced that these were 'dead accurate' in two dimensions and covered the range of depths by twelve depth settings ranging from 50 to 700 feet.[12] These attacks included a three-ship attack of seventy charges, with *Starling* in the middle not using her throwers which might well have pitched their charges right on the quarter decks of her wingers. Walker reported that:

'The teamwork of the three ships was pretty to watch and their interpassing reminded me of a first-class three-quarter line... They carried out a large number of attacks and I would have bet my shirt that these were dead accurate in plan.'

What confidence these commanding officers had in the training and discipline of their teams, and what risks they took! This was no time for a fumbled pass.

Nevertheless, with the approach of darkness, even Walker admitted to being a bit bothered and to blaming himself for an inordinate expenditure of depth charges. He sent off *Bentley* and *Gore* six miles ahead. If the U-boat surfaced and made off on the surface behind a cloud of Gnats, it would get a hot welcome from these two ships.

Sixteen minutes before midnight the U-boat increased to her full submerged speed and turned a complete circle. This presented a pretty problem for the three hunting ships close alongside each other, trying to creep along behind it at dead slow speed. Walker signalled: 'I think the crisis must be near'.

At midnight the Group had been in contact for fifteen hours, their longest chase to date.

The U-boat surfaced at 0014 on 6 May. Walker reported that it then provided: 'the most exhilarating twenty minutes that the Group has had yet in a far from dull career. The target was illuminated immediately and was shot to ribbons by the three ships in commendably quick time, despite drastic high-speed zigzagging by the Boche. Early on it was difficult to see the target in the smoke and spray of battle, but soon the evil glow of fire round the conning tower provided a perfect aiming mark... At least one torpedo passed down *Wren*'s port side but the prudent Herrenvolk soon took to the water, leaving their boat circling to port at high speed. In a most abandoned manner it tried to ram me and then sank nearby at 0033. Two small explosions were heard at 0035 (probably scuttling charges); and at 0042 a very heavy explosion, doubtless marked the very fitting end of *U-473*. Thirty prisoners were fished out.'

In the last moments of its life, it made for *Starling*, who had to take violent evasive action. It then charged straight at *Wild Goose* before sinking 300 yards short. Thus did retaliation descend on the assailant of U.S.S. *Donnell*.

Walker issued no orders during this battle until the enemy sank, when he ordered: 'Cease Firing. Gosh, what a lovely battle'.

With the U-boat on its way to join the other nineteen that he had despatched, and U.S.S. *Hopping* escorted by *Whimbrel* and *Magpie* towing the damaged *Donnell* back to Glasgow, the objective had been achieved, but at considerable expense, not only in expenditure of depth charges, but also of four-inch shells. When *Wren* opened fire the range from her radar was 2940 yards: her first hit, blowing the U-boat's gun over the side, was from the fourth of her rapid salvoes. *Starling* was illuminating the scene with starshell from B mounting and at the same time fired 133 rounds of four-inch from 'A' mounting in the twenty minutes of action, scoring twelve hits. Her after mounting was loaded with the latest weapon 'Shark'[13], but this was not used since the guns could not be brought to bear before the U-boat sank.

The prisoners confirmed that their maximum safe diving depth was 820 feet. In emergencies they went lower. Whereas Walker blamed himself in unambiguous terms for not appreciating that his charges were exploding above the U-boat, his ships still had no accurate 850 and 900 feet depth settings on their heavy charges and the light charges could only be set to 800 feet. Prisoners said that all the charges had been exploding above them.

After this long chase — the Group's longest — *Tracker* came back to spend the whole of the next day, from 0930 until 2230, refuelling the sloops, providing 513 tons of oil, divided between Starling (190), Wild Goose (175) and Wren (148).[14]

In the morning watch on 8 May a frightened sentry reported to the Officer of the Watch that he had just wounded one of the prisoners. He was not accustomed to handling small arms and, while on watch guarding the prisoners, he had been experimenting with his revolver which went off and hit a sleeping German. Walker disciplined the two Able Seamen involved, apologized formally to the prisoner in front of the senior German rate on board and obtained a signed statement describing the circumstances. The prisoner was not seriously hurt, but Walker did not take the incident lightly.

The Group swept off to the north-west in a strong westerly wind and a big swell, and spent another four wet and uncomfortable days chasing a weather reporter stationed 1000 miles west of Ireland, in strong winds and big swells, before setting course for home at 13 knots on 14 May, arriving in Gladstone Dock at 0815 on the 17th.

Walker was summoned straight to Derby House for a conference with the Commander-in-Chief about the coming Normandy landings. To us who were with him day by day, he seemed to need some respite, but the change visible to Eilleen when he came back from sea was much more noticeable and alarming.[15] This was also Admiral Horton's reaction. Horton was a very hard man, but, nevertheless, most aware of the needs of his commanding officers: he had a particular empathy with and admiration for Walker. He promised him, as had the First Lord after the February patrol, a period of rest before he went to the next task that the Admiralty had planned for him — command of an aircraft carrier and promotion to Flag rank for duties in the Pacific. This career pattern meant that he would be knighted in due course.

But first the Navy had a job to do securing the passage of the Allied landings on the Normandy beaches, in which he was to play a major role in keeping the U-boats out of the English Channel.

CHAPTER NINE

THE NORMANDY LANDINGS

The large number of Allied escorts now at sea, the air offensive from aircraft carriers and UK bases, the efficiency of radar and HF/DF, the impact of Ultra since February, 1943, contrasted with the gloomy picture which Dönitz had now to face. His glider bombs had failed, his acoustic torpedoes had not achieved the results that he expected, the Allied airmen had beaten him in straight gun battles on the surface, the convoys could not be located and his losses, including milch cows and surface supply ships, were crippling.

Nevertheless Dönitz had enormous resilience. He had plans that could again tip the balance of the Battle of the Atlantic in Germany's favour and enable him to put a final strangle-hold on the trade routes supplying the UK.

On 8 July, 1943, he had persuaded Hitler to authorize maximum concentration on the building of the revolutionary Type XXI 1600-ton U-boats, capable of sustaining eighteen knots for an hour and a half and twelve to fourteen knots for ten hours under water. These were formidable vessels which could finally bring the Allies to their knees. The smaller Type XXIII boats were also approved. The programme (the Merker plan) envisaged a production of forty boats per month, and large numbers were to be ready by the autumn of 1944, prefabricated inland. Ultra had intercepted traffic between the Japanese and the Germans that detailed the development and production plans of these boats. This was not an impossible endeavour. Ninety-eight were commissioned in the second half of 1944 and eighty-three in the first three months of 1945.[1]

Meanwhile, intelligence reports and the lull in attacks on the Atlantic convoys indicated very clearly that the U-boats were regrouping in the Bay of Biscay ports ready for an attack on the invasion forces as soon as they put to sea. A substantial force was also assembled off the coast of Norway. Hitler still feared that this would be the area where the first landings would take place and kept some of his best troops there until well after the Normandy landings were firmly established.

This released a large number of escort vessels from convoy and support duties and made them available for work in the defence of the landings.

In the sloops in the Second Support Group hardships and perils shared over a year at sea had now built a team that ran smoothly and efficiently with a minimum of orders. Walker had frequently boarded and taken temporary command of other ships in the Group at sea without notice, so carrying out informal but thorough inspections, while their commanding officers had gone to *Starling* to see first-hand how things were done there. Walker knew intimately the strengths and weaknesses of each ship, and each of his commanding officers knew his peculiarities and understood what he required of them. By his example and personality, he had impressed on them the policy and action appropriate in any emergency.

There was an equally high standard of efficiency among the officers and men of the ships' companies. Each ship had no doubt that her performance was equal to, or better than, all the others, including *Starling*. With the old familiars around, all hands felt secure and unruffled by the emergencies that arose. Torpedoman Frank Clarke says, 'We had no fear . . . . We believed sinking U-boats was our right.'

Sadly, these great advantages would now be diluted, since the requirements for the final stage of naval operations during the landing were quite different from those needed in defending ocean convoys. Because most of the Western Approach escorts lacked the strong anti-aircraft armament mounted in the sloops, the Second Support Group split up. *Starling, Wild Goose* and *Wren* remained together and were joined by the frigates *Loch Killin, Loch Fada* and *Dominica*, thus leaving the Group with a main armament that still boasted eighteen four-inch anti-aircraft guns as well as a large number of close range anti-aircraft guns.

The ships detached were *Woodcock*, after completion of extensive repairs following the winter Atlantic storms, *Magpie* and *Whimbrel*. *Kite* never came back to the Group after the February patrol.[2] Of the new ships that replaced them, *Loch Killin* was the most notable, fitted with 'Squid',[3] the most advanced, ahead-throwing, anti-submarine weapon, designed to replace depth charges, but still to be proved in action.

The lull in the U-boat activity was not solely caused by the need to regroup and prepare to repulse the landings. The mass fitting of Schnorkel, approved in November, 1942, had started. This was a big pipe containing an air inlet and exhaust, the top of which projected above the U-boat. In suitable sea conditions a U-boat could come up to periscope depth, raise the Schnorkel and cruise on diesel engine or charge its batteries without the need to surface. The device could only be spotted by radar or by observation from the air in the right conditions when the surface of the sea was fairly smooth. As waves began to form or visibility was affected by cloud or mist, the chances of detection were very much reduced. In shallow inshore waters the U-boats could even in some cases lie on the bottom while charging their batteries. The first of these had been fitted in *U-264*, but its trials were brought to an untimely end when it was sunk by *Starling* and *Woodpecker* on 19 February, 1944, but Biscay-based U-boats had been carrying out trials in the western part of the Channel at the end of May. The intention was to fit all the Mk VIIC boats in the Bay of Biscay with Schnorkels by the end of the month.

In the two years and seven months since going to sea in *Stork*, Walker had brought two groups up to the highest standard of efficiency and had sunk twenty U-boats. He had been continuously at sea for the past twelve months. He was now faced with the break-up of his well-loved Second Support Group, the creation of another, and a vital role in an unfamiliar type of warfare in the support of the largest landing operation that had ever been attempted.

To prepare the ships for the type of fighting which might be expected and to liven them up after the slower pace of specialized ocean convoy duty, all the escorts of the Western Approaches were put through an energetic battle training course in the Irish Sea. Operational British submarines cooperated with aircraft firing live ammunition, and with high-speed motor torpedo boats, to provide realistic imitations of the conditions that were expected in the Channel. Landing parties, collision drills, breakdown and fire drills, air-to-sea communication exercises and gun actions against surface and air attacks were simulated.

In the last week of May these training exercises came to an end. This was the only period in the Group's history when all the ships were lying idle, not actually on patrol or being patched up in dock. We lay at anchor off Lough Foyle waiting for the operation to start. It was a pleasant rest in lovely weather. We filled in the time with routine tasks and chipping off paint that might catch fire. In the afternoon the whalers were taken away for sailing races or for picnics, provided that they stayed within sight of the ships to see any recall signals that might be flown. Lying on the sand in the sun, it was hard to imagine the hundreds of thousands of soldiers who must now be tensed up, waiting to board their landing craft.

On a fine summer's day the seals were broken and the orders for Operation Neptune were revealed. We had expected a vast operation, but this surpassed our wildest ideas. The large bound book covered every aspect of the plan from the exact time and route for each ship to the towing arrangements for the artificial harbours, fuel pipe lines and mine-sweeping arrangements. A prerequisite in the first stages was air supremacy. The whole of the English Channel and its approaches was to be swamped by 350 Allied aircraft from No. 19 Group,[5] which would attack and blast anything that moved outside the routes designated for the use of the vast fleet of vessels carrying the invasion forces and their supplies. This great force of aircraft would keep the U-boats off the surface and so restrict their movements to rather less than one hundred miles a day, the best they could achieve when submerged.

By the time the Germans realized that the main landings were committed to the Normandy beaches, the Western Approach ships had established deep lines of patrols to the west of Ushant and the Scilly Isles. The function of these patrols was to prevent the submerged U-boats from getting amongst the invasion convoys.

Dönitz was relying on the use of the U-boats which had been fitted with Schnorkel. His plans had not progressed very fast because of the disruption caused by the bombing of the points of production and then more bombing and sabotage in the course of transit across France. The U-boat patrols in May showed that Schnorkels enabled them to remain in the area, even if they were detected by airborne radar, but they were not yet familiar with their use.[6] For example, if the valves designed to keep the sea-water out closed unexpectedly while the diesels were running, the air below decks was gulped out, leaving the crew members in great distress and pain. The squalor and stink down below was made even worse because the problem of getting rid of waste had not yet been solved.

Apart from these familiarization sorties, Dönitz had not been maintaining regular patrols in the vicinity of the Normandy landing beaches and was therefore unable to make any immediate response. There were twenty U-boats lying in Norwegian waters, twelve deployed on distant operations and four weather-reporting. The operational boats able to interfere with the landings were disposed as follows:[7]

Seventeen on passage from Norway, of which five were sunk and one damaged by aircraft on the way, leaving five fitted with Schnorkel.

Seventeen at Brest, of which eight were fitted with Schnorkel.

Nineteen at St. Nazaire, Lorient and La Pallice. Only one was fitted with Schnorkel.

The orders for Operation Neptune were not opened until the ships involved were at sea, to make certain that careless talk could not endanger security. The actual day on which the operation was to start, D-Day, was withheld until the last possible moment. So much depended on the weather and the forecasts. Meantime all the anti-submarine ships were gathering together in Moelfre Bay, off the coast of Wales to the west of Anglesey.

That evening, as we sailed from Lough Foyle to join the rest of the Fleet, the wind started to rise and had reached gale force by the time we reached the anchorage: the assembled fleet was half-hidden in rain and flying spray. Captain Walker was senior officer of this gathering of about forty ships, and many vital points of detail had still to be clarified. In the gale Starling's motor boat went round the fleet distributing orders and collecting commanding officers for conferences on board. By nightfall it was all done and the ships were ready to go. However, Moelfre is not the ideal anchorage, and the wind force increased steadily. To stop them dragging their anchors, the ships steamed at slow speed into their cables.

In the morning it was still not time to go. *Starling's* motor boat, which had been tied up astern, had disappeared; all that remained was the frayed end of its securing painter. *Dominica's* first job in the Second Support Group was to find it and bring it back, much to the relief of her ship's company who then had good cause to think that things went wrong even in Walker's ship.

The weather showed no signs of improving and there seemed to be no chance of the invasion starting. The sloops took their whalers away for sailing races around the fleet, but otherwise there was nothing to do except make a final check on every item of equipment.

Hands went to prayers on the quarterdeck. Walker was conducting the service, reading from the prayer book which was propped on the oerlikon gun about ten feet directly below the muzzles of X gun. In the middle of a period of silent prayer, there were two muffled explosions and two small puffs of smoke: two bags fell from the heavens either side of his feet, bursting and spraying his shoes with sand. Leading Torpedoman Profitt had managed to get himself excused from prayers so that he could test the gun-firing circuits. He had forgotten to take the sandbags from the ends of the barrels before firing the test charges.[8]

He was saved from the wrath to come by the executive order to move into our positions for Operation Neptune. Still in a strong wind the invasion was on, for better or for worse.

Groups of ships started to move away from their anchorages and to manoeuvre into line ahead. Soon we too heard the clanking of our cable shortening in as we made ready to weigh anchor. A cluster of flags broke out from *Starling's* yardarm and came running down. The ships steamed to their appointed stations. Signal lamps flickered.

'GOODBYE, GOOD LUCK AND GOOD HUNTING.'

The return journey to Europe had started.

Captain Walker was never again to spend an uninterrupted night in his bunk at sea. The ships that were responsible for keeping the U-boats out of the Channel were almost all trained and indoctrinated ocean convoy escorts. Many of them were manned by commanding officers and men who had spent all their time at sea in the wastes of the Atlantic Ocean with plenty of deep water and leagues of sea room. Narrow shoal waters with rocks, wrecks, tides, sandbanks and proximity of land were strange to them.

There were 4000 vessels involved in the landings, including five support groups and 200 other ships from the Western Approaches, charged with keeping the U-boats away from the landing beaches and the approach routes from the west. With so many ships crowded into the narrow bottlenecks of the entrances to the Channel and to the Irish Sea, the risks of collision, of stranding, wrecking and mistaken identity were added to the dangers of assaults by the enemy. These ships were accustomed to working with reconnaisance aircraft but not with the swarms of Coastal Command aircraft that blanketed the area into which they were moving. The pilots were as keen as mustard, but many of them were lacking in experience: their keenness itself created problems. Every swirl in the water was a diving U-boat, every broom handle a periscope or a Schnorkel.

There was no possibility of detailed control of these operations from shore. Without any staff except his specialists, Walker relied more and more on his young 24-year-old First Lieutenant John Filleul to handle and run the ship, and on Arthur Ayers, the Pilot, to keep him clear of shoals, rocks, wrecks and minefields, but he had problems controlling his own Group with three new ships, of cooperation with aircraft, and of working with the other ten groups operating in the Western Patrol area and the neighbouring anti-submarine area to the east. Day or night, on every encounter, Walker was the Senior Officer on the spot who had to make the decisions. He had no relief on his return to harbour: a car would whisk him off to conferences with the Commander-in-Chief to discuss solutions to the many problems which he had just experienced at sea.

As soon as we reached our area, reports flowed in of U-boats at sea making for the western entrances to the Channel. Many of these reports were correct: there were forty-nine boats in the Biscay ports of which fourteen were not ready for sea, but thirty-five sailed on the first day of the landings and set course for the invasion area. They were attacked fifty times by aircraft on the first night.[9] Although there were scores of aircraft sighting reports, generated by the enormous enthusiasm of Coastal Command, there was no means of separating the true reports from the false.

The U-boats not equipped with Schnorkels had been ordered to intercept the invasion fleets coming down from the Irish Sea, but the most immediate threat to the landings came from the eight Schnorkel-equipped boats from Brest, only two hundred miles from the landing beaches.

The Second Support Group's days and short midsummer nights became one headlong chase from one sighting position to the next. The first echo classified as a submarine was picked up when two lines of escorts were passing through each other at right angles. The subsequent mêlée, as one group went into a pre-arranged encircling movement to prevent the U-boat escaping, while two ships went in for an attack, and the other group tried to clear the pitch — all in complete darkness without lights — required the highest level of seamanship, alertness and experience to prevent collision and tragedy, without the presence of U-boats and torpedoes. Situations such as this demanded the personal involvement of the commanding officers who could seldom leave the bridges of their ships. The ships' companies were at action stations all through the nights and often for the greater part of the daylight hours.

After several days of this hectic activity, the Group went into Plymouth to refuel and to get at least one full night of uninterrupted sleep. The first part of the task had been successfully accomplished. General Eisenhower had asked for two weeks clear of U-boats and this had been achieved. While his men slept and relaxed, Walker went off to a conference with Coastal Command, to work out a better system of communication between ships and aircraft.

Although this part of the operation had gone well, it was still vital to maintain control of the entrances to the Channel, and this could only be achieved by a continuation of the pressure from aircraft and surface ships. If the U-boats ever got through to the Normandy beaches, or to the swept channels leading to them, there could be the most appalling slaughter. Dönitz was very much aware of this opportunity and had issued orders to his U-boat commanders to carry out 'kamikaze' attacks in implementation of a calculated decision that all U-boats, except the new Type XXI and XXIII boats, were to be treated as expendable. In his Memoirs he argues that a U-boat with a few men on board was the sole means of really harming the enemy was by sinking a ship laden with soldiers and weapons of war, even if the U-boat was itself sunk. It is hard to understand his argument: even if the U-boat was expendable, the U-boat crew was not, but he went on to order:

'Every vessel taking part in the landing, even if it has but a handful of men or a solitary tank on board, is a target of the utmost importance which must be attacked regardless of risk. Every effort will be made to close the enemy invasion fleet regardless of danger from shallow water, possible minefields or anything else. Every man and weapon destroyed *before* reaching the beaches lessens the enemy's chances of ultimate success. Every boat that inflicts losses on the enemy while he is landing has fulfilled its primary function, *even though it perishes in so doing.*'[10]

Walker had no time to rest. He was involved without a break in forming searches in response to aircraft reports, redirecting other Groups and writing up his Reports of Proceedings and recommendations. His sense of urgency intensified and he was continuously warning against the danger of a moment of carelessness or misjudgement that might permit four or five U-boats to get through. The stakes were high. In this small area the greater part of the Western Approaches Fleet was concentrated against the U-boat Fleet using the benefits of the Schnorkel and opportunities to hide submerged in shoal waters.

On the second night of the second patrol, it was already pitch black when Walker staggered off the bridge into the chart house. In the dim red light, for the thousandth time he leant over the plot for an instant and asked the usual question: 'Everything OK, Pilot?'

As he took off his oilskins, a dark shape appeared from behind: 'Cup of kye, sir?'

'Thankyou, Gardner.'

He went into his sea-cabin and sat on the bunk, leaning back against the bulkhead to steady himself against the never-ending movement of the ship. He closed his eyes and dozed off. The ship rolled and the kye went all over the deck.

John Filleul handed over the middle watch to stan Baulcomb. There was a glimmer of light in the sky over to the east and an occasional break in the cloud. The Group was weaving along at twelve knots in line abreast. Pilot appeared:

'John, we're due for an Easy Item turn[11] starting at 0430. I'll be on watch. Do you want to tell the Captain?'

'I'll tell him on my way down. Guns has got the weight. Have a nice watch.'

John disappeared into the gloom at the rear of the bridge and clambered down the ladder to the wheelhouse, grateful for a little warmth. He rapped lightly on the door of the Captain's sea cabin, which was as usual on the hook.

Walker's cup was rolling around the deck, where it had fallen. Walker was slumped back against the pillows on the bunk where he had immediately fallen asleep.

'Captain, sir. Easy Item to 180 degrees due at 0430. That's in twenty-five minutes. Pilot's got the watch. He'll call you. There might be a star later on.'

'Very good, Number One'.

John went back to the wheelhouse.

'Bosun's mate, clear up that mess on the deck of the Captain's sea-cabin, but do it quietly.'

'Aye, aye, sir.'

The Pilot and Stan Baulcomb, who had kept every morning watch together on every day *Starling* was at sea since she commissioned, settled down to endure the coldest time that signalled the end of the night. They didn't like the English Channel. There were too many ships scurrying around the constricted waters between the Lizard and Ushant. The sky was rarely clear of patrolling aircraft, and the loudspeaker on the bridge crackled continuously with their reports. Asdic conditions were at their worst in the tide rips stirred up by the eternal ebb and flow of the Channel in shoal waters. Wrecks accumulated over the centuries added to the abundance of false echoes. It was very difficult and sometimes impossible to keep track of all the ships in the area in which Walker was operating. They preferred the empty wastes of the broad Atlantic.

Pilot took a last look at his plot. Five minutes to go. How many times had the Group carried out this manoeuvre! It was a neat simple operation, first devised by *Woodpecker*, not difficult with all the sea-room of the Atlantic Ocean in which to manoeuvre, but he had to be even more certain than usual in these constricted waters. Time to tell the Captain. He'd had a bit of sleep. Still pretty dark: better use the voice-pipe.

'Captain, sir. Easy Item to 180 degrees at 0430. Dark night, but clear. It's 0425 now and five minutes to go.'

'Carry on, Pilot. Execute when you're ready. I'll be up.'

'Aye aye sir. Yeoman, make to the Group "From *Starling* prepare to alter course Easy Item 180 degrees".'

Pilot smiled to himself as he imagined four weary commanding officers swinging their legs over the sides of their bunks and calling for more kye before pulling on their wet oilskins and climbing back up to the bridge. Serve the silly sods right, they didn't have to keep a standing morning watch.

'0430 sir.'

'Execute. Log that please, Guns.'

He went over to the PPI and saw with relief that the little blip representing the first ship to alter course was already starting to move across the rear of the line of sweeping sloops. One more and it would be *Starling's* turn.

He looked through the blackness to the rear of the bridge for the tall outline of the Captain. Funny, he must have gone back to the wheelhouse to look at the plot. The Gunner peered over the binnacle.

'Pilot, I reckon we should put our wheel over when *Wren* bears 285 degrees. That should be in about eight minutes.'

This was fun. If they got it exactly right (not simple, because the speed of turning varied with every sea and wind condition), then it wasn't necessary to make any further alteration in the engine revolutions so as to keep station on the new course. If they weren't in station for an instant, then there would be all sorts of 'private' rude messages from OOW to OOW as soon as it was light enough to permit the use of signal lamps. These 'private messages' were not logged and not seen by the Captain, but their contents were common knowledge in the privileged circles of the communications messes and the Chief and Petty Officers' messes. 'Subby made a real mess of it this morning. He had to juggle around with revs for best part of half-an-hour. The OOW of *Wren* didn't half give him the stick.' And Petty Officer Dyson in his lair down below would not be pleased at having to adjust his valves time and time again.

The watch was passing quickly and a faint horizon was starting to show with occasional glimpses of clear sky.

'Have you got the weight, Guns? I might be able to get a couple of stars. Bosun's mate, bring up my sextant and deck watch, and stand by to take some times.'

Pilot walked over to the binnacle and bent over the voice-pipe to Walker's sea cabin.

'Captain, sir, one or two stars coming through and there's a chance of a good horizon.'

'Very Good, Pilot. Carry on. I'll be up shortly.'

After breakfast that morning, when he had discussed the business of the day with the Chief Bosun's Mate and detailed the hands, John Filleul made his way along the upper deck and climbed up the ladder to the bridge, where he knew that he would find Walker pacing slowly up and down the starboard side, ten paces forwards and ten paces back. He made his usual report, answered a few questions, saluted and turned to leave.

'One moment, Number One. The officers on the morning watch are becoming lazy. According to the log, the Group altered course at 0430. Furthermore, Pilot has put in a new position based on a fix during the morning watch which means that there was a horizon and stars. I was not called on either occasion. I want you to have a word with them and make it very clear that I am not at all pleased.'

John went straight back to the wardroom where Pilot, the Gunner, the non-watchkeepers and the middle-watchmen had just finished their breakfasts. He closed the hatch to the wardroom pantry. White in the face with rage, he recited what Captain Walker had said and asked for an explanation.

There was a deathly and prolonged hush, broken by the entry of the Chief Bosun's Mate for further orders. The morning watch officers went with John to his cabin across the passageway. The matter was never mentioned again.

For much of the time a light mist lay on the surface of the sea, but the skies above were clear and swarms of Allied aircraft could be seen going over towards France. Sometimes the Group was operating close enough to the French coast for us to see the houses ashore: the blown-up bodies of dead airmen floated past: the radar became badly affected by the hot damp weather and started to produce very odd echoes to add to the confusion.

When the Group was carrying out a sweep within sight of the Ushant lighthouse, a light blinked from *Wren*: 'Radar reports twenty-one unidentified aircraft approaching from 180 degrees, range twenty-six miles.'

As the guns swung round to the bearing, a long line of black objects detached themselves from the mist just above the surface of the sea, coming straight towards us. They looked like a swarm of angry bees and covered the whole horizon as far as the eye could see. When the guns opened up there would be no chance of missing them because they were so close together, but there were so many that there was little chance of survival. No one was surprised. It had been too good to last. The German air force was at last going to make up for these impertinent patrols off their doorstep. We would just have to do the best we could against this overwhelming force. The shells went home and the 'Gun Ready' lamps glowed, waiting for the order to open fire. Then Walker's voice sounded loud and clear over the speakers: 'Friendly Aircraft. Secure from Action Stations.'

A babble of excited and relieved chatter broke out as the guns' crews unloaded the guns and stowed away the ammunition.

This was only one of the false alarms. There were so many that they became tedious and aggravating. The level of activity was as high or higher than it had ever been but the only signs of U-boats were the sighting reports from aircraft. No ship, even *Wild Goose*, achieved a single Asdic contact. The men of the Second Support Group were used to the real thing and were rapidly getting frustrated, edgy and tense.

After three weeks, aircraft sightings became less frequent. U-boats using Schnorkels and sometimes lying on the bottom for rest and concealment began to penetrate the invasion area. Although the Group had moved further to the east and was now operating west of a line from Start Point to the Channel Islands, Walker tried without avail to persuade the C-in-C to move the Group even closer to the action on the Normandy beaches, but the combined effects of the saturation of the air and the deep lines of surface patrols had served their purpose. The great fleet of landing craft and supporting services had established their foothold ashore and had survived the vital first weeks.

The U-boats had tried simultaneously to cover the possibility of the main landings taking place in the Bordeaux area and in Norway, as well as trying to move in to attack the actual invasion beaches in the Seine Bay. As planned, if they remained on the surface they were immediately blasted by aircraft. When they submerged they were vulnerable to the great concentration of surface vessels: instead of the hundred miles per day range which they had anticipated, their mobility had been reduced to sixty miles or less per day. Their whole system of centralized control was disrupted. U-boats were not reporting back and Dönitz had little idea where they were or even whether they had been sunk or were still operational.

Out of his fleet of 450 U-boats, of which 182 were supposed to be operational, Dönitz only managed to deploy twelve U-boats fitted with Schnorkels against the Normandy landing.

So effective was the screen set up against these boats that they achieved nothing until 15 June, when *U-764* sank *Mourne* and *Blackwood*, and *U-621* sank a landing craft. The same boat fired torpedoes at two bombarding battleships of the *King George V* and *Valiant* class, all of which exploded prematurely.[12] After this the U-boats achieved nothing for a further two weeks.

Starling arrived in Liverpool on 2 July, where Walker learnt from the *London Gazette* of 20 June that he had been awarded his fourth DSO.

On the very same day, a month after the first Allied troops had landed on French soil, Dönitz ordered all his U-boats back to harbour. Twenty-six U-boats were sunk during the four weeks from D-Day until 2 July, of which twelve were sunk in the approaches to the Normandy beaches, six by aircraft, four by ships and two by the combined efforts of aircraft and ships.[13]

Captain Walker's 'Thousand British Tars' would have the satisfaction of knowing that they had added another chapter of honour to their glowing record. They had played their part in making sure that the troops in the landing craft did not have to worry about the U-boats before they even got ashore as well as weather, mines, aircraft and shore batteries.

But Captain Walker would never know.

We looked forward to spending the week in harbour to replenish stores, fuel and ammunition, and to enjoy the luxury of uninterrupted sleep and the shelter of Gladstone Dock, the scene of our triumphant entry a few weeks before. The packed and frantic rush of the English Channel seemed a world away.

Johnnie and Eilleen Walker went off for a few days' leave with their family, during which he was able to spend some time getting to know his youngest son Andrew, who was now five years old. On Friday, Commander D.E.G. Wemyss came on board to say goodbye: for the first time *Wild Goose* would not be coming back to sea with the Group, as it was her turn for a refit. Like Walker, he had served in the battleship *Valiant* as a midshipman in the First World War twenty-five years before, and in the past year they had done great deeds together.

Wemyss said: 'It was with a heavy heart that I visited the Boss to say goodbye. I found him in very good form, after having admitted for the first time some days earlier that he was tired, which, since we had all been out of bed for three nights in succession, had not caused much surprise. He was trying out a special recording of *Starling's* hunting tune, and seemed completely back in form.'[14]

Captain and Mrs. Walker lunched with some of the officers in the Adelphi Hotel. He was given two signals. The first confirmed the death of his eldest son Timothy in the submarine *Parthian* which had gone down in the Mediterranean on 10 August the year before. The second ordered the Group to sea on the following day.

That evening he was taken to the Royal Naval Hospital in Seaforth. The Group sailed the next day under Commander N. A. Duck, who had taken over temporary command in *Starling*, expecting Walker to rejoin in Devonport.

During the middle watch of Sunday 9 July, the ships were at sea on patrol in the Channel when they received the following signal:
'The Admiralty regrets to inform you of the death of your Senior Officer which took place at 0200 today.'

The coffin containing Walker's body was taken to the Flotilla Chapel in Gladstone Dock to lie in state with a guard of Able Seamen.

On the morning of the 11th, after a short family service, the coffin was taken to Liverpool Cathedral and rested there until the ceremony in the afternoon, attended by many hundreds of mourners from the three services, the merchant service and from the people of Liverpool. During the night, the Commander-in-Chief, Admiral Sir Max Horton, had composed a Solemn Acknowledgement which he read out:

> 'They that go down to the sea in ships, that do business in great waters; these see the works of the Lord and his wonders in the deep.
>
> 'On the day when the waters had well-nigh overwhelmed us, our brother here departed, apprehending the creative power in man, set himself to the task to conquer the malice of the enemy.
>
> 'Solemnly we acknowledge the working of God's spirit in His son and servant. In our hour of need he was the doughty protector of them that sailed the seas on our behalf. His heart and his mind extended and expanded to the utmost tiring of the body even unto death; that he might discover and operate means of saving our ships from the treacherous foes.
>
> 'Truly many, very many, were saved because he was not disobedient to his vision.
>
> 'Victories have been won and should be won by such as he. All praise be to the most high for such perfection of skill and rare knowledge added to determination and daring leadership.
>
> 'May there never be wanting in this realm a succession of men of like spirit in discipline, imagination and valour, humble and unafraid.
>
> 'Not dust, nor the light weight of a stone, but all the sea of the Western Approaches shall be his tomb.'[15]

The coffin, draped with the Union Flag, was carried down the steps of the Cathedral to the waiting gun carriage and hauled by bluejackets through the lined streets to Prince's Pier, flanked by eight Captains, followed by Eilleen, Nicolas and Gillian. The mourners took their places on the quarterdeck of

Hesperus as *Starling's* tattered battle ensign was hoisted and half-masted while the coffin was piped on board.

As she reached the Bar Light Vessel marking the entrance to the Mersey river, *Hesperus* passed between two lines of merchant ships from an outward and a homeward bound convoy, whose crews lowered their red ensigns and lined the rails bare-headed in a final salute to the man who had so often protected them. Not a single man was lost and not a single merchant ship was sunk due to enemy action while under the protection of the Second Support Group with Walker in command.

When clear of the entrance channel, the body was committed to the deep and a single wreath was thrown after it by Eilleen.

'Be pleased to receive into thine Almighty and most gracious protection the persons of us thy servants and the Fleet in which we serve. Preserve us from the dangers of the sea, and from the violence of the enemy; that we may be a safeguard unto our most gracious Sovereign Lord, King GEORGE, and his Dominions, and a security for such as pass upon the seas upon their lawful occasions; that the inhabitants of our Island may in peace and quietness serve thee our God; and that we may return in safety to enjoy the blessings of the land.'

The signal stunned the sloops. Commander Duck had ordered all ships to trail their lifelines over the side from their sea boats, a traditional mark of respect paid by merchant seamen to a departed colleague; they continued through the oily seas with ensigns at half-mast but otherwise showing no outward signs of the grief that had struck them down. It would be some while before the full impact hit them, but as the day went on groups of men paced the decks talking in twos and threes. The usual cheerful banter had ceased; their spirit had gone and they were bitter at the injustice of the blow; a heavy hush of mourning lay over all. There was a strong feeling that *Starling* should now be on her way back to bury her Captain and accompany him on his last journey.

The Group completed its patrol and returned to Plymouth where Commander Wemyss, who had been present at the funeral and the burial at sea, came on board to speak to the assembled ships' companies. He told us of the burial service in Liverpool Cathedral and described the commitment of Walker's body to its final resting place, far beyond the Bar Light Vessel.

When Commander Wemyss had spoken, Mrs Walker came down to the messdeck. It was hard for us to lose our Captain and to see his wife so badly hit; how much harder it must have been for her to come down to say goodbye to us and to his ship. She did not speak on the quarterdeck, as was the custom, but came down to the mess deck where the men ate and slept. She was the only woman ever to address the assembled ship's company and we felt that it was fitting and right that this should be so, though it must have taken a great deal of courage. Her action meant much to those who had so often seen her first of all standing on the jetty to welcome us all back after our sea trips.

Eilleen Walker wrote later to my mother: 'My husband loved the ship so much and everybody in her individually. He was so proud of them all, and I think that in the last six months his great happiness was not in the awards that he received, but in his terrific pride in everyone on board.'

After this sorrowful period the Group went back to the Channel patrols determined to keep up its record.

The Group had been trained to such a high peak of efficiency that the performance of the ships at sea and the results that they continued to achieve were unaffected. But three Commanding Officers were sent to *Starling* in quick succession, making a total of eight Commanding Officers to hold this position in the few months since the ship had gone to sea. Each of them had their own ways, particularities and styles of leadership, but none of them, almost by definition, could inherit the professional skill, the genius for leadership, and the empathy that Walker had built up with his officers and key ratings, who continued instinctively to do things in Walker's way and to operate his priorities. Even that doughty warrior Wemyss was highly critical of some aspects of the discipline on board which were not in line with his own views. There was a strong feeling that John Filleul should have taken over command. He, of all people, knew Walker's ways and was determined to keep the old tradition going, supported by the battle-hardened ship's officers and ship's company who remained unchanged in their appointments and imbued with the ideas implanted by Walker during his command. But the Royal Navy had not the flexibility of the Royal Air Force where an outstanding officer could and did sometimes rise from the rank of Flight Lieutenant to Group Captain during the course of the War.

Although the results continued to be achieved, the spirit had changed. Before, the tussle had not been a vengeful and personal struggle, but every man on board knew that Walker's death had been caused by the increasing strain of his endless fight against the U-boats; it was this, combined with the atrocious physical conditions which he had borne without complaint, that had killed him just as surely as if he had died in the blast of a German torpedo's explosion.

The Group did not have long to prove its resolve. Before the end of the month, *Starling* and *Loch Killin* had sunk *U-333*, a veteran boat that had caused the Allies much trouble off Florida and the West Coast of Africa. A week later the same two ships sank *U-736*, using *Loch Killin's* latest weapon, the Squid, which caused a submarine to surface right under her stern and become entangled in her quarterdeck where it hung for five minutes with Germans pouring on board *Loch Killin*. The next day *Wren* and Liberator C/53 sank and picked up all the crew of *U-608*, and on 10/11 August the Group opened fire on *U-385* which was sunk early the next morning by *Starling's* and the Group's gunfire, directed by Sunderland P/461. This made a healthy total of four U-boats sunk in ten days and one hundred and ten prisoners taken. *Starling* was detached and joined 22nd Escort Group which sank *U-482*. There was then a quiet spell before *Wild Goose*, *Loch Fada*, *Labuan* and aircraft H/112 sank *U-1208*[16], and finally *Loch Killin* sank *U-1063*, making a total of eight more U-boats destroyed by ships from Walker's Groups after his death. (*U-683*, originally thought to have been sunk by *Wild Goose* and *Loch Ruthven* on 12 March, 1945, was later found to have been the wreck of a previous sinking.)

CONCLUSION

There were half a dozen outstanding Senior Officers who did great deeds in this struggle and a score of Commanding Officers of escort vessels who fought right through from the darkest days to final victory.

Why, then, did the Admiralty say, in a communiqué issued in 1950 that 'Captain Walker, more than any other, won the Battle of the Atlantic. His methods had amazing success and more than any other factor gave the Royal Navy supremacy'?

The reply lies in his record of sinking twenty U-boats, and a further eight sunk within a year of his death by ships from his Group. In the first six months of the Second Support Group's career he sank on average one U-boat every fortnight.

He achieved these results by a combination of technical competence, leadership and good fortune, backed by a commanding presence.

Scores of men who served in his ships contributed to this book, speaking or writing from their personal recollections. Not one of them found grounds for criticism of his competence or his character.

From the time that he went to sea in *Stork*, he was given the best ships, armaments and equipment that the Royal Navy could offer. Although these facilities were inadequate at the start of his sea time and seriously lacking in important respects right up to the end of his career, he used them in a most imaginative way, developing new applications which were not in the mind of the designers, and rejecting any innovations that might fail in action conditions.

He was given the best people to man his ships, some of whom followed him from ship to ship. He did not always make the most obvious choices among the officers and men who held the key positions. The most obvious cases were his young First Lieutenant, John Filleul, his Navigator, Arthur Ayers (a salesman), his Chief Yeoman of Signals, Roland Keyworth (a farmer) and his Chief Petty Officer Telegraphist, Tommy Teece.

He was awarded total loyalty by all his men. His secretary, Bill Johnson (a bank manager), said that he would have jumped over the side if told to by Walker. One of his quartermasters, Walter Riley, who steered both his ships, today spends all his working hours running the unique Captain Walker's Old Boys Association that still keeps his memory alive by monthly meetings and an annual reunion in Bootle.

The loyalty that he received from his people was a return for the loyalty that he gave to them. When Eilleen Walker said — 'My husband loved the ship so much and everybody in her individually. He was so proud of them all,' she was expressing something that we all knew to be true.

At sea, he led by an example of perfectionism and total dedication. He was without doubt a modest man, never claiming personal credit and always underlining his own mistakes when others could benefit. He gloried in delegation, never interfering, even in action, when the battle was being waged in the right way by his trained officers and men.

Where he succeeded when others might have failed was in his determination and persistence. After many cold and miserable hours on the bridge, when others faltered, his determination and alertness never weakened, long after his body and his mind had told him to give up.

Above all he had a great respect for human lives, particularly the lives of British seamen. He took many decisions and did many things that appeared at the time to be very risky. In retrospect they were seen to be calculated courses of action, even though taken in the heat of battle, and they were successful.

Fifty years after the event, Sir Roger Young, who was then a midshipman RNVR (the lowest form of animal life) remembers the time that Captain Walker climbed up the rope ladder from the sea boat and boarded *Wren* for a short visit.

'So, for that week's mission, I actually served directly under Walker – as a midshipman, apprentice navigator, Officer of the Watch. He left a deep impression on me. He said very little; he was a quiet man. He did very little in any obvious sense. But he had a tremendous presence through his sheer commitment, professionalism and devotion to the task; and his clear-cut integrity – combined with charm – not in the superficial sense of that latter word, but in the sense of that quality in someone's personality which gives grace to all he does, thus inspiring one to trust and follow him. One knew he was in total control, with a sure grasp of tactics, strategy and the minutiae of the operation. Everyone knew exactly what was expected of them – and dreaded letting him down by not doing it.

'He seemed tireless and sleepless, though in fact he spent quite some time in his cabin, trusting people to get on with the job, yet available at a second's notice and fully in command again. I remember keeping watch while he stood at one corner of the bridge, silently looking out into the night. No one has ever given me such a sense of being trusted, so that he refused to take any part in the ordinary business of the watch; that was up to me, even though as a mere midshipman I had no real authority or experience. It gave me remarkably mixed feelings; of alarm lest I should not be up to the job; but also of confidence because if he trusted me then all was well. There was remarkable reassurance in that silent strong, attractive figure.

'It was only a week, but a memorable one.'

Frederic John Walker was a man of his age. His whole life had been a technical preparation for his wartime achievements. When the call came, he demonstrated that he was motivated solely by the need to keep Britain's Trade Routes open by destroying U-boats. He carried out his task with dignity and total conviction, and was deeply missed by his 'Thousand British Tars'.

> What if some little pain the passage have
> That makes frail flesh to fear the bitter wave?
> Is not short pain well borne, that brings long ease
> And lays the soul to sleep in quiet grave?
> Sleep after toil, port after stormy seas,
> Ease after war, death after life, does greatly please.
>
> Edmund Spenser

Johnnie Walker Memorial Appeal

As you will have discovered from reading this book, Captain Johnnie Walker was an outstanding hero of the Battle of the Atlantic, which was so crucial to Britain's survival in World War II. As a belated commemoration of Walker, it has been decided to commission a memorial to him and his ships' companies. A statue will be erected at the Pier Head in Liverpool, close to from where he sailed so often. Donations should be sent to The Billington Group, Cunard Building, Pier Head, Liverpool L3 1EL, with cheques made out to the Walker RN Memorial Appeal. Any excess would be sent to benevolent funds for Royal and merchant seamen.

Vice Admiral M P Gretton CB, 1998
Johnnie Walker Memorial Fund
Registered Charity No 266982

U-BOATS SUNK BY CAPTAIN F. J. WALKER RN

These lists of U-boats destroyed by his ships are a tribute to his methods of training and his ability to inspire the officers and men who served under him. They show an achievement which was unsurpassed by any officer at sea in the history of anti-submarine warfare. Between 3 September, 1939, and 8 May, 1945, 206 U-boats were sunk by British ships (plus thirty-seven by US ships and three shared). Of these, twenty were sunk by ships under Captain Walker's command at sea, and a further eight after his death by ships which were part of the Second Support Group during the period of his command.

He developed tactics in his Groups (in particular the creeping attack) which proved so successful in the final destruction of U-boats that they were adopted throughout the Western Approaches Command.

The first list shows twenty U-boats sunk by ships in the Groups under Captain Walker's command during his lifetime.

The second list shows eight U-boats which 'his' ships went on to sink after his death.

LIST NUMBER ONE
36th ESCORT GROUP

Reference	Date	U-Boat Number	Ships Involved (See Note 1)
1	17/12/41	U-131	Blankney, Exmoor, Penstemon, Stanley, Stork and 802 Squadron (Audacity).
2	18/12/41	U-434	Blankney and Stanley.
3	19/12/41	U-574	Stork.
4	21/12/41	U-567	Deptford and Samphire.
5	14/4/42	U-252	Stork and Vetch.

SECOND SUPPORT GROUP

6	1/6/43	U-202	Starling.
7	24/6/43	U-119	Starling.
8	24/6/43	U-449	Kite, Wild Goose, Woodpecker, Wren.
9	30/7/43	U-504	Kite, Wild Goose, Woodpecker, Wren.

	30/7/43	U- 462	Scuttled after damage by aircraft and gunfire from ships of 2 SG. (See Note 2)
10	6/11/43	U-226	*Kite, Woodcock, Starling.*
11	6/11/43	U-842	*Starling, Wild Goose.*
12	31/1/44	U-592	*Magpie, Starling, Wild Goose.*
13	8/2/44	U-762	*Wild Goose, Woodpecker.* (See Note 3)
14	9/2/44	U-238	*Kite, Magpie, Starling.* (See Note 3)
15	9/2/44	U-734	*Starling, Wild Goose.* (See Note 3)
16	11/2/44	U- 424	*Wild Goose, Woodpecker.*
17	19/2/44	U-264	*Starling, Woodpecker.*
18	15/3/44	U-653	*Starling, Wild Goose,* A/825 *(Vindex).*
19	29/3/44	U-961	*Starling.*
20	5/5/44	U- 473	*Starling, Wild Goose, Wren,* (sunk 6/5/44)

NOTES

1. The "Ships involved" column is largely from Admiralty official attributions, which are sometimes a bit arbitrary. For example, the rest of the Group, and *Kite* in particular, were involved in the destruction of *U-202*, which was credited to *Starling* as a single-handed kill. The MOD is still investigating various sinkings.
2. *U- 462* was badly damaged by Halifax S/502 on 30 July, 1943, so that it was unable to dive. It then came under fire from ships of the Second Support Group. According to its captain, he then scuttled, I imagine to avoid the danger of being boarded and his boat captured by the ships of the Second Support Group which were in hot pursuit.
3. The Second Support Group sank three U-boats *U-762, 238* and *734*, on 8 and 9 February, 1944, but there is no way of telling the order in which they were sunk since there were no survivors.

The list does not include *U-127*, which was sunk by HMAS *Nestor* on 15 December off Cape St Vincent, on its way to intercept convoy HG 76.

There were no warships or merchant ships sunk in the convoys supported by the Second Support Group in this period, except *Woodpecker*, all of whose crew were safely transferred to other ships.

Captain Walker died on 9 July, 1944.

LIST NUMBER TWO

U-boats sunk after Captain Walker's death.

21	31/7/44	*U-333*	*Loch Killin, Starling.*
22	6/8/44	*U-736*	*Loch Killin, Starling (Squid attack).*
23	9/8/44	*U-608*	*Wren,* Liberator C/53.
24	11/8/44	*U-385*	*Starling,* Sunderland P/461.
25	16/1/45	*U- 482*	*Amethyst, Hart, Loch Craggie, Peacock, Starling* (in 22nd Escort Group).
26	27/2/45	*U-1018*	*Loch Fada (Squid attack).*
27	27/2/45	*U-1208*	*Wild Goose, Labuan, Loch Fada,* Liberator (Originally thought to have been *U-327*).
28	15/4/45	*U-1063*	*Loch Killin.*

OUR LOSSES

19/12/41 H.M.S. *Stanley* sunk by *U-574.*
21/12/41 H.M.S. *Audacity* sunk by *U-751.*
20/02/44 H.M.S. *Woodpecker* torpedoed by *U-764; sunk 27/2/44.*
21/08/44 H.M.S. *Kite* sunk by *U-344.*

APPENDIX TWO

THE ESCORT VESSELS

Inadequate funds were made available for building escort vessels in 1939. Even at that date the approval given under that year's programme, and the War Emergency Programme that followed, covered less than half the minimum number of ships then considered to be essential by the Admiralty. These two programmes included only two Black Swan Class sloops, and concentrated instead on 116 Flower Class corvettes and fifty-six Hunt Class escort destroyers whose construction and design did not come anywhere near the minimum standards for ocean convoys work. The destroyers were unstable and had not enough endurance; the corvettes were too slow and inadequately armed.

THE FLOWER CLASS CORVETTES

The corvettes were small single-screw ships of 925 tons, developed from a design of Smith's Dock, Middlesbrough, for their whale-catcher, *Southern Pride*. Their length was 205 feet, limited by the maximum that could be fitted into the building yards with spare capacity in the UK. Their maximum designed speed was 16 knots, but in practice more like 14 to 15 knots, whereas some of the U-boats now joining the operational fleet in the Atlantic could do 18½ knots on the surface and all of them could outpace the corvettes. Their anti-aircraft armament, when it arrived − it had to be delivered from Switzerland (20mm Oerlikons) and Sweden (40mm Bofors) − was scarcely adequate to take care of their own close-range defence, let alone the protection of a convoy that could cover thirty square miles or more.

However, they were splendid little ships. Their main advantages stemmed from the initial simplicity and seaworthiness of the overall design, driven by extremely reliable engines. These ships were cheap to build; the first to take the water cost £66,000; they could be mass-produced and the designs were available. As new equipment was produced and operational requirements changed it was simple to introduce quite major modifications. In the course of the Second World War no less than twenty major Alterations and Additions were approved, one of which covered their conversion for tropical service and another increased the number of the ship's company from twenty-five to ninety-six.

Initially, their endurance (3,450 miles at twelve knots) was quite good but as the years passed and refuelling at sea became commonplace, the limiting factor proved to be the ability of the crew to endure the worst seas that the Atlantic Ocean could throw at them. The officers and men who manned them worked throughout the Battle in conditions of extreme discomfort with many moans and groans, sustained only by a sense of humour and the belief that their little ships were indomitable. Corvettes rolled on wet grass and were said to be 'A way of life'. They were the cause of many love/hate relationships.

THE HUNT CLASS DESTROYERS

Whereas the corvettes were adaptations of a basic practical commercial working design, the Hunt Class destroyers were little mini-thoroughbreds, small replicas of the glamorous Fleet destroyers. They displaced 1000 tons with a maximum speed of just under 30 knots and were well armed with twin four-inch guns mounted in two turrets, carrying 60/70 depth charges. However, they were severely hampered by an inadequate range of 2500 miles at 20 knots. This limitation meant, for example, that, in convoy HG 76, one of the shorter ocean routes, the fully bunkered *Blankney* and *Exmoor* had to leave their stations on the afternoon of the fourth day out from Gibraltar, just before the convoy came into the second stage and main area of attack.

They also tended to be top-heavy and needed to be ballasted. A request for a basic crow's nest to accommodate the masthead lookout could not be met as it would have needed a ton removed at deck level to compensate.

THE MODIFIED BLACK SWAN CLASS SLOOPS

The first specialized escort ship, a sloop of the Black Swan Class, was laid down on 20 June, 1939, at Yarrow's yard and completed on 27 January, 1940, nineteen months later. In the 1940 and 1941 programmes another twenty-seven were laid down. Ships from the first batch were to be commissioned at the end of 1942 and the beginning of 1943.

These ships were 300ft overall, beam 38ft, drawing 8ft 9in, with a maximum speed of 20 knots. They carried 390 tons of oil fuel, with an endurance of 7500 miles at twelve knots, sacrificing speed for a greater range of operation. They were designed to carry a complement of 181, but by the time they were commissioned forty to sixty extra men had to be fitted into the same accommodation.

They were armed with ten 20mm Oerlikons and six mark XVI* four-inch guns on Mark XIX mountings, which could be used for surface or anti-aircraft firing: to provide a stable gun platform they were designed for a long slow period of roll and fitted with Denny Brown stabilizers. Aft, they carried four depth-charge throwers with two sets of rails and, when first launched, 110 depth charges. This was increased to 180 or however many more could be accommodated.

Whereas the Flower Class corvettes were built to commercial specifications, the Modified Black Swan Class sloops and the Hunt Class destroyers retained full warship specifications. Consequently they were built in yards which had experience of warship construction.

Because of the length of time that they take to build, all warships are out-of-date before they start their working lives. These sloops were no exception, but as far as possible they reflected the most advanced thinking of the Naval Staff for escort vessels that would spend their time in the defence of ocean convoys against U-boat and aircraft attack in the Atlantic Ocean.

Modified Black Swan Class Sloops
In the Second Support Group

H.M. Ship	Builder	Job Number	Building Time	Completed
Starling	U66 Fairfields	J11701	17m 4d	1/4/43
Wild Goose	U45 Yarrow	J1862	13m 14d	13/1/43
Kite	U87 Cammell Laird	J3467		16/2/43
Magpie	U82 Thorneycroft	J6082	20m 0d	30/8/43
Wren	U28 Denny	J1260	23m 5d	4/2/43
Woodpecker	U08 Denny	J1259	23m 10d	11/2/43
Woodcock	U90 Fairfields	J1170	9m 8d	25/5/43

APPENDIX THREE

CLOSE ESCORTS FOR CONVOYS

In the tight screens stationed around and close to the ships of the convoys there was a great danger that the Officers of the Watch, in heavy weather and bad visibility, became so intent on avoiding collision that they were unable to concentrate their full attention on the main job, the detection and destruction of the enemy. As the size of the escorting forces increased, there were many ships zigzagging together and holding station relative to each other. In each ship the Officer of the Watch had to ensure that the correct zigzag was made at the right time: he had to keep exact station on the guide of the Fleet: he had to watch the escorts next to him on the radar screen in case they made a mistake. He had to watch for unwieldy merchant ships veering out of position and for sudden breakdowns. His Asdics were rendered less efficient by numerous underwater sounds all around, and sometimes by interference from other ships' transmissions; his radar set was cluttered up by the many ships in company and by spurious echoes caused by their proximity.

Only when the OOW had sorted out all these extraneous distractions could he concentrate on the problems of detecting U-boats, which had freedom of manoeuvre until, in the last 1500 yards or less, they came within Asdic range. If he did get an echo it would be only just outside the range at which the U-boat could fire at the convoy, and his freedom to put in an effective counter-attack would be severely hampered by the proximity of the ships around him. If his attack failed, the U-boat could be right inside the screen and could pass clear underneath the convoy, or worse still, surface right in the middle, between two columns.

APPENDIX FOUR

THE GERMAN U-BOATS

By far the greatest number of U-boats operating in the Second World War were Type VIIs which were the workhorses of the Atlantic groups. There were three variations of the Type VIIs, of which the main characteristics were great strength and manouevrability. They were limited by their endurance to about 9,000 miles at ten knots if they could stay on the surface, but this was reduced to about one hundred miles submerged at two/four knots, before recharging their batteries. Their displacement was 750 tons, length 220 feet and beam twenty feet. They were manned by a crew of forty-four, and had a maximum surface speed of seventeen to eighteen knots.

THE MILCH COWS AND SUPPLY BOATS

From 1943, Type IX U-boats started to operate. These boats displaced over 1000 tons with their endurance increased to over 16,000 miles on the surface. The largest were the Type IXD U-cruisers, and the Type XIV 1,700-ton supply U-boats. Ten of the Type XIV were commissioned; their function was to replenish operational boats and so keep them on station for much longer periods. They carried an additional 700 tons of fuel.

In the Bay of Biscay in the summer of 1942, *U- 459* was sunk by Wellington Q/172 on 24 July. *U- 461* and *U- 462* were sunk by aircraft and the Second Support Group on 30 July. By 4 August, 1943, the Germans had lost seven of their ten milch cows and so the chance of effective operations in distant waters. There were several U-boats now lying off the Azores so short of fuel that they could not get home.

Eleven U-boats were sunk while attempting to cross the Bay of Biscay between 20 July and 3 August, including the four refuellers (nine between 29 July and 3 August). These losses were described by Dönitz as an 'appalling total' and caused him to give up the attempt to fight his way through on the surface and to cancel all sailings from the Atlantic bases for the time being, until the new radar search receivers became available at the end of August.

APPENDIX FIVE

THE ASDIC SYSTEM

The system of detection used by Allied Navies during the Second World War was referred to in the Royal Navy as ASDICS, derived from the

Anti-Submarine Detection Investigation Committee set up to develop the methods used in the First World War. The Americans called it SONAR.

A beam of sound waves was transmitted from a dome below the hunting vessel's hull. When these sound waves hit a submerged object an echo came back to the ship. From this, the range and bearing, but not the depth, of the object could be established reasonably accurately in normal sea conditions.

The Asdic system on which the Royal Navy pinned its faith had many severe limitations, some of which are listed below.

—The range was limited to 1500/2000 yards at about fifteen knots in moderate sea conditions.

—This range was reduced as the speed of the ship increased.

—Since the large convoys could cover an area of more than sixty square miles it was evidently impossible to build, man and equip the number of escorts required to provide a full screen for the thousands of ships travelling in convoy.

—The performance fell away as surface sea and swell conditions deteriorated.

—Several types of submerged objects could send back echoes, such as wrecks, tidal rips, artifical decoys emitted from the U-boat to confuse the hunter (submarine bubble targets or S.B.T.s), shoals or rocks or other ships operating Asdics in the vicinity. (Today, a more refined system is widely used for locating fish.)

—In certain water conditions, particularly in calm weather conditions, layers of water at different temperatures could deflect the Asdic transmissions, effectively hiding the target (layering).

—In the opening years of the battle, Asdics gave no reliable and accurate measure of the depth of the target, which was estimated according to the range at which contact was lost.

—Asdics lost contact with a deep U-boat at a range of about 750 yards, or a shallow U-boat at about 150 yards, after which the attacking ship had no means of knowing what evasive action the U-boat might be taking (the Blind Period).

—While in contact, the only way of estimating the course and speed of the target was by the rate of change of angle and range, combined with the Doppler effect. This was a matter of subjective human judgement which could only be refined and improved by practical experience in real conditions. The effective use of Asdics was a skill not easily or quickly acquired.

—At the outbreak of war only about 200 escorts were fitted with the Asdic system.

—Given the exact location of the U-boat, it could dive below the maximum range of our depth charges. As the battle progressed, experience would show that it might take several hours to ensure the destruction of a U-boat, using several ships and scores (even hundreds) of depth charges. Analysis of many attacks showed that the U-boat often survived as many as seven attacks and was most likely to succumb after the eighth attack.

– There were many chances of Asdics losing contact for any of these reasons, or because the escorts might be forced to abandon the chase for tactical reasons, in which case the U-boat would live to fight another day.

– The system had not been exhaustively tested in convoy conditions. Not one exercise had been carried out between the two wars to test out the working of the convoy system, which depended largely for its protection on Asdics.

– When the Germans introduced the Gnat (acoustic torpedo), escorts were fitted with Foxers, bundles of iron trailed over the stern, which made enough noise to distract the torpedoes. When these were in use, they interfered so much that the Asdics were rendered useless and the ship was blinded.

Finally, Dönitz had trained and was training his U-boat crews to attack by night on the surface at speeds which could not be equalled by the merchantmen or many of the escorting warships. Asdics was of no practical value against U-boats on the surface by night or by day.

On 15 June, 1938, Churchill went to sea to observe Asdics in action, with Lord Chatfield the First Sea Lord, and admits that 'I overrated, as they did, the magnitude of their achievements, and forgot for a moment how broad are the seas'. An error of judgement shared by almost all naval planners, except Captain Walker, which was so nearly fatal.

APPENDIX SIX

CREEPING ATTACK

Extract from Second Support Group Operation Instructions

'The "creeping attack" will normally be used against a deep U-boat, as follows:-

(b) The directing ship (normally the Senior Officer) is to take station astern of the U-boat at convenient range for keeping Asdic contact, i.e. about 1500-2000 yards. She is to keep astern and pointed at the U-boat.

(c) When ordered by the directing ship, the attacking ship is to proceed at about five knots and take station about 1000 yards ahead of the directing ship, i.e. between the latter and the U-boat. She is then to attack at about five knots. She is NOT to operate Asdic.

(d) Meanwhile the directing ship is to pass ranges and bearings of the U-boat continuously to her by R/T, and is to inform her exactly when and what courses to steer; in other words the directing ship cons the attacker over the

U-boat. A Stuart's distance meter or one meter range-finder is a convenient method of keeping the range of the attacking ship.

(e) When the attacking ship is over (or preferably just short of) the U-boat, the directing ship is to order her to "stand-by" and then "fire".

(f) The attacking ship is then to fire 26 depth charges setting as previously ordered; distance between dropped charges 25 yards i.e. 9 seconds at 5 knots.

(g) Immediately the attacking ship has fired her pattern she is to report by R/T and clear the range at full speed. The directing ship is then to increase to full speed and drop a pattern of 22 charges spaced 25 yards apart setting "E for Easy" over the U-Boat or over the area of the first attack if the U-Boat's position is not known. This pattern is to be eighteen charges from the rails and four from throwers.'

This method of attack had the following advantages:

1. It gave no warning to the U-boat of an impending attack and thus no opportunity to take last-minute evading action.

2. The attack was carried out at a speed where the noise of the screws could not be picked up by a Gnat.

3. It was extremely accurate as to bearing and range.

4. It had been proved to be most effective by Walker's practical experience.

A devastating variation of the creeping attack was the 'Plaster' attack, in which three ships, stationed close abeam, delivered the attack.

REFERENCES AND NOTES

Chapter One
(pp. 4-12)

1. Padfield, *Dönitz* p. 92.
2. Personal letter to author.
3. The Commander in a big ship is second in command responsible to the commanding officer for running the ship. The equivalent in a destroyer or escort vessel is the First Lieutenant (Number One).
4. Arbuthnot was appointed Fourth Sea Lord and a member of the Board of Admiralty in 1937.
5. Timothy Walker left the English College, was a stretcher bearer at Dunkirk, and became an ordinary seaman in the RNVR.
6. R. W. Roskill, *The War at Sea*, v. 1 p. 50 (hereinafter RWR).
7. RWR v. 1, p. 50.
   Forty-seven of these would be put out of action in May and June 1940.
8. Padfield, *Dönitz* p. 194.
9. HMSO 1946 Cmd 6843.
10. RWR vol. 1, p. 228.

Chapter Two
(pp. 13-39)

1. Sloops *Stork* and *Deptford*. Flower Class Corvettes *Convolvulus, Gardenia, Marigold, Penstemon, Samphire* and *Vetch*.
2. Many Admirals on the retired list came back to do great work at sea and ashore. 'Monkey' Stephenson was one of them. Some of them were in charge of the convoys and ranked as Commodores. Twenty-one Commodores went down with their ships, of whom twelve were Admirals and nine were Captains RNR.
3. 'Operation Haggis' is described on p. 192.
4. *German Naval History: The U-Boat War, 1939-1945*, HMSO, 1989 (hereinafter GNH). Diag. 31.
5. Dönitz commandeered a château at Kernéval from which he could watch the U-boats going in and out of Lorient. Whenever possible he would welcome each boat personally and bestow decorations there and then. He stayed there until the Commando Raid on St Nazaire, which so

alarmed the German High Command that he was ordered to skedaddle back to Paris.

6. *British Intelligence*, Vol. II, p. 270.
7. Brit Int: v. 1 p. 163.
8. GNH, diag. 13 section 153/154.
9. *Walker RN*, Terence Robertson, p. 47 (hereinafter WRN).
10. It should have been two to nil, *U-131* and *U-127*.
11. *U-574, 575, 434, 107*, and *108* were up with the convoy. *U-71, 567* and *751* were on their way from their bases in the Bay of Biscay.
12. There had been a blind period between February and early December, after which BP started once more to penetrate the cypher code-named Triton.
13. After this convoy, Walker's ships never returned to the convoy in a direct line, in case U-boats were following at a distance.
14. Chief Petty Officer Kelly was awarded a DSM and three bars, the largest number of DSC awards in World War Two.
15. In his report, Walker shouldered full blame for the loss of *Audacity*. The C-in-C commented that no blame could be attributed. See Chapter 3.
16. Letter from George Dyson to the author.
17. Letter from Captain E. Palmer RN to the author.
18. GNH, section 153.

Chapter Three
(pp. 40-53)

1. *Price of Admiralty*, John Keegan, pp. 42-44.
2. Nearly forty years after Johnnie Walker died, the Captain Walker's Old Boys Association, whose members and associate members all served at sea with him in HM Ships *Stork* or *Starling*, the 36th Escort Group or the Second Support Group, still meet in the spring of each year in Liverpool for a reunion and to attend a memorial service in Liverpool Cathedral.
3. Asdic — see Appendix 5.
4. Commercial oil stocks fell to two and a half months' cover in 1942 and remained at that low level for many months, (RWR, vol. 2, p. 217) but this shortage was not apparent to warships at sea. This was very close to final starvation.
5. ADM, 199, 1257.
6. Walker's orders were over-ridden from on high, but his commanding officers tended to do what he told them, irrespective of other suggestions.
7. GNH, section 184.
8. GNH, diag. 16 and sections 196 and 206.

9. WRN, pp. 69 to 84.

10. GNH diag. 16, point 44, section 206.

11. In the sloops, unless the ship was perfectly upright when firing ahead — particularly at long range — a significant error was introduced into the gunnery for which the instruments did not compensate. It was a matter for the Director gunlayer's judgement. This was Petty Officer Bungy Williams in *Starling*. Since his father and his grandfather had both been gunners in their time, he rarely got a word in when he tried to tell them of his deeds at sea.

12. Subsequent records showed that no U-boats were sunk on that day.

13. GNH, section 206 and diag. 16.

14. Milch cows. See Appendix 4.

15. U-boats *U-84, 89, 134, 437, 552, 571, 575*.

Chapter Four
(pp. 54-81)

1. Captain Walker was appointed in command of HMS *Starling*, and Captain (D) Second Support Group. The Group, even in official documents, was sometimes referred to as the Second Escort Group, but in this book, to avoid confusion, it is always referred to as the Second Support Group (SG 2). See also note 6 below.

2. RWR, vol. 1, p. 456.

3. The Hedgehog was a form of mortar that threw twenty-four charges ahead of the firing ship. It depended on direct hits.

4. *Business in Great Waters*, John Terraine, p. 436 (hereinafter BIGW).

5. GNH diag. 31 and 32, September 1942.

6. See note 1 above. Escort Groups normally provided close escorts to a convoy with responsibility for the safe and timely arrival of the merchantmen. Support Groups adopted an aggressive hunting role, not tied down to the same extent.

7. The source of much of this information about Liverpool is Brian Perrett's book *Liverpool, City at War*.

8. The description 'old hands' is relative. Anyone who had completed a couple of years on Atlantic convoys qualified as an 'old hand'.

9. CWOBA archives.

10. CWOBA archives.

11. GNH, diag. 31.

12. BIGW, p. 569.

13. GNH, diag. 21 and sections 333 and 3353.

14. Churchill, *The Second World War*.

15. The gun mountings were trained and the guns were loaded by hand. The

delay in opening fire was determined by the length of time that it took to swing the mounting on to the target. The bearing of a U-boat moving fast on opposite course at very short range could change almost as fast as the four-inch guns could be swung round. With constant drilling the standards set became maxima and crews competed fiercely to beat the record for the prize of a bar of nutty. *Starling*'s normally achieved standard when in cruising watches was to fire six rounds within thirty seconds of getting the target in the sights and to set and fire a pattern of ten depth charges within fifteen seconds.

16. As normally pronounced.
17. 'Haggis' was a detailed SG2 drill for boarding a U-boat, bottling up the Germans inside, taking it in tow and getting it back into harbour intact. A copy of the orders are to be found in CWOBA's archives.
18. The Intelligence people considered that an attempt should have been made to board during this time, but this was not accepted by the C-in-C for the reasons given here by Walker.
19. See Appendix 6 for more details of the 'creeping attack', its development and use.
20. By 1940, all U-boats could dive to 160m (530ft) or 180m (600ft) without danger. Newer types of U-boat – Type V11Cs – standard depth was 200m (660ft) and 300m (990ft) in an emergency.

Chapter Five
(pp. 82-108)

1. GNH, section 357.
2. Frank Clarke wrote 'We all thought we had a right to sink U-boats'.
3. There was not much time to raise the dome and this might have prejudiced his chance of regaining contact if the ramming had failed. Nevertheless, not content with sinking the U-boat, Walker blamed himself for not remembering this possible action.
4. *Harvester* had rammed a U-boat and had been torpedoed by its mate while lying damaged and stopped after the impact.
5. Able Seaman Jack Moss of *Wren*, loader on the right gun of B mounting claims it was his gun. He says, 'I was loading on right, B gun ... I still reckon it was B gun that took *Starling*'s bullring that successful day in Biscay. A great rate of fire but known to have moments of inaccuracy.'
6. Wemyss and Walker both served in the battleship *Valiant* in World War One.
7. In the 1950s the author went to *Osprey* for his annual RNVR training, where the Instructor attempted to teach him this method of attack.
8. The Second Support Group did 88 ship days at sea in the month of June.

Adm. 199, 1406, pp. 428-433.

9. In the seventeenth century, rigid rules called The Fighting Instructions governed the conduct of the Fleets. In the eighteenth century, the signal 'General Chase' was introduced and flown, for example, at the battles of Cape Finisterre and Quiberon Bay. This signal meant basically 'Get On With It', which was more Walker's style.

10. The sinking of *U- 462* was attributed to Halifax S No. 502 Squadron, and therefore does not appear in the appendix of U-boats sunk by ships under Walker's command.

11. GNH section 359, diag. 23, points 7 and 99.

12. This account that follows of the real life situation may have been the inspiration for the central scene in *The Cruel Sea*, in which the Commanding Officer was faced with the same dilemma.

13. GNH sections 359 and 360.

14. The Admiralty was wiser. During these operations a cruiser, either *Scylla* or *Bermuda*, was lurking in support just below the horizon. It would have made an interesting battle.

15. RWR, vol. 3, p. 29.

16. RWR, vol. 3, p. 29.

17. ADM 199, 1406.

Chapter Six
(pp. 109-123)

1. Nearly always the ships of the Group were under wheel continuously, weaving about a mean course to make their movements less predictable to the enemy.

2. Walker knew more than anyone the limitations of Asdic and that its performance could vary greatly and unpredictably. (See Appendix 5.)

3. Adlard Coles, *Heavy Weather Sailing*, Appendix 1:
   'Beaufort Scale, Force Ten. Wind speed up to 60 mph; very high waves with long overhanging crests. The resulting foam in great patches is blown in dense white streaks along the direction of the wind. On the whole the surface of the sea takes a white appearance. The tumbling of the sea becomes heavy and shocklike. Visibility affected. Waves of 60 feet in height are to be expected.' Also *Admiralty Manual of Seamanship*, Vol. 2.

4. The maximum roll recorded by *Tracker* was fifty-two degrees from the vertical. Most domestic staircases are angled at forty-five degrees. Try propping a plank on the stairs and standing on it!

5. Letter from Jack Moss, CWOBA's archives.

6. GNH, section 399.

7. ADM, 199, 1406.
8. ADM, 199, 1406.
9. ADM, 199, 1406.
10. This was an unusual but a quarterly occurrence – an expression of his greatest rage and frustration.
11. The human remains were packaged by Doc Fraser and sent to D.A/S.W with a covering note: 'Enclosed are specimens of human remains picked up after sinking of enemy U-boat by H.M.S. *Starling* and H.M.S. *Wildgoose* (sic) on November 6/43. With the compliments of Captain F. J. Walker RN.' Walker received a rap over the knuckles. D.A/S.W's staff did not find it amusing to unwrap items of this sort in the morning mail. ADM, 199, 1406, p. 506.
12. ADM, 199, 1406, p. 514.
13. Walker said that he had just begun to realize how jerry-built these ships really were. ADM, 199, 1406. A little unfair: they were tested beyond limits that could normally be expected.
14. GNH, section 395.
15. The force of the seas on the breakwater across the forecastle had torn this welded steel structure away from the deck in places.

Chapter Seven
(pp. 124-143)

1. This was the average daily distance covered by Nelson's fleet of square-riggers.
2. GNH, section 376 diag. 32. The Allied bombing, shortage of manpower in the repair yards and the long training periods for crews accounted for the low percentage of U-boats operational. Dönitz hadn't got the balance right.
3. GNH, diag. 24.
4. See Glossary.
5. ADM 199 2061. The cause of this explosion, which missed *Starling* by a whisker, has never been satisfactorily explained. Walker thought that the U-boat had probably come up to a hundred feet and fired a Gnat that had exploded at the end of its circling run just before connecting with *Starling*'s ship side. The plot showed that *Starling* was immediately over the U-boat when the explosion took place. Buzzes started on the lower deck about a new German mine released by the U-boat when it was right underneath the attacking ship. Walker dismissed this possibility; a mine released from a U-boat was as likely to hit the bottom of a ship as a single depth charge dropped over the side was to find a U-boat.
6. Blondie Mockridge was awarded the DSM.

7. This was before the days of the Plan Position Indicator which gave all round coverage.
8. See note 10 below.
9. See Plate 11 of *Kite* dwarfed by a near miss. The pyramid of water makes her look like a rowing boat.
10. Three U-boats, *U-762, 794* and *238*, were definitely sunk by the Second Support group on 8 and 9 February, 1944, but since there were no survivors it is not possible to say which ships sunk which U-boats. Letter from MOD Historical Branch to the author, and War Diary ADM, 199, 2289.
11. Wemyss, *Relentless Pursuit*.
12. ADM, 199, 1096, p. 196.
13. The other Schnorkel boat at sea at this time was sunk on 17 March, 1944, GNH, diag. 25, point 2.
14. Long-Serving Ratings served for twelve years, and always bemoaned the fact, however much they enjoyed themselves.
15. Walker had pointed out that a sloop's propeller below seven knots was not audible above the normal water noise level.
16. ADM, 199, 1096 AUD 238/44.

Chapter Eight
(pp. 144-159)

1. Honours and Awards Committee Minutes.
2. RWR, vol. 3/2, p. 433.
3. Convoy JW-55B at the end of December had tempted the 32,000-ton battle cruiser *Scharnhorst* to her destruction at the hands of the Home Fleet. Admiral Sir Bruce Fraser, perhaps with his tongue in his cheek, had declared that the safety of the convoy was his prime objective. True to his word, the convoy reached its destination without loss, but meantime his cruisers and destroyers had intercepted *Scharnhorst* just short of the convoy, beaten her off and brought in the battleships for the kill. This was one of the most brilliant actions in the history of the Royal Navy, in which the battleship *Duke of York* crippled the *Scharnhorst* by gunfire at night in typical Arctic weather. She was finally sunk by the cruisers and destroyers as their fuel ran dangerously low. One of the seamen in the attacking destroyer *Scorpion*, which closed within 3000 yards of the *Scharnhorst*'s full broadside of nine 11-inch, twelve 5.9-inch and fourteen 4.1 inch guns is reported to have said:
'Get out wires and fenders. We're going alongside the bastard!' (RWR, vol. 3, p. 87).
4. ADM, 199, 327, p. 780.

5. See Appendix 5: The Asdic System (p. 185).
6. Signalling positions 180 degrees in error.
7. *Tirpitz* and her destroyers were only as good as their crews who had been given no chance to put in any sea time; they were poorly led by their High Command, who tried to avoid all risks which did little for the officers' and men's morale. Even Hitler despised them. They had a rotten war.
8. RWR, vol. 3/1, p. 273.
9. RWR, vol. 3/1, p. 273.
10. RWR, vol. 3/1, p. 273.
11. *Starling*, as Captain (D)'s ship, always sported a black band round her funnel as a badge of rank. When Walker transferred to another ship at sea, it was always a challenge to have the black band painted before the seaboat could be rowed across and he scrambled up the rope ladder.
12. Even at this stage of the war the depth charges did not have settings below 700 feet.
13. 'Shark' was a huge projectile of low muzzle velocity, designed to be fired from the four-inch guns and to penetrate a U-boat's hull below the waterline. It was a very destructive weapon but difficult to handle and cumbersome. We experimented using it as a mortar in a creeping attack but with no success.
14. ADM, 471.
15. WRN, p. 136.

Chapter Nine
(pp. 160-175)

1. GNH, chap. XI, p. 83 onwards, and section 463.
2. On 21 August, 1944, *Kite* was sunk by U-344 in the Norwegian sea while supporting convoy JW 59. At the time she was disregarding three of Walker's standard procedures, rigidly enforced while he was in command: (a) She had been steering a steady course for several minutes; (b) the need to attend to her Foxers was dictating her speed and taking up too much attention; (c) Lifelines were not worn by many of the oil-covered survivors in the water, which made it much more difficult, and sometimes impossible, to pull them out.
3. Squid was a heavier version of the ahead-throwing Hedgehog, it could throw three charges weighing 350 lbs. 700 yards ahead of the ship.
4. GNH, section 420.
5. BIGW, p. 646.
6. GNH, section 437 and 432.
7. GNH, section 433.

8. As a safety measure and to save the gun sweepers work, the smart polished brass tampions adorned with *Starling*'s crest were put away when the ship left harbour and replaced by small sandbags tied on by a bit of line to stop the sea water getting down the barrels.

9. The full story of the Normandy landings are beyond the scope of this book. They are described elsewhere in very great detail, particularly in RWR, vol. 3, pt. 11, chapters XIV and XV.

10. Dönitz, *Memoirs*, p. 422.

11. S.G.M.4. 'A method of altering line of advance from line abreast formation designed by *Woodpecker*. The signal used will be "Easy Item" followed by three numeral flags to denote new course. The ship furthest from the direction of alteration takes guide and alters immediately to new course. The remainder proceed on the old course and each in turn alters to the new course when she is on the beam of the guide'. CWOBA Archives.

12. GNH, section 441/2.

13. HMSO, Cmd. 6843.

14. Wemyss, *Relentless Pursuit*.

15. CWOBA archives.

16. Originally thought to be *U-327*. See Appendix 1 — List of U-boats sunk.

BIBLIOGRAPHY

Barnett, C. *Engage the Enemy More Closely*, Hodder & Stoughton, 1991.

Bekker, C. *Hitler's Naval War*, Macdonald and Janes, 1974.

Buckheim, L. G. *U-boat*, William Collins, 1974.

Calvocoressi, P. *Top Secret Ultra*, Cassell, 1980.

Chalmers, W. *Max Horton and the Western Approaches*, Hodder & Stoughton 1954.

Coles, K. A. *Heavy Weather Sailing*, Adlard Coles, 1967.

Costello, J., and Hughes, T. *Battle of the Atlantic*, William Collins, 1977.

Gretton, P. *Crisis Convoy*, Peter Davies, 1974.

Gibbs, N. *Grand Strategy* Vol. 1, H.M.S.O., 1976.

Hesler, G. *German Naval History,The U-boat War*, H.M.S.O., 1989.

Hinsley, F. *British Intelligence in the Second World War*, 1979.

Keegan, J. *Price of Admiralty*, Hutchinson, 1988.

Lamb, R. *Drift to War*, W. H. Allen, 1989.

Lewin, R. *Ultra Goes To War*, Hutchinson, 1978.

Morison, S. *History of United States Naval Operations* Vol. VI, Oxford University Press, 1948.

Noli, J. *Admiral's Wolfpack*, Fayard Publishers, 1970.

Padfield, P. *Dönitz*, Victor Gollancz, 1984.

Perrett, B. *Liverpool, A City At War*, Robert Hale, 1990.

Poolman, K. *Escort Carrier*, Leo Cooper, 1983.

Preston, A. *U-boats*, Arms and Armour Press, 1978.

Robertson, T. *Walker, R. N.*, Evans Brothers, 1956.

Roskill, R. W. *War At Sea* (Three Volumes), H.M.S.O., 1954-1961; *The Navy at War* (US Naval Institute), Collins, 1960.

Sainsbury, A. and Shrubb, R. *Royal Navy Day by Day*, Centaur Press, 1979.

Showell, M. *U-boats under the Swastika*, Ian Allan, 1987; *Fuehrer Conferences on Naval Affairs*, Greenhill Books, 1990.

Terraine, J. *Business in Great Waters*, Leo Cooper, 1989.

Wemyss, D. *Relentless Pursuit*, William Kimber, 1955.

Van Der Vat, D. *Atlantic Campaign*, Hodder & Stoughton, 1988.

Winterbotham, F. *Ultra Secret*, Weidenfeld & Nicolson, 1974.

Winton, J. *Ultra at Sea*, Leo Cooper, 1988.

INDEX

Acoustic Torpedoes, see Gnats.
Africa, 16, 17, 46, 55, 96.
Afrika Korps, 17.
Algeçiras, 18.
Altenfjord, 153.
America, see United States of America.
Anglo-German Naval Agreement, 8.
Arbuthnot, Captain G. S. RN, 7.
Arctic Convoys, 146-155.
Argentia, 111, 117, 118.
Aubrey, Commander, 107.
Ayers, Lieutenant A.C. see Pilot.
Azores, 43, 97, 105, 120, 184.

Baltic, 8, 15.
Bar Light Vessel, 139, 173.
Battle of the Atlantic, 4, 10, 41, 42, 54, 55, 69, 145, 160.
Baulcomb, Stan – The Gunner, 66, 91, 167.
Baumann, 22, 23.
Beatty, Admiral, 8.
Beaufighter aircraft, 83.
Beobachter Dienst, 17, 70.
Berliner Tageblatt, 8.
Bidston Dock, 122.
Bigalk, 34.
Birkenhead, 123.
Biscay, Bay of, (The Bay), 16, 46, 50, 53, 81, 83, 88-102, 105, 106, 111, 114, 145, 160, 184, 189.
Bishop Rock Lighthouse, 91.
Bletchley Park, 16, 17, 18, 25, 56, 145.
Bootle, 58, 81.
Bordeaux, 16, 19, 43, 46, 88, 96, 170.
Boyer, Lieutenant F.L. 98.
Bramble, Chiefie – The Engineer Officer, 66, 67, 75, 87, 107, 121.
Bray, Able Seaman Clem, 16, 98, 110.
Brest, 16, 165.
British Intelligence, 5.

Bunkers, U-Boat, 4, 146.
Burn, Lieutenant Alan, 14, 92, 93.

Cadiz, 18.
CAM, (Catapult Aircraft Merchantman), 47.
Canary Islands, 17.
Canadian Navy, Royal, 57.
Caribbean, 53.
Catalina aircraft, 52, 95, 99, 105.
Channel Islands, 170.
Chiefie, see Bramble.
Churchill, Winston, 8, 11, 56, 71.
C-in-C, Commander-in-Chief, 32, 33, 37, 40, 42, 53, 81, 91, 100, 104, 117, 119, 121, 122, 132, 133, 136, 140, 141, 165, 170.
Clarke, Torpedoman Frank, 161.
Coastal Command, 54, 82, 83, 84, 92, 105, 106, 165.
Commando Raid on St Nazaire, 188, 189.
Creasy, Captain George, RN, 12, 40.
Creeping Attack, 2, 49, 76, 81, 89, 92, 97, 114, 115, 127-134, 142, 145, 149, 152, 157, 178, 186, 191.
Cruel Sea, The, 192.
Cunningham, Admiral, 17.
C.W.O.B.A., Captain Walker's Old Boys' Association, 189, 190, 191.

Dartmouth, Royal Naval College, 5.
Dalrymple-Hamilton, Admiral, 147.
D-Day, see Normandy Landings.
Derby House, 54, 121.
Devil's Point, Intr, 91.
Devonport, 63, 172.
D/F (or HF/DF), Direction Finding, 23, 25, 48, 67, 74, 79, 95, 114, 115, 117, 120, 129, 130, 138, 145, 146, 151, 152, 157, 160, Glossary.
Director of Anti-Submarine Warfare, 193.
Director of Naval Intelligence, 70.

Etrib, 50.
Exmoor, 18, 26, 27.

Falmouth, 6.
Forester, 136.
Furious, 154.

Gore, 157.
Grenville, 102.

Harvester, 191.
Hesperus, 172, 173.
Hopping, 158.

Irwell, 123.

Keppel, 148, 152.
King George V, 171, 194.

Lady Madeleine, 138.
Landguard, 102.

Malakand, 58.
Mermaid, 5.
Milwaukee, 147.
Mourne, 170.

Nairana, 1, 125, 126, 142, 143.

Onslow, 147.
Osprey, 6, 191.

Parthian, 102, 171.
Pelavo, 46.
Pelican, 40.
Philante, 140, 142.

Revenge, 6.
Rother, 141.
Royal Oak, 10.
Ruckinge, 30.

Sarpedon, 5.
Scharnhorst, 194.
Scylla, 192.
Shikari, 6, 11.
Southern Pride, 181.
Spero, 19.
Stanley, 18, 21, 25-31, 37, 43.
Storm King, 138, 142.

Tirpitz, 147, 153, 154, 195.

Towey, 128.
Tracker, 109-120, 125, 147, 150, 155, 156, 159.
Tyne, 147.

Queen Elizabeth, 6.

Valiant, 6, 7, 171, 191.
Victorious, 140, 154.
Vindex, 144.

Western Isles, 13.

U-BOAT INDEX
* U-boats sunk by Captain Walker's ships.
** U-boats sunk by Captain Walker's ships after his death.

U-29, 10.
UB-68, 5.
U-82, 46.
U-127, 20, 179.
U-119*, 85, 92.
U-131*, 22, 23.
U-202*, 71, 74, 79-81, 83.
U-226*, 113, 115.
U-238*, 179.
U-252*, 44, 46, 55.
U-262, 121.
U-264*, 135, 136, 142.
U-288, 153.
U-333**, 174.
U-344, 195.
U-360, 152.
U-385**, 175.
U-424*, 142.
U-434*, 25, 26.
U-449*, 92, 142.
U-454, 99.
U-459, 52, 184.
U-460, 52, 184.
U-461, 96, 97, 184.
U-462, 96, 97, 179, 184.
U-473*, 156, 158.
U-482**, 175, 180.
U-504*, 96, 97, 142.
U-542, 121.
U-552, 50, 52.
U-567*, 34.
U-571, 34.
U-574*, 27, 29.
U-587, 46.